ALWAYS REFORMING

Reflections on Martin Luther and Biblical Studies

ALWAYS REFORMING

Reflections on Martin Luther and Biblical Studies

Edited by **CHANNING L. CRISLER**
and **ROBERT L. PLUMMER**

STUDIES IN HISTORICAL AND SYSTEMATIC THEOLOGY

LEXHAM PRESS

Always Reforming: Reflections on Martin Luther and Biblical Studies
Studies in Historical and Systematic Theology

Copyright 2021 Channing L. Crisler and Robert L. Plummer

Lexham Press, 1313 Commercial St., Bellingham, WA 98225
LexhamPress.com

Print ISBN 9781683594697
Digital ISBN 9781683594703
Library of Congress Control Number 2020951969

Lexham Editorial: Todd Hains, Elizabeth Vince, Danielle Thevenaz, Kelsey Matthews
Cover Design: Bryan Hintz
Typesetting: Fanny Palacios

To Mark A. Seifrid
Scholar, Teacher, Colleague,
Doktorvater, Christian Brother, Friend

CONTENTS

ABBREVIATIONS

—

BC   *The Book of Concord: The Confessions of the Evangelical Lutheran Church.* Edited by Robert Kolb and Timothy J. Wengert. Translated by Charles Arand et al. Minneapolis: Fortress, 2000.

BSELK   *Die Bekenntnisschriften der Evangelisch-Lutherischen Kirche.* Edited by Irene Dingel. Göttingen: Vandenhoeck & Ruprecht, 2014.

LW   *Luther's Works* [American Edition]. 82 vols. projected. St. Louis: Concordia; Philadelphia: Fortress, 1955–1986, 2009–.

TAL   *The Annotated Luther.* 6 vols. Edited by Hans J. Hillerbrand, Kirsi I. Stjerna, and Timothy J. Wengert. Minneapolis: Fortress, 2015–2017.

WA   *D. Martin Luthers Werke, Kritische Gesamtausgabe: [Schriften].* 73 vols. Weimar: Hermann Böhlaus Nachfolger, 1883–2009.

WABr   *D. Martin Luthers Werke, Kritische Gesamtausgabe: Briefwechsel.* 18 vols. Weimar: Hermann Böhlaus Nachfolger, 1930–1983.

WADB   *D. Martin Luthers Werke, Kritische Gesamtausgabe: Deutsche Bibel.* 12 vols. Weimar: Hermann Böhlaus Nachfolger, 1906–1961.

CONTRIBUTORS

—

Gregg R. Allison (PhD, Trinity Evangelical Divinity School) is professor of Christian theology at The Southern Baptist Theological Seminary. He is the author of numerous books, including *50 Core Truths of the Christian Faith: A Guide to Understanding and Teaching Theology*, *Roman Catholic Theology and Practice: An Evangelical Assessment*, and *Historical Theology: An Introduction to Christian Doctrine*.

Oswald Bayer (PhD, University of Tübingen) is professor emeritus of systematic theology at the Evangelical Theological Faculty of the Eberhard Karls University of Tübingen, Germany. He is the author of numerous books, including *Theology the Lutheran Way*, *A Contemporary in Dissent: Johann Georg Hamann as a Radical Enlightener*, *Martin Luther's Theology: A Contemporary Interpretation*, and *Freedom in Response: Lutheran Ethics*.

D. A. Carson (PhD, University of Cambridge) is emeritus professor of New Testament at Trinity Evangelical Divinity School and co-founder of The Gospel Coalition. He is the author of more than fifty books, including *Learning to Pray Like Paul*, *Jesus the Son of God: A Christological Title Often Overlooked, Sometimes Misunderstood, and Currently Disputed*, *The God Who Is There: Finding Your Place in God's Story*, and *How Long, O Lord: Reflections on Suffering and Evil*.

Channing L. Crisler (PhD, The Southern Baptist Theological Seminary) is associate professor of New Testament at Anderson University and the Clamp School of Divinity in South Carolina. He is the author of *Echoes of Lament and the Christology of Luke* and *Reading Romans as Lament: Paul's Use of Old Testament Lament in His Most Famous Letter*, and the co-author of *The Bible Toolbox*.

A. Andrew Das (PhD, Union Theological Seminary) is professor of religious studies at Elmhurst University. He is the author and editor of numerous books, including *Paul and the Stories of Israel: The Grand Thematic Narratives of Galatians*, *Galatians: A Theological Exposition of Sacred Scripture*, *Solving the Romans Debate*, *Paul and the Jews*, and *Paul, the Law, and the Covenant*.

Robert A. Kolb (PhD, University of Wisconsin-Madison) is professor emeritus of systematic theology at Concordia Seminary, St. Louis. He is the author of several books, including *Martin Luther as He Lived and Breathed: Recollections of the Reformer*, *Martin Luther and the Enduring Word of God: The Wittenberg School and Its Scripture-Centered Proclamation*, *Luther and the Stories of God: Biblical Narratives as a Foundation for Christian Living*, and *Martin Luther: Confessor of the Faith*.

Timo Laato (PhD, University of Göttingen) is associate professor of New Testament at the Lutheran School of Theology in Gothenburg, Sweden. He has contributed articles and essays to numerous journals and edited volumes. He is also the author of multiple books, including *Paul and Judaism: An Anthropological Approach*, *Matti Väisänen: The Bible and the Office of Pastor*, and *Justification in James: A Comparison with Paul*.

Benjamin L. Merkle (PhD, The Southern Baptist Theological Seminary) is professor of New Testament and Greek at Southeastern Baptist Theological Seminary. He is the author of numerous books, including *Exegetical Gems from Biblical Greek*, *Greek for Life*, *Going Deeper with New Testament Greek*, and *Ephesians: Exegetical Guide to the Greek New Testament*.

Robert L. Plummer (PhD, The Southern Baptist Theological Seminary) is the Collin and Evelyn Aikman Professor of Biblical Studies at The Southern Baptist Theological Seminary. He has written, co-written, or edited several books, including *Getting Started with New Testament Greek*, *Greek for Life: Strategies for Learning, Retaining, and Reviving New Testament Greek*, *Going Deeper with New Testament Greek*, *Held in Honor: Wisdom for Your Marriage from Voices of the Past*, and *40 Questions about Interpreting the Bible*. Plummer is perhaps most widely known for his role in founding and hosting the screencast, The Daily Dose of Greek (www.dailydoseofgreek.com).

Thomas R. Schreiner (PhD, Fuller Theological Seminary) is the James Buchanan Harrison Professor of New Testament Interpretation and associate dean of the School of Theology. He is the author and editor of several books, including *Handbook on Acts and Paul's Letters*, *Romans* (BECNT), *Galatians* (ZECNT), *The King in His Beauty: A Biblical Theology of the Old and New Testaments*, *40 Questions about Christians and Biblical Law*, and *New Testament Theology: Magnifying God in Christ*.

Brian J. Vickers (PhD, The Southern Baptist Theological Seminary) is professor of New Testament interpretation. He is the author of *Justification by Grace through Faith: Finding Freedom from Legalism, Lawlessness, Pride, and Despair*, and *Jesus' Blood and Righteousness: Paul's Theology of Imputation*.

FOREWORD

—

The pilgrimage of Mark Seifrid has been along two axes, differentiable but interrelated, with one being more important than the other.

On the one hand, Mark has progressively recaptured his German roots. When he first arrived at Trinity Evangelical Divinity School as a student, both he and everyone else pronounced his last name *Seefrid*; today it is unambiguously *Sīfreed*. The distinction is in line with his growing fluency in German and his deepening appreciation for his German cultural heritage, purchased in part by study leaves spent in Germany.

The second (and more important) axis is theological. Following his doctoral studies at Princeton Theological Seminary, Mark began to teach at Southern Baptist Theological Seminary, where he became the Ernest and Mildred Hogan Professor of New Testament Interpretation. In 2015, however, his Lutheran roots recaptured him, and he was appointed to teach New Testament at Concordia Seminary in St. Louis, Missouri.

The link between these two axes is not hard to find. The focus of Dr. Seifrid's studies has been the letters of Paul, and especially the theme of righteousness or justification, contributing an impressive list of essays and books not only on the δικ- word group but on related themes. As he wrestled ever more deeply with some of the voices in the camp of the New Perspective on Paul, he could not help but observe how they chose to distance themselves from the Reformers, especially Luther, and then his own studies in Luther showed him how badly Luther was misunderstood, which in due course drew him closer to the Reformer. And hence the appropriateness of a Festschrift to honor Dr. Seifrid, with the theme of this volume.

Even a casual reading of the Table of Contents discloses how Mark Seifrid has forged and maintained links of friendship and scholarship with Baptists, Lutherans, and Calvinists. In his own pilgrimage, he has plied his way to confessional Lutheranism, but not at the expense of abandoning an admirable theological ecumenicity.

Quite a few of the contributors to this volume do an admirable job of taking us back to Luther and forward to the present world of scholarship, without making either Luther or the contemporary world of scholarship the test of all things. There is a place for trajectories, for an early anticipation of later developments, a recognition that sometimes the later developments are saying very similar things but in slightly different categories. Taken as a whole, the essays in this volume maintain this tension better than many similar efforts, and thus constitute a worthy tribute to our honoree.

In multos annos!

D. A. Carson

INTRODUCTION

—

"Comfort yourself with *the Word of God*, the pre-eminent consolation."[1] In this way, Martin Luther consoled a father and husband suffering the loss of both his wife and newborn. Similarly, to a woman troubled by recurring outbursts of anger, Luther reassured her with the words: "Your sin is forgiven. Rely resolutely on this. Do not revive your own notions. Give heed to all that your pastor and preacher tell you from *the Word of God*."[2] To one stricken by unbelief, Luther recommended, "For at such a time you must accustom yourself not to wrap yourself up in your misfortune and sink into your own thoughts, without *the Word of God*, as if you proposed to wait until the terror subsides. On the contrary, you must remember at that very time to hear nothing but prayers and *the Word of God*."[3] After observing a woman stricken by a mixture of spiritual and physical maladies, he wrote to her husband: "In a word, her illness is not for the apothecaries (as they call them), nor is it to be treated with the salves of Hippocrates, but it requires the powerful plasters of the *Scriptures* and *the Word of God*."[4] Indeed, for Luther, the word of God was like "powerful plaster," offering healing properties for the soul. In his many consolations to the afflicted, without fail, Luther prescribed the word of God for any and every malady.

However, Luther did not prescribe the word without hermeneutical instruction. He knew that to truly hear the word, one needed interpretive assistance. While Luther did not eschew the role of reason, rhetoric, and language in biblical interpretation, such things did not stand at the

---

1. Theodore G. Tappert, ed. and trans., *Luther: Letters of Spiritual Counsel* (Vancouver: Regent College Publishing, 1960), 63.
2. Tappert, *Luther: Letters of Spiritual Counsel*, 103.
3. Tappert, *Luther: Letters of Spiritual Counsel*, 121.
4. Tappert, *Luther: Letters of Spiritual Counsel*, 83.

heart of interpretation.[5] Instead, Luther stressed the importance of one's disposition toward the word. This emphasis is encapsulated in Luther's instructions to his dear friend George Spalatin, who asked for advice about the study of Scripture:

> In the first place, it is most certain that one cannot enter into the Scriptures by study or skill alone. Therefore, you should begin by praying that, if it pleases the Lord to accomplish something through you for his glory, and not for your own glory or that of any other man, he may grant you a true understanding of his words. For there is no master of the Scriptures other than Him who is their author. Hence it is written, "They shall all be taught of God." You must completely despair of your own industry and ability, therefore, and rely solely on the influx of the Spirit. Believe me, for I have experience in this matter.[6]

For Luther, exegesis begins with despair and a cry for help, which could only be answered by the Spirit. Those who approach the Scriptures must confess to God their inability to truly understand. Luther had experience in this matter, and he found that only the "influx of the Spirit" could lead to an understanding of the word.

While Luther underscores the inward disposition of the interpreter, he does not end his interpretive advice to Spalatin there. He continues his instructions to Spalatin by underscoring that the interpreter must be familiar with the biblical stories and humble enough to seek exegetical help:

> Then, having achieved this despairing humility, read the Scriptures in order from beginning to end so as to get the substance of the story in your mind (as I believe you have already done long since). Saint Jerome's epistles and commentaries will be of great help in this. But for an understanding of Christ and the grace of God (that is, for the hidden knowledge of the Spirit) Augustine and Ambrose seem to me far better guides, especially because it appears to me that Jerome Origenizes (that is, allegorizes) too much. I say this

---

5. As Luther puts it, "Faith then is aided by reason, rhetoric, and language which were such great obstacles before [we had] faith." *The Disputation concerning Man* (1536), LW 34:144.

6. Tappert, *Luther: Letters of Spiritual Counsel*, 112.

although it is contrary to the judgment of Erasmus. But you asked
for my opinion and not for his.[7]

It is not surprising that, in just a few lines of advice, we find those elements
that define Luther's entire approach to Scripture. For example, he recom-
mends a reading of the text that captures the "substance" of the larger
scriptural story. Individual texts could then be interpreted in relation to
the whole of Scripture. We also see that Luther does not forego the help of
biblical commentators. He prefers those commentators whose interpretation of the text illuminated the "hidden knowledge of the Spirit," that
is, "Christ and the grace of God."[8] However, Luther warns against excess
allegorizing in the vein of Origen. He still preferred the "plain" meaning
of the text.

Luther's preference for the "plain" meaning of the text includes his
reading of the Old Testament, which he often used to comfort the Christian.
In this way, he takes the apostle Paul at his word: "For as much as was written beforehand, it was written for our instruction, in order that through
endurance and through the encouragement of the scriptures we might have
hope" (Rom 15:4). Luther puts Paul's description of the Old Testament into
pastoral use. As one witness recalls from one of those famed table talks:

> I held a Psalter in my hand and he [Luther] inquired whether I found
> pleasure in it. "Do you find joy or sorrow in it?" I replied, "I have
> often derived consolation from it, but then Satan comes and asks
> what the psalms have to do with me." He said, signing himself with
> the cross, " 'Whatsoever things were written aforetime were written
> for us that we through,' etc. Abraham, Isaac, Jacob, the dear Joseph,
> Rebecca, and Leah have no idea whatsoever that we are today read-
> ing narratives about them. David does not know that we now have
> his psalms in Germany and that we find comfort in them even as he
> did long ago. The Lord helped David, who put his trust in God. So
> he will also aid us who hope in him, for his word is yea and amen."[9]

---

7. Tappert, *Luther: Letters of Spiritual Counsel*, 113.

8. Luther specifically suggests Andreas Bodenstein von Karlstadt's commentary on
Augustine's *De spiritu et litera*.

9. Tappert, *Luther: Letters of Spiritual Counsel*, 87–88.

Here we see that Luther encouraged readers to see themselves in biblical figures, especially afflicted figures. As he wrote to a father grieving the loss of his son, "The Scriptures do not prohibit mourning and grieving over deceased children."[10] In this way, Luther's admonition to capture the "substance" of the scriptural story did not gloss over an individual's pain. He did not advise the afflicted to find their place in the grand narrative— rather, he advised them to find their salve in the way God healed the pain of those found in the sacred text.

Of course, in his reading of either Testament, the crucified and risen Christ stood at the center of Luther's hermeneutic. The centrality of Christ shines brightest when Luther consoles those afflicted by God's wrath. As Luther wrote to a man who had been imprisoned and lost his wife, "What must distress us most is that God himself seems to be smiting us; yet it is from him that all our comfort is to come."[11] Moreover, Luther acknowledges that Christian suffering must look like divine wrath to an unbelieving world: "Thus it appears as if God has now attacked you, and your enemies can boast and say, 'So fare these Christians; this is the reward of your new gospel.' This is more than suffering and dying; it is being buried and descending into hell."[12] In these instances, Luther consoles the afflicted by accentuating the centrality of Christ in the word.[13] For instance, in rebuking a brother's sharp tongue, he wrote:

> Therefore, my dear brother, learn Christ and him crucified. Learn to pray to him and, despairing of yourself, say: "Thou, Lord Jesus, art my righteousness, but I am thy sin. Thou has taken upon thyself what is mine and hast given to me what is thine. Thou has taken upon thyself what thou wast not and hast given to me what I was not."[14] Beware of aspiring to such purity that you will not wish to be looked upon as a sinner, or to be one. For Christ dwells only in sinners. On this account he descended from heaven, where he dwelt

---

10. Tappert, *Luther: Letters of Spiritual Counsel*, 68.
11. Tappert, *Luther: Letters of Spiritual Counsel*, 66.
12. Tappert, *Luther: Letters of Spiritual Counsel*, 66.
13. Tappert, *Luther: Letters of Spiritual Counsel*, 109.
14. Tappert, *Luther: Letters of Spiritual Counsel*, 109.

among the righteous, to dwell among sinners. Meditate on this love
of his and you will see his sweet consolation.[15]

If ever Luther's words consoled those afflicted by fears of divine wrath,
surely the dictum "Christ dwells only in sinners" did just that. One has to
"learn" Christ and him crucified. Such learning takes place when one hears
the word in affliction.

While Luther's consolations through the word are embedded in the
muck and mire of medieval Europe, it turns out that his historical setting and hurts are not the sort of hermeneutical obstruction that some
modern interpreters have railed about.[16] As we near the completion of
the first quarter of the twenty-first century, we find remarkable overlap
between earliest Christianity, Luther's day, our own day, and all the days in
between.[17] That is because, for believers of all eras—including our own—
the Christian experience unfolds between the tension of hope in a crucified and risen Christ on the one hand and a world full of darkness and
divine wrath on the other.[18] It was within this tension that Luther penned
his letters, which are teeming with timely correctives for those who critically engage in biblical interpretation and theological formation today, if
they are willing to hear him.

Martin Luther routinely consoled the afflicted. He consoled bereaved
parents, widows, convalescents, and those engulfed by depression. He
consoled those afflicted by uncertainties about doctrine, faith, forgiveness, the interpretation of Scripture, ecclesiastical practices, marriage,
the politics of the day, and the like. In short, Luther consoled those whose

---

15. Tappert, *Luther: Letters of Spiritual Counsel*, 109.

16. I am thinking here of New Testament scholars such as Krister Stendahl and N. T.
Wright, who have thrived on their criticism of Luther. For a criticism of their criticism, see
Stephen Westerholm, *Pespectives Old and New on Paul: The "Lutheran" Paul and His Critics* (Grand
Rapids: Eerdmans, 2003).

17. Even as I pen this introduction in the spring of 2020, the entire world is gripped by
fear and anxiety over the outbreak of the COVID-19 virus, a virus to which Christians are
obviously not immune. In this way, I am reminded that Luther lived, ministered, and wrote
in a world gripped by fear and anxiety over the plague.

18. As Luther put it in a letter to Justus Jonas (May 15, 1542), "The wrath of God is greater
than even we who are godly readily believe." Yet Luther did not want afflicted Christians to
misunderstand divine wrath in the world. As he wrote to John Reneck, who had recently lost
his wife (April 18, 1536), "Are you afraid, then, that the Lord took your son in wrath? Such an
opinion is not from God." Tappert, *Luther: Letters of Spiritual Counsel*, 50, 69.

bodies, minds, and hearts were racked by pain stemming from a variety of sources. The counsel he offered did not ignore or downplay his recipients' hurt, present them with trite solutions, bombard them with a litany of biblical citations, or drag them through a labyrinth of theological speculation. Instead, Luther leaned into their pain with the acumen of a biblical scholar, the deductive powers of a theologian, the heart of a pastor, and the empathy of one often embroiled in his own *Anfechtung* (agonizing struggle). This Bible professor from Wittenberg chose clarity for the sake of consolation rather than sophistry for the sake of sophistication.[19]

In this way, Luther has something to teach those laboring in the twenty-first century fields of biblical and theological studies. We, of all people, must comfort the afflicted the way that Luther did. Whatever the malady, Luther prescribed the same remedy: the word of God. Luther challenges the academic guild's tendency to speak only to itself, albeit with its historical preciseness, literary ingenuity, and theological profundity. But to what end, to whose benefit, and, above all, to whose consolation? Luther does not bid us to take leave of rigorous academic work, but he does dare us to address more than one another. He reminds us that we are servants of the word, even physicians, who must humble ourselves for the sake of those who suffer from God's hiddenness. We must learn to console others with the word so that they might hear and see God in Christ and Christ in the word. As Luther asserted, "Christ will lead you to the hidden God."[20] May Luther teach those in biblical and theological studies afresh how to lead in this way.

Channing L. Crisler

Domine memento mei

---

19. In reflecting on Luther's attitude toward scholarship, H. G. Haile notes: "To our way of thinking, there is a vast difference between the popular, devotional writing exemplified by *A Simple Way to Pray* and serious scholarship. Luther was not unacquainted with this point of view. He associated it with Scholasticism, which he contemptuously called 'sophistry.' He consciously broke away from this kind of scholarship." H. G. Haile, *Luther: An Experiment in Biography* (New York: Doubleday, 1980), 59.

20. Tappert, *Luther: Letters of Spiritual Counsel*, 133.

1

—

THE PERSPICUITY OF SCRIPTURE ACCORDING TO MARTIN LUTHER

The Early Development of His Doctrine, 1520–1521

Gregg R. Allison[1]

Whereas most treatments of Luther's doctrine focus mostly or exclusively on his articulation and defense of perspicuity in his treatise *On the Bondage of the Will* (1525), this essay focuses on the inchoate development of his view in three prior works (1520-1521): (1) *To the Christian Nobility of the German Nation*, (2) *Answer to the Hyperchristian ... Book by Goat Emser*, and (3) *Confutatio Rationis Latomianae*.[2]

---

1. As a New Testament scholar, Mark Seifrid teaches and writes to assist Christians in their understanding of Scripture, a task not unlike that which his hero, Martin Luther, undertook five hundred years ago. For Luther and Seifrid, the duty to help others interpret the Bible is based on a fundamental truth: as the inspired word of God, Scripture is perspicuous, or clear. In appreciation of the life and career of my friend Mark, I offer this essay on Luther's doctrine of the clarity of Scripture.

The perspicuity of Scripture was one of the doctrines that contributed to the divide between Roman Catholicism and Protestantism at the time of the Reformation. Gerald Bray, *Biblical Interpretation: Past and Present* (Downers Grove, IL: InterVarsity Academic, 1996), 192. Sadly, this doctrine has received only marginal treatment since that time. Contemporary writings on the doctrine include: James Callahan, *The Clarity of Scripture: History, Theology, and Contemporary Issues* (Downers Grove, IL: InterVarsity Press, 2001); Larry D. Pettegrew, "The Perspicuity of Scripture," *The Masters Seminary Journal* 15, no. 2 (Fall 2004): 209-25; Mark D. Thompson, *A Clear and Present Word* (Downers Grove, IL: InterVarsity Press, 2006); Wayne Grudem, "The Perspicuity of Scripture," *Themelios* 34, no. 3 (November 2009): 288-308; and Richard M. Edwards, *Scriptural Perspicuity in the Early English Reformation in Historical Theology*, Studies in Biblical Literature (New York: Peter Lang, 2009).

2. Resources for the study of Luther's doctrine of perspicuity include: Paul Althaus, *The Theology of Martin Luther* (Philadelphia: Fortress, 1966); Cornelius Augustijn, "Hyperaspistes I: La Doctrine d'Erasme et de Luther sur la *'claritas scripturae,'* " in *Colloquia Erasmiana Turonensia*, J.-C. Margolin (Toronto: University of Toronto Press, 1972), 2:737-48; Friedrich Beisser, *Claritas scripturae bei Martin Luther* (Gottingen: Vanderhoeck & Ruprecht, 1966); Ulrich Duchrow,

LUTHER'S VIEW OF PERSPICUITY ACCORDING
TO HIS TREATISE *TO THE CHRISTIAN*
NOBILITY OF THE GERMAN NATION

The year 1520 saw the publication of three momentous works by Luther, the first of which was *To the Christian Nobility of the German Nation*.[3] In this tractate, Luther overthrows three "walls" that had for centuries buttressed the position and power of the Church, and he calls for a reform of the Church by the civil authorities.[4] The first wall was the secular-spiritual divide, which Luther insisted must be torn down. The second wall was the Church's claim that the interpretation of Scripture belongs to the pope, and to the pope alone. The third wall was the pope's claim to possess the sole prerogative to convene a church council, a strategy that Luther favored as a plan to rehabilitate the Church. Our attention will be focused on the second of the three walls torn down by Luther: the Church's claim that the pope alone could interpret Scripture.

Luther affirms that the crucial factor in the correct interpretation of Scripture is not ecclesiastical position but the character of the interpreter. Qualities mentioned by Luther include having a pious heart and being a true or good Christian who has "the true faith, spirit, understanding, word, and mind of Christ."[5] Chief among the characteristics noted by Luther is "possess[ing] the Holy Spirit."[6] Thus, it is not the interpretation of Scripture by the pope, but its interpretation by Christians—even the most

---

"Die Klarheit der Schrift und die Vernunft," *Kerygma und Dogma: Zeitschrift für theologische Forschung und kirchliche Lehre* 15 (1969): 1–17; Rudoph Hermann, *Von der Klarheit der Heiligen Schrift: Untersuchungen und Erörterungen über Luthers Lehre von der Schrift in De servo arbitrio* (Berlin: Evangelische Verlagsanstalt, 1958); Ernst W. Kohls, "Luthers Aussagen über die Mitte, Klarheit und Selbsttätigkeit der Heiligen Schrift," *Luther Jahrbuch* 41 (1973): 46–75; Robert Kolb, Irene Dingel, and L'Ubomír Batka, *The Oxford Handbook of Martin Luther's Theology* (New York: Oxford University Press, 2014); Otto Kuss, "Über die Klarheit der Schrift," *Theologie und Glaube* 60 (1970): 273–321; Mark D. Thompson, *A Sure Ground on Which to Stand* (Eugene, OR: Wipf & Stock, 2004); E. Wolff, "Über 'Klarheit der Schrift,' nach Luthers 'De servo arbitrio,'" *Theologisches Literaturzeitung* 92 (1967): 721–30; A. Skevington Wood, *Luther's Principles of Biblical Interpretation* (London: Tyndale Press, 1960), 17–21.

3. Martin Luther, *To the Christian Nobility of the German Nation*, LW 44:115–217.

4. One should recall that at this historical juncture, only one Church—what today would be called the Roman Catholic Church—existed in the West. It is against this Church that Luther writes.

5. *LW* 44:134–35.

6. *LW* 44:134–35.

insignificant believers—possessing the above listed qualities that should be followed:

> If it were to happen that the pope and his cohorts were wicked and not true Christians, were not taught by God and were without understanding, and at the same time some obscure person had a right understanding, why should the people not follow the obscure man? Has the pope not erred many times? Who would help Christendom when the pope erred if we did not have somebody we could trust more than him, somebody who had the Scriptures on his side? ... The Romanists must admit that there are among us good Christians who have the true faith, spirit, understanding, word, and mind of Christ. Why, then, should we reject the word and understanding of good Christians and follow the pope, who has neither faith nor the Spirit?[7]

Luther also develops the doctrine of the perspicuity of Scripture as foundational for approaching and understanding Scripture. Luther maintains that each and every Christian has the responsibility "to test and judge what is right and wrong in matters of faith" and to ascertain "what is consistent with faith and what is not." This discernment is carried out on the basis of one's "believing understanding of the Scriptures."[8] Scripture itself is clear and understandable: it is fit to be the intelligible standard against which all else is to be measured. Luther maintains that it is the duty for each believer in Jesus Christ, armed with perspicuous Scripture and the proper characteristics, "to espouse the cause of the faith, to understand and defend it, and to denounce every error."[9]

---

7. *LW* 44:135.
8. *LW* 44:135.
9. *LW* 44:136.

LUTHER'S VIEW OF PERSPICUITY
ACCORDING TO *ANSWER TO THE*
HYPERCHRISTIAN ... BOOK BY GOAT EMSER

One of the most substantial critiques of Luther's *To the Christian Nobility of the German Nation* was published in December of 1520. Mockingly entitled *Against the Unchristian Book of the Augustinian Martin Luther, Addressed to the German Nobility*, it was written by Jerome (Hieronymus) Emser (1477-1527). Luther dubbed him "the goat in Leipzig" because Emser's coat of arms—a shield and helmet adorned with a goat—appeared on the title page of his writings. Moreover, he was Luther's former professor, with whom the Reformer had already tussled.[10] This publication sparked Luther to issue a series of four writings against Emser throughout 1521. The longest and most thorough reply to Emser's *Against the Unchristian Book* is entitled *Answer to the Hyperchristian, Hyperspiritual, and Hyperlearned Book by Goat Emser in Leipzig—Including Some Thoughts Regarding His Companion, the Fool Murner.*[11] Two points concerning Luther's view of the perspicuity of Scripture appear

---

10. Emser had instructed the young Luther when Luther was a student at the University of Erfurt. For a discussion, see Ernst Ludwig Enders, *Luther und Emser Ihre Streitschriften aus dem Jahre 1521* (Halle: Druck von Ehrhardt Karras, 1891), 2:179; Martin Brecht, *Martin Luther 1521-1532: Shaping and Defining the Reformation* (Philadelphia: Fortress, 1990). Emser, an observer at the Leipzig debate of 1519, had defended Luther in a letter dated August 13, 1519, against the charges that he had committed the "Hussite heresy." Having read that letter, Luther concluded that Emser was attempting to trick him by placing him on the horns of an unpleasant dilemma. In response, Luther wrote *An Addition to Goat Emser* in September, 1519, accusing the man of deceit and betrayal. Two responses followed: the first, by Johann Maier von Eck (for English purposes, John Eck), came on October 28, 1519, and was entitled *An Answer for Jerome Emser against Luther's Mad Hunt*; the second, by Emser himself, was *An Assertion of the Goat against Luther's Hunt*, which also appeared in the fall of 1519. One year later, Emser wrote his response to Luther's *To the Christian Nobility of the German Nation*. LW 39:107-10.

11. The first of Luther's four writings against Emser, *To the Goat in Leipzig*, came out in January of 1521 and was a short response to only the initial pages of the "in publication" work *Against the Unchristian Book*. A rejoinder by Emser immediately followed: *To the Bull in Wittenberg* (January of 1521). Luther replied with his second brief response, entitled *Concerning the Answer of the Goat in Leipzig* (January or February of 1521). Emser answered this response with a brief *Reply to the Answer of the Raging Bull in Wittenberg*. Finally in possession of the completed publication of *Against the Unchristian Book*, Luther composed the third work against Emser: *Answer to the Hyperchristian ... Book*. To this writing, Emser responded with *Quadrupica to Luther's Recent Answer, Concerning His Reformation*. This long and drawn out battle of words finally wound down with Luther's fourth writing, entitled *Dr. Luther's Refutation of the Error Forced upon Him by the Most Highly Learned Priest of God, Sir Jerome Emser, Vicar in Meissen*. It is a biting, sarcastic reply in which Luther ironically agrees with Emser. The final installment in this feud came with the publication of Emser's *Reservation to Luther's First Retraction*, a work that displayed the author's misunderstanding of Luther's ironical and final reply. *LW* 39:110, 119, 139-41.

in this work: his denial of the need for the Church's clarifying interpretations of Scripture, and his dismissal of multiple meanings of Scripture. Both rejections are grounded on Luther's doctrine of Scripture's clarity.

LUTHER'S REJECTION OF THE CLARIFYING
INTERPRETATIONS OF THE CHURCH

One of Emser's main points in his *Against the Unchristian Book* is that Christians can rely on three weapons in theological sword fighting: (1) the "sword," or Scripture; (2) the "long spear," or tradition and ecclesiastical usage; and (3) the "short dagger," or the interpretations of Scripture by the church fathers. Luther is disturbed by Emser's insistence on this trinity and critiques the implication that Scripture is obscure and therefore stands in need of the Church's clarifying interpretations.

Luther challenges this view of Scripture and hermeneutics with five points. First, it is futile to imagine that something that is more obscure (i.e., the church fathers' interpretations of Scripture) can effectively illuminate something that is already less obscure (i.e., Scripture): "If the Spirit spoke in the fathers, he spoke even more in his own Scripture. And whoever does not understand the Spirit in his own scripture—who will believe that he understands him in the writings of someone else? ... If one does not grasp it [Scripture] as it is by itself, but rather through human words and glosses, it will soon be blunt and more obscure than before."[12] Luther ties the inspiration of Scripture by the Holy Spirit to its clarity. He then draws the corollary that if the Spirit has communicated clearly in his Scripture, even if one grants the Spirit's work in the interpretations (the "human words and glosses") of the church fathers, the church fathers' interpretations are still less clear than Scripture. Logically, then, if one interprets Scripture by the church fathers, the result can only be that Scripture ends up being more obscure than it was at the outset.

Second, the church fathers themselves operated on the principle that "Scripture without any glosses is the sun and the whole light from which all teachers receive their light, and not vice versa."[13] Thus, the church fathers themselves acknowledged the relative obscurity of their own teaching in

---

12. *LW* 39:164.
13. *LW* 39:164.

comparison with Scripture itself: "This can be seen from the following: when the fathers teach something, they do not trust their own teaching. They are afraid it is too obscure and too uncertain; they run to Scripture and take a clear passage from it to illumine their own point."[14]

Third, the church fathers themselves acknowledged the relative obscurity of their own biblical interpretations in relation to Scripture itself, as demonstrated by their exercise of the principle of the *analogia fidei*: "In the same way, when they interpret a passage in Scripture they do not do so with their own sense or words (for whenever they do that, as often happens, they generally err). Instead, they add another passage which is clearer and thus illumine and interpret Scripture with Scripture."[15] Thus, it is wrong, concludes Luther, "to attribute to the fathers the light with which to illumine Scripture," for this is contrary to the attitude of the church fathers themselves, who "confess their own obscurity and only illumine Scripture with Scripture."[16]

Fourth, one application of the Pauline command to "test every doctrine and hold fast to what is good" (1 Thess 5:21) is that the church fathers' teachings should be evaluated. If this is so—and Luther places himself in opposition to both Emser and Eck on this point[17]—then there is an important implication for the clarity of Scripture: "If, however, we should test them, as St. Paul says here, what kind of touchstone should we use other than Scripture? It must really be clearer and more certain than the fathers' teaching, for how else could we use it as a test to judge what is right or wrong?"[18]

Fifth, Luther appeals to Aristotle who, through the writings of Thomas Aquinas, had become an important voice in Catholic theology and practice:

---

14. *LW* 39:164.

15. *LW* 39:164.

16. *LW* 39:164. Indeed, the "best father" is the one who correctly "gather[s] Scripture." Thus, "One should read the books of all the fathers with caution, not believing them but rather watching out whether they cite also clear passages and illumine Scripture with clear Scripture" (*LW* 39:165). This practice is supported by no less a figure than Augustine: "St. Augustine did the same thing, and writes that he would believe no teacher, no matter how godly and learned he might be, unless he proved his teaching with Scripture or clear reason. From this we learn how the fathers should be read, namely, that we should not consider what they say but whether they use clear Scripture or reason" (*LW* 39:166).

17. At the Leipzig debate of 1519, Eck disagreed with Luther on this matter (*LW* 39:165).

18. *LW* 39:165.

Aristotle had written—and nature, without Aristotle, also teaches it to the peasants—that one cannot prove something obscure and uncertain with something obscure and uncertain, even less, light with darkness. Instead, whatever is obscure and uncertain must be illumined with something clear and certain. Since, then, all the fathers prove their point with Scripture, it is incredible that they could have been so mad and nonsensical (as follows from Emser's philosophy and short dagger [the interpretation of Scripture by the church fathers]) as to consider Scripture an obscure fog (as Emser scolds and blasphemes) with which they clarified and illumined their teaching. Rather, they most certainly considered Scripture the principal light and the greatest clarity and certainty, to which they appealed and upon which they relied as upon the most obvious and the clearest teaching to judge and to test all teaching.[19]

Aristotelian logic undermines Emser's hermeneutical position.

Luther extensively argues against the position that Scripture is obscure and therefore stands in need of the clarifying interpretations of the church fathers.

LUTHER'S REJECTION OF MULTIPLE MEANINGS OF SCRIPTURE

Luther also critiques the notion that Scripture has a twofold or fourfold meaning.[20] These expressions are used interchangeably. The expression "twofold" refers to the distinction between the literal and the spiritual meanings of Scripture, and the expression "fourfold" refers to the literal, allegorical, anagogical, and tropological senses. (These last three are simply the three divisions of the spiritual meaning employed in the twofold scheme of classification.) This hermeneutic was a cornerstone of scholastic theology, and Emser promoted it with appeals to 2 Corinthians 3:6 ("the letter kills, but the Spirit gives life") for scriptural warrant, and to Origen, Dionysius, and others for support from Church tradition. Luther's objections to this multiple-sense hermeneutic are as follows.

---

19. *LW* 39:166. Aristotle discusses this principle in *Prior Analytics* (2:16) and *Topics* (5:2).

20. For discussion of the historical development of the multiple senses of Scripture in the Church, see Gregg R. Allison, *Historical Theology: An Introduction to Christian Doctrine* (Grand Rapids: Zondervan, 2011), 162–84.

As a starting point, such an interpretative scheme wreaks havoc with Scripture itself. Luther demonstrates the absurdity of the position with respect to Galatians 4:22–24 and Romans 7:7 and 14.[21]

Additionally, Scripture would be rendered null and void without the "literal" meaning, but it survives fine without the "spiritual" sense. Luther affirms that the "literal" understanding is "the highest, best, strongest, in short, the whole substance, nature and foundation of Scripture. If one abandoned it, the whole Scripture would be nothing."[22]

Luther offers two reasons for this insistence on the "literal" sense of Scripture. The first has to do with the Holy Spirit's inspiration of Scripture: "The Holy Spirit is the simplest writer and adviser in heaven and on earth. That is why his words could have no more than the one simplest meaning which we call the written one, or the literal meaning of the tongue."[23] The second reason goes to the very nature and logic of effective communication itself: "But [written] words and [spoken] language cease to have meaning when the things which have a simple meaning through interpretation by a simple word are given further meanings and thus become different things [through a different interpretation] so that one thing takes on the meaning of another."[24]

Luther nuances his position in two important ways. With a nod to Aquinas (who maintained that God signifies meaning by both the *verba* [words] of Scripture—this is its "literal" sense—and by the *res* [things] of Scripture—this is its "spiritual" sense),[25] Luther specifies the following:

> Even though the things described in Scripture mean something further, Scripture should not therefore have a twofold meaning. Instead, it should retain the one meaning to which the words refer. Beyond that we should give idle spirits permission to hunt and seek the manifold interpretations of the things indicated besides the words. But they should beware of losing themselves in the hunt or the climb, as happens to those who climb after chamois [goat-like

21. *LW* 39:176–77
22. *LW* 39:177.
23. *LW* 39:178.
24. *LW* 39:178.
25. Thomas Aquinas, *Summa Theologica*, 1.1.10.

bovids], and as also happened to Origen. It is much more certain and much safer to stay with the words and the simple meaning, for this is the true pasture and home of all the spirits.[26]

A further nuance has to do with the distinction between figurative language found in Scripture and the spiritual or figurative interpretation of Scripture. Figurative language is a linguistic phenomenon and is commonly found in Scripture (e.g., Jesus identifies himself as "the door" and as "the vine"; John 10:7, 9; 15:1). A literal understanding of such figures of speech is not to be confused with a wooden, literalistic interpretation, but refers instead to an appreciation for the author's intent that is "dress[ed] up" in "flowery" speech; as Luther argues, even "boys in school" are taught how to understand figurative language, and thus it should not prove to be a stumbling block to literal interpretation.[27] It is not against figurative language, but rather figurative interpretation, that Luther dissents, noting that there is no scriptural support for such a hermeneutic. Thus, Luther rejects the spiritual meaning of Scripture; he argues that there is no basis for a twofold or fourfold sense of Scripture. There is only one sense: the literal meaning or, as Luther prefers, the "grammatical, historical meaning."[28]

Luther affirms the perspicuity of Scripture over against the church fathers. Their interpretations are obscure, relatively speaking, in comparison with Scripture and thus cannot be used to shed a clarifying light on the word of God. Also, the Reformer expends great effort to overthrow the scholastic hermeneutical system of multiple senses of Scripture, arguing instead that there is one, and only one, meaning of Scripture: the simple, plain, natural, literal or "grammatical, historical" meaning.

---

26. *LW* 39:179.

27. Luther supplies a pointed and uncomplimentary illustration of the difference between a wooden, literalistic interpretation of a figure of speech and a literal understanding of the same: "For example if I said, 'Emser is a crude ass,' and a simple man following the words understood Emser to be a real ass with long ears and four feet, he would be deceived by the letter, since through such veiled words I wanted to indicate that he had a crude and unreasonable mind." *LW* 39:180.

28. *LW* 39:181.

LUTHER'S VIEW OF PERSPICUITY
ACCORDING TO *AGAINST LATOMUS*

In similar fashion, Luther responded to Jacob Latomus, a professor of theology at the University of Louvain. The theologians at this institution were some of the first to attack Luther, condemning him in 1519 (*Facultatis theologiae Lovaniensis doctrinalis condemnatio Martini Lutheri*). Following a response by Luther in March of 1520 (*Responsio Lutheriana ad condemnationem doctrinalem per magistros nostros Lovaniensis et Coloniensis*), Latomus defended the university's condemnation of the Reformer in *Articulorum doctrinae fratris M. Lutheri per theologo Lovaniensis damnatorum ratio ex sacris literis et veteribus tractoribus* (1521). This writing reached Luther in March of 1521 while he was sequestered at the Wartburg. Disturbed by the interruption that it caused in his translation of the Bible, Luther nonetheless responded to Latomus's arguments with *Against Latomus*.[29] Although this response focuses on the issues of sin and grace, law and gospel, justification and sanctification, and the like, Luther also sets forth some ideas regarding the clarity of Scripture. It is those that interest us now.

Against Latomus's recasting of the Pauline concept of sin in Romans 6 in terms of weakness, penalty, and things pertaining to human mortality, Luther underscores the perspicuity of Scripture: "Nevertheless it is stupid of us to labor with so many words over such obvious things when we have the Apostle asserting sin and evil passion with such clear and distinct words. Who, if he is not satisfied with Paul's words, would be persuaded by ours?"[30] Against Latomus's appeal to the church fathers as support for his position, Luther argues: "[On the one hand] even if the fathers appear to favor them [Latomus and the other theologians of Louvain], we must not adhere to them but rather to Paul; and if, [on the other hand,] they spoke the truth, [we still must adhere to Paul] because they speak more obscurely and less forcefully than he does. Paul's words are too clear to need any gloss; indeed, interpretation rather obscures them."[31] As he does in his reply to Emser, Luther also underscores the violation of an Aristotelian principle in Latomus's appeal to the Fathers:

---

29. *LW* 32:135–36.
30. *LW* 32:214.
31. *LW* 32:215.

Consequently I might say this to our sophists who fight against me with the statements of the fathers: You discuss and demonstrate the clearest of divine matters with what is human and obscure. Therefore, since even your Aristotle forbids the demonstration of the unknown through the unknown, the obscure through the obscure—much less the manifest through the obscure—I conclude that you are clumsy disputants who constantly and in everything beg the question.[32]

Luther anticipates a number of objections to his rebuff of the church fathers and responds by means of pointed questions. To the charge that he does not believe the church fathers, he asks: "Should I believe? Who has commanded that I believe them? Where is the precept of God regarding such belief?"[33] To the rejoinder that the church fathers were holy men who illumined Scripture by their interpretations, Luther queries: "Who has shown that they made the Scriptures clearer—what if they obscured them? By whose pronouncement do you prove that they threw light on Holy Writ?"[34] With an appeal to 1 Thessalonians 5:21 ("Test everything; hold fast to what is good"), Luther insists that "the fathers are to be tested by the judgment of the divine Scriptures so that it may be known who has clarified and who has obscured them."[35] Luther's reasoning is that the Scriptures, not the church fathers, are perspicuous. In a concluding comment, he rejects the church fathers' clarification of the Scriptures and affirms the Scriptures' perspicuity: "Miserable Christians, whose words and faith still depend on the interpretations of men and who expect clarification from them! This is frivolous and ungodly. The Scriptures are common to all, and are clear enough in respect to what is necessary for salvation, and are also obscure enough for inquiring minds."[36]

Luther also turns to a discussion of the use of dogmatic terminology (e.g., *homoousion*) employed in the Church's creeds. Luther expresses a certain reluctance about the use of such words—not because he denies

---

32. *LW* 32:215.
33. *LW* 32:216.
34. *LW* 32:217.
35. *LW* 32:217.
36. *LW* 32:217.

the creeds or their contents, but because these theological terms are not derived from Scripture itself. His caution with regard to such terms reflects his view of the clarity of Scripture as opposed to the obscurity of human formulations:

> The integrity of Scripture must be guarded, and a man ought not to presume that he speaks more safely and clearly with his mouth than God spoke with his mouth. He who does not understand the Word of God when it speaks of the things of God, ought not believe that he understands the word of a man speaking of things strange to him. No one speaks better than he who understands; but who understands the things of God better than God himself? Indeed, how much does a man really understand of the things of God?[37]

Thus, Luther maintains the perspicuity of Scripture over the obscurity of human words because the one who communicates through Scripture understands himself better than any human being does. Accordingly, God is able to communicate clearly those things that he reveals about himself.

CONCLUSION

Building on this early articulation and defense of the perspicuity of Scripture, Luther will compose what is generally considered to be the centerpiece of his doctrine in his 1525 treatise *On the Bondage of the Will*.[38] In that work, he affirms a twofold perspicuity: an external and an internal.[39] With regard to the external clarity of Scripture, "pertaining to the ministry of the Word"—that is, to Scripture as it is taught and proclaimed—Luther maintains that "nothing at all is left obscure or ambiguous, but everything there is in the Scriptures has been brought out through the Word into the

---

37. *LW* 32:244.

38. Martin Luther, *On the Bondage of the Will*, in *Luther and Erasmus: Free Will and Salvation*, Library of Christian Classics 17 (Philadelphia: Westminster Press, 1969), 101–334.

39. This internal clarity of Scripture, which this essay will not treat, is Luther's focus on "the understanding of the heart," or the readers/hearers of Scripture. Because of the darkness of the heart of every reader/hearer, Luther emphasizes the necessity of the illumination of the Holy Spirit for the understanding of Scripture: "If you speak of the *internal* clarity, no man perceives one iota of what is in the Scriptures unless he has the Spirit of God. ... For the Spirit is required for the understanding of Scripture, both as a whole and in any part of it." *On the Bondage of the Will*, 112.

most definite light, and published to all the world."[40] He further avers that "it ought above all to be settled and established among Christians that the Holy Scriptures are a spiritual light far brighter than the sun itself, especially in things that are necessary to salvation."[41]

Though the doctrine of the perspicuity of Scripture is axiomatic for Luther—thus, from a philosophical standpoint, this "first principle of ours" does not and cannot require proof—he offers support for it because of the calumny of his opponents.[42] This support includes biblical passages that associate Scripture with light and enlightenment (e.g., Pss 19:8; 119:105, 130; 2 Pet 1:19), the apostles' appeal to Scripture as proof of their preaching, Christ's own urging to "search the Scriptures" (John 5:39), and the example of the Bereans (Acts 17:11), as well as theological and philosophical warrant. Moreover, Luther anticipates possible objections to his presentation of Scripture's clarity and offers rejoinders.

Accordingly, Luther championed the doctrine of the perspicuity of Scripture. Other Reformers followed him—for example, Huldrych Zwingli and John Calvin[43]—thereby fixing this doctrine as a major point of division between Catholicism and Protestantism. Following the lead of Martin Luther who, as one of the Protestants championing this doctrine, developed it during the early years of the Reformation, may we eagerly read, study, memorize, and meditate upon Scripture with the expectation that we will be able to understand and apply it because it is the perspicuous word of God.

---

40. *On the Bondage of the Will*, 112.

41. *On the Bondage of the Will*, 159.

42. *On the Bondage of the Will*, 159.

43. Huldrych Zwingli, *Of the Clarity and Certainty of the Word of God*, in *Zwingli and Bullinger*, Library of Christian Classics 24 (Philadelphia: Westminster Press, 1953), 59–95; John Calvin, *Institutes of the Christian Religion*, Library of Christian Classics 20–21 (Philadelphia: Westminster Press, 1960); John Calvin, *Calvin: Commentaries* Library of Christian Classics 22 (Philadelphia: Westminster Press, 1958).

2

—

CONTRA ORIGEN

Martin Luther on Allegorizing the Biblical Text

Robert L. Plummer

In recent years, several prominent biblical scholars have promoted the practice of allegorical exegesis, often citing Origen as an inspiring model of the art.[1] The purpose of this essay is to ask how Martin Luther would assess this recent trend. How would the Reformer's statements about allegorical interpretation and his personal exegetical practices help us evaluate the recent reappearance of allegory within the scholarly guild? We will begin by surveying contemporary academic voices advocating allegory. We will then attempt to understand Luther's complex and seemingly contradictory approach to allegorical interpretation with the goal of informing the hermeneutical discussions of our day.[2]

THE RECENT SHIFTING TASTE FOR ALLEGORY

Four decades ago, pro-allegorical interpretive rivulets began to trickle into the hinterland of the academy. One of the most significant streams of thought was David C. Steinmetz's seminal article in *Theology Today* entitled "The Superiority of Pre-Critical Exegesis." If the title is not sufficient

---

1. E.g., Peter J. Leithart, *Deep Exegesis: The Mystery of Reading Scripture* (Baylor: Baylor University Press, 2009); Hans Boersma, *Scripture as Real Presence: Sacramental Exegesis in the Early Church* (Grand Rapids: Baker Academic, 2017); Keith D. Stanglin, *The Letter and Spirit of Biblical Interpretation: From the Early Church to Modern Practice* (Grand Rapids: Baker Academic, 2018). See also the introduction by the translator in Origen, *On First Principles: A Reader's Edition*, trans. John Behr, Oxford Early Christian Texts (Oxford: Oxford University Press, 2020).

2. On the topic of Martin Luther as a guide for modern-day biblical faithfulness, I can think of no greater living example than Mark Seifrid. It is fitting, then, to offer this essay as a token of appreciation to my former doctoral supervisor, my colleague, and my beloved friend. I am so grateful for Mark and Janice Seifrid and their influence on my life.

to clue you in to the author's meaning, the concluding summary of the work leaves no ambiguity:

> The medieval theory of levels of meaning in the biblical text, with all its undoubted defects, flourished because it is true, while the modern theory of single meaning, with all its demonstrable virtues, is false. Until the historical-critical method becomes critical of its own theoretical foundations and develops a hermeneutical theory adequate to the nature of the text which it is interpreting, it will remain restricted—as it deserves to be—to the guild and the academy, where the question of truth can be endlessly deferred.[3]

Disaffection with the sterile and often ostensibly irrelevant detailed studies produced by modern-day biblical scholars strengthened in the 1990s and coalesced into a broad movement that came to be called "The Theological Interpretation of Scripture" (TIS) movement. Self-identified practitioners of TIS are both conservative and liberal Protestants, as well as Catholics. Yet the group loosely shares some characteristics:[4]

(1) Practitioners of TIS are generally disillusioned with the historical-critical method and traditional author-oriented principles of interpretation. To recent scholarly work on the Bible, TIS advocates would give two assessments: "Not enough" (by leaving theology in the cerebral realm), and "Not faithful to the nature of Scripture and our identity as Christians" (by not reading as followers of Jesus who encounter God in the words of the Bible).[5]

---

3. David C. Steinmetz, "The Superiority of Pre-Critical Exegesis," in *The Theological Interpretation of Scripture: Classic and Contemporary Readings*, ed. Stephen E. Fowl, Blackwell Readings in Modern Theology (Oxford, UK: Blackwell, 1997), 37. The essay originally appeared in *Theology Today* 37, no. 1 (1980): 27–38.

4. The list below is an edited and condensed version of my reflections on TIS from my book *40 Questions about Interpreting the Bible* (Grand Rapids: Kregel, 2010), 313–20. See also Brian C. Collins's revised (2012) PhD dissertation for a more detailed description and assessment of the TIS movement ("Scripture, Hermeneutics, and Theology: Evaluating the Theological Interpretation of Scripture," available at www.exegesisandtheology.com).

5. Kevin J. Vanhoozer, "Imprisoned or Free? Text, Status, and Theological Interpretation in the Master/Slave Discourse of Philemon," in *Reading Scripture with the Church: Toward a Hermeneutic for Theological Interpretation*, ed. A. K. M. Adam, Stephen E. Fowl, Kevin J. Vanhoozer, and Francis Watson (Grand Rapids: Baker, 2006), 92. Similarly, Joel B. Green

(2) Practitioners of TIS respect external theological parameters as
     guides for interpretation. If one writes in and for the church,
     it is legitimate to be bound by ecclesiastical confessions, argue
     TIS authors. For example, one can unashamedly appeal to the
     "rule of faith" as a prism for one's interpretation. The "rule of
     faith" (or *regula fidei*) is the "oldest term used by the Ante-
     Nicene fathers, Ignatius, Polycarp, and in particular Irenaeus
     and Tertullian, to refer to the sum content of the apostolic
     teaching."[6] One can also legitimately appeal to creeds, con-
     fessions, and the contours of the Christian canon.[7]

(3) Practitioners of TIS look to the early church fathers and medi-
     eval exegetes as helpful hermeneutical tutors.[8]

The appropriation of the early and medieval fathers' exegetical methods is most relevant to our current discussion. Within the TIS movement,
numerous scholars have advocated a return to the church fathers' allegory as a Christ-centered and spiritually-enriching method of reading and
expositing the Scriptures. For example, Peter J. Leithart, in his 2009 book
Deep Exegesis: The Mystery of Reading Scripture, writes:

---

favors "interpretive practices oriented toward shaping and nurturing the faith and life of
God's people"; Joel B. Green, *Seized by Truth: Reading the Bible as Scripture* (Nashville: Abingdon,
2007), 79.

    6. Kathryn Greene-McCreight, "Rule of Faith," in *Dictionary for Theological Interpretation
of the Bible*, ed. Kevin J. Vanhoozer (Grand Rapids: Baker; London: SPCK, 2005), 703.

    7. Daniel Treier's description of the Brazos Theological Commentary on the Bible series
illustrates the TIS commitment to doctrinal parameters: "The series 'presupposes that the
doctrinal tradition of the church can serve as a living and reliable basis for exegesis.' This tradition, more specifically, is that doctrine surrounding the Nicene Creed. The series promotes
'intratextual analysis' as its key 'method,' along with drawing upon 'the liturgical practices
and spiritual disciplines of the church as a secondary dimension of the canonical context
for exegesis of scriptural texts.' Such an approach can lead to various senses of Scripture,
including 'allegorical' readings, and requires that contributors engage the history of exegesis, not in order to provide readers with a summary of past interpretation, but in order to
shape exegetical judgments in conversation with the tradition.' " Daniel J. Treier, *Introducing
Theological Interpretation of Scripture: Recovering a Christian Practice* (Grand Rapids: Baker,
2008), 40. The quotations within Treier's remarks are from an undated Brazos document
describing the purpose of the series to contributors.

    8. In recent years, one can point to both popular and scholarly fascination with the early
church (e.g., Brian D. McLaren, *Finding Our Way Again: The Return of the Ancient Practices*
[Nashville: Thomas Nelson, 2008]; The Ancient Christian Commentary on Scripture Series
[IVP Academic]).

The hermeneutical method offered here is very similar to the four-fold method developed by medieval Bible teachers. For the medievals, the literal sense of the text opened out into a christological allegory, which, because Christ is the head of his body, opened out into tropological instruction and, because Christ is King of a kingdom here yet also coming, into anagogical hope.[9]

More recently, Hans Boersma, in his 2017 book *Scripture as Real Presence: Sacramental Exegesis in the Early Church*, repeatedly praises Origen's hermeneutical brilliance and modern-day relevance. In reference to the writings of Origen and other church fathers, he writes, "It is this same sacramental sensibility that still has the vitality to renew the life of the church today."[10] Boersma, for example, suggests that Origen's allegorical interpretation of Joshua 9 provides a solution to the morally objectionable report that Israel enslaved the Gibeonites. Boersma writes,

> Modern exegetes who advocate a strictly literal reading of the text are faced with a stark choice: to justify the violence inherent in the Old Testament or to abandon the Old Testament as Christian Scripture. Since either option seems to me detrimental to the church, I suggest that a serious look at the third-century exegesis of Origen is well worth our while.[11]

The hermeneutical rivulets of Steinmetz and the interpretive streams of his followers have now coalesced into a mighty allegorical river (*fluvius*

---

9. Leithart, *Deep Exegesis*, 207. Similarly, see Stephen E. Fowl, "The Importance of a Multivoiced Literal Sense of Scripture: The Example of Thomas Aquinas," in *Reading Scripture with the Church: Toward a Hermeneutic for Theological Interpretation*, ed. A. K. M. Adam, Stephen E. Fowl, Kevin J. Vanhoozer, and Francis Watson (Grand Rapids: Baker, 2006), 35–50; R. R. Reno, "'You Who Were Far Off Have Been Brought Near': Reflections on Theological Exegesis," *Ex Auditu* 16 (2000): 169–82.

10. Boersma, *Scripture as Real Presence*, 279.

11. Boersma, *Scripture as Real Presence*, 111. Boersma notes, "[Origen] ... provides a spiritual interpretation of the Gibeonites' identity as people who go through all the right motions in church while making no effort to restrain their vices and to cultivate virtuous habits" (110). See, similarly, Keith D. Stanglin, *The Letter and Spirit of Biblical Interpretation*, 170–71. Craig A. Carter offers a more nuanced approach, looking to Calvin as a key interpretive model. Carter confesses, "I am probably more enthusiastic about the Fathers than [D. A.] Carson is, although I might be slightly less enthusiastic about them than Boersma is" (*Interpreting Scripture with the Great Tradition: Recovering the Genius of Premodern Exegesis* [Grand Rapids: Baker Academic, 2018], 207).

allegoricus), which threatens to erode the dominant evangelical approach to hermeneutics—one that looks to the biblical author's consciously-intended meaning as a touchstone of hermeneutical faithfulness.[12] Iain Provan, in his insightful *The Reformation and the Right Reading of Scripture*, has responded to this rapid hermeneutical climate change.[13] Yet, in recent years, the number of significant academic publications advocating allegorical exegesis have far exceeded those answering the trend.

LUTHER ON ALLEGORY

We turn now in the next section of this essay to consider what Luther says about allegory. If the Reformer were alive today and fully informed of the current hermeneutical discussion, what would he say? How does Luther's own wrestling with the early church fathers and their allegorical methods inform our situation?

As we launch this historical inquiry, it is important to register a caveat. Luther wrote much over many years. He developed his own thought. He was provocative. It's possible that he was inconsistent. One could supply a sentence from Luther that could be used to support almost any modern-day theological, ethical, or hermeneutical position. There is always a danger of reading one's views back into historical figures, but this is especially true of Luther. For example, in comparing Frederic Farrar's Oxford lectures on biblical interpretation (1885) and Robert Kolb's more recent treatment of Luther's approach to Scripture (2017), one finds that they reach contradictory views. Perhaps not surprisingly, in both cases, their concluding assessments are in continuity with their respective theological commitments. Farrar confidently affirms that Luther was not so small-minded as to get hung up on the infallibility of the biblical text.[14] On the other hand,

---

12. For a passionate defense of the human author's conscious intent as the touchstone of hermeneutics, see E. D. Hirsch Jr., *Validity in Interpretation* (New Haven: Yale University Press, 1967).

13. Iain Provan, *The Reformation and the Right Reading of Scripture* (Baylor: Baylor University Press, 2017).

14. Farrar recognizes some inconsistency in Luther's statements, but the Cambridge don is eager to side with Luther's comments that imply contradiction in the Bible. He apparently sees such high-mindedness as a model for his own day: "'When a contradiction occurs in Holy Scripture,' [Luther] says, 'so let it go.' … Some of these views were doubtless rash; they were caused by an almost inevitable deficiency in the nascent science of Biblical criticism; nor did he desire to press them upon others. And yet it would have been well for the peace

Kolb, professor of exegetical theology at Concordia Theological Seminary (St. Louis), cites many examples of Luther's reverence for the "flawless" and authoritative word of God.[15] So, as we turn to Luther's view of allegory, we need to be especially cautious about the problem of "confirmation bias."

---

of Christendom, it would have robbed many controversies, even in our own lifetime, of their miserable bitterness, if Christians had acquired the strong spiritual confidence which enabled Luther to seize essentials without being troubled by minor details. 'The eagle that soars near the sun does not worry itself how to cross the rivers' " (Frederic W. Farrar, *History of Interpretation: Eight Lectures Preached Before the University of Oxford in the Year MDCCCLXXXV* [London: Macmillan, 1886], 337). Roland Bainton seems to follow Farrar here, though he does not cite him: "[Luther] did not attempt any minor harmonization of discrepancies because trivial errors gave him no concern. If on occasion he could speak of every iota of Holy Writ as sacred, at other times he displayed blithe indifference to minor blemishes, such as an error in quotation from the Old Testament in the New Testament. The Bible for him was not strictly identical with the Word of God. God's Word is the work of redemption in Christ which became concrete in Scripture as God in Christ became incarnate in the flesh; and as Christ by the incarnation was not denuded of human characteristics, so the Scripture as the medium of the Word was not divested of human limitations" (Roland H. Bainton, *Here I Stand: A Life of Martin Luther* [reprint; Peabody, MA: Hendrickson, 2011], 340–41; cf. Farrar, 336–38). Bainton also affirms the "canon within a canon" idea espoused by Farrar: "[Luther's approach to the canon] was a hierarchy of values within the New Testament. First Luther would place the Gospel of John, then the Pauline epistles and First Peter, after them the three other Gospels, and in a subordinate place Hebrews, James, Jude, and Revelation. He mistrusted Revelation because of its obscurity. 'A revelation,' he said, 'should be revealing' " (Bainton, 341; cf. Farrar, 336). Timothy J. Wengert also enlists Luther against inerrancy, writing, "In contrast to a (nonbiblical) insistence on an 'inerrant and infallible' text, Luther's treatment of the book of James, clouded by centuries of misconstrual, may help guide us to hear anew the authoritative center of Scripture as Luther experienced it: '*Was Christum triebet*' (what pushes Christ). This interpretive key to Scripture, best summarized by the phrase *solus Christus* (Christ alone), contrasts with Luther's reticence concerning and occasional rejection of the phrase *sola Scriptura* (Scripture alone), which some later Christians invoked to support more literalistic approaches to Scripture" (*Reading the Bible with Luther: An Introductory Guide* [Grand Rapids: Baker Academic, 2013], vii). Roy A. Harrisville and Walter Sundberg wrongly wrest a rhetorically-charged and humorous comment by Luther from its context and compare it to later post-Enlightenment rejections of Scripture on the basis of reason or personal preference (*The Bible in Modern Culture: Theology and Historical-Critical Method from Spinoza to Käsemann* [Grand Rapids: Eerdmans, 1995], 15–16; cf. LW 41:28).

15. Erik Herrmann, "Luther's Absorption of Medieval Biblical Interpretation and His Use of the Church Fathers," in The *Oxford Handbook of Martin Luther's Theology*, eds. Robert Kolb, Irene Dingel, and L'Ubomír Batka (Oxford: Oxford University Press, 2014), 71–90; Robert Kolb and Carl R. Trueman, *Between Wittenberg and Geneva: Lutheran and Reformed Theology in Conversation* (Grand Rapids: Baker Academic, 2017). See especially Kolb's quotes and summaries of Luther's approach to the Bible on pages 5–15. I am self-aware enough to know that I am also a member of Kolb's interpretive camp. I confess that I would find it disappointing if Luther denied the inerrancy of Scripture. Yet, after revisiting many of Luther's own statements, I'm also convinced that Kolb is fundamentally correct. John Woodbridge quotes Luther on inerrancy: "It is impossible that Scripture should contradict itself; it only appears so to the senseless and obstinate hypocrites" (John D. Woodbridge, *Biblical Authority: Infallibility and Inerrancy in the Christian Tradition* [Grand Rapids: Zondervan, 2015], 53).

There can be little doubt as to what Luther thought of the allegory of Origen, Jerome, and many other church fathers. He repeatedly blasts their allegorical exegesis as unfaithful twisting of Scripture.[16] Farrar offers a nice medley of the Reformer's excoriations:

> An interpreter ... must as much as possible avoid allegory, that he may not wander in idle dreams. ... Origen's allegories are not worth so much dirt. ... Allegories are empty speculations, and as it were the scum of Holy Scripture. ... Allegory is a sort of beautiful harlot, who proves herself specially seductive to idle men. ... To allegorise is to juggle with Scripture. Allegorising may degenerate into a mere monkey-game. Allegories are awkward, absurd, invented, obsolete, loose rags.[17]

For a more extended example of his rejection of allegory, consider Luther's lectures on Deuteronomy (delivered 1523–1525), where he writes,

> This admonition I have often given elsewhere I repeat here and shall give again: that the Christian reader should make it his first task to seek out the literal sense, as they call it. For it alone is the whole substance of faith and Christian theology; it alone holds its ground in trouble and trial, conquers the gates of hell (Matt. 16:18) together with sin and death, and triumphs for the praise and glory of God. Allegory, however, is too often uncertain, and is unreliable and by

---

16. William Baird states, "More significant than texts and tools of exegesis was the development of the Reformation hermeneutic. For the reformers, the biblical text had essentially one meaning—the literal. Allegorical interpretation was only allowed when the biblical author intended it. The medieval notion of the four senses was attacked as both wrong and dangerous. According to Luther, heresies had been fostered by the failure to follow the simple, literal meaning of the text. The Bible, as word of God, had a unified message; thus Scripture was to be interpreted by Scripture: *scriptura scripturae interpres*" (*History of New Testament Research: From Deism to Tübingen*, vol 1 [Minneapolis: Fortress, 1992], xvii). Harrisville and Sundberg observe, "The artificial medieval system of allegorization, with its four senses of literal, allegorical, anagogical, and tropical [tropological] interpretation, was largely although not entirely abandoned by Luther in favor of the right of the biblical text, literally interpreted, to speak for itself" (17). Jerry K Robbins writes, "Luther believes that we should always seek the plain, historical sense of the text. In discussing the days of creation, for example, Luther rejects Augustine's allegorical method in favor of a literal reading of Moses, who 'calls a spade a spade' " (*The Essential Luther: A Reader on Scripture, Redemption, and Society* [Grand Rapids: Baker, 1990], 19).

17. Farrar, *History of Interpretation*, 328. Most of these quotes are drawn from Luther's lectures on Genesis. See Farrar, *History of Interpretation*, 328n3.

no means safe for supporting faith. Too frequently it depends on human guesswork and opinion, and if one leans on it, one will lean on a staff of Egyptian reed (Ezek. 29:6). Therefore we should beware of Jerome, Origen, and similar fathers or read them with independent judgment. Yes, we should beware of that whole Alexandrian school, which the Jew Philo extols, according to the testimony of Eusebius and Jerome, for having once excelled in the pursuit of such allegorical interpretation. For later writers unhappily imitated their example, which was adopted with excessive praise. They constructed and taught arbitrarily from Scripture according to their liking, until some shaped the words of God into the most absurd monstrosities; and, as Jerome also complains about his own time, they drag Scripture into contradiction with itself by citing proofs that do not apply, a crime of which he himself was also guilty.[18]

In light of the Reformer's strong words, it is ironic that we find many examples of allegory in Luther's own exegesis.[19] In the published preface to the same lectures on Deuteronomy (just cited above) where Luther condemns allegory, he notes, "I have added brief allegories, almost for every chapter." For example, after giving a factual recounting of the golden calf incident described by Moses in Deuteronomy 9, Luther provides these allegorical reflections:

> The calf made of gold is the doctrine of works, which is a perversion of the words and the Law of Scripture, a distortion carried out through the ministry and artifice of priests, who ought to lead the

---

18. *LW* 9:24–25.

19. Harrisville and Sundberg note: "Calvin is one with Luther in affirming the right of Scripture to interpret itself over against the ecclesiastical ideology of allegorical exegesis. Indeed, if anything, Calvin is more disciplined than Luther in his rejection of allegory. Whereas Luther allows allegory insofar as it 'embellishes and illustrates [the historical sense] as a witness' [*LW* 6:125], Calvin admonishes the biblical expositor that 'there is nothing more profitable than to adhere strictly to the natural treatment of things' " (19). Jerry K. Robbins remarks, "Although Luther rejects the fourfold method of interpretation, he cannot completely exorcise it from his thinking. He frequently allegorizes and spiritualizes the text: the creation of heaven is a sign of eternal life; the fact that we are made in the image of God is a promise of the incarnation; and the creation of woman is evidence of the establishment of the household. Most striking is Luther's style of baptizing the Old Testament, finding Christ or the church on many of its pages" (20–21).

people instead of doing this. This doctrine is worshiped when the conscience glories and trusts in it rather than in the true God alone; this is what the self-righteous must do. Moses, however, seizes it, and when he has burned it with fire and crumbled and pulverized it, he throws it into a stream which flows down the mountain; that is, the true service of the Law teaches that sin should be acknowledged, and that works, together with their teachings, are nothing, but that what is necessary is the grace of God, which justifies. Therefore this whole teaching is ground up and thrown out; it is devoured by the stream of the Gospel, which flows from the mountain that is Christ and fills the earth. From it Moses gives the people to drink as he shows the Gospel to be necessary and drives them towards it through the knowledge of sin.[20]

Luther both repeatedly condemned allegory and extensively practiced it.[21] What are we to make of this apparent contradiction?

MAKING SENSE OF LUTHER'S
USE OF ALLEGORY

We will now consider a few responses with an eye to modern relevance. First, it is important to note that Luther changed and developed as an interpreter and theologian. We have more than thirty years' worth of Luther's writings or transcribed lectures, and it is not fair for us to assess the younger Luther alongside the more mature Luther. Luther himself decries his early days of unguarded allegorical flights of fancy.[22] He writes:

---

20. *LW* 9:108-9.

21. C. Clifton Black observes, "Scholars remain divided over the significance Luther accorded to allegorical exegesis. Some think he continued to view allegories positively, albeit cautiously (Gerrish, 'Biblical Authority and the Continental Reformation,' 346; Kooiman, *Luther and the Bible*, 220); others, that he regarded them as trivial or dangerous (Pelikan, *Luther the Expositor*, 89; Bornkamm, *Luther and the Old Testament*, 262). Part of the problem is that Luther said and did different things at different times in his life; his later estimation of allegory as 'tomfoolery' (*LW* 54:406) can be squared neither with his exercise of it in his commentaries nor with positive assessments he made of it elsewhere (*WA* 42:347). Regarding his commentaries on Ps 51, we can say that Luther does not reject allegory when trying to illumine the text or edify his audience, but pivotal points are not made to turn on allegorical interpretation" (*Reading Scripture with the Saints* [Eugene, OR: Cascade, 2014], 122n15).

22. Timothy George observes, "Throughout his lectures on Romans, Luther still makes use of the fourfold interpretive grid. Even later, when he had abandoned its use as standard

The ridiculous procedure which Origen and Jerome follow in [the first three chapters of Genesis] is well known. Everywhere they depart from the historical account, which they call the "letter that kills" and "the flesh"; and they bestow lofty praise on the "spiritual meaning," of which they have no actual knowledge. In fact, Jerome followed Origen as his teacher. The same thing happens in our time; those who are influential, either through their native ability or through their eloquence, strive with all their power to persuade their hearers that the historical accounts are dead matter and useless for building the churches. Thus it came about that with common zeal we rashly strove for allegories. When I was a young man, my own attempts at allegory met with fair success.[23] It was even permissible to come up with foolish ideas, since these great teachers of the churches, such as Jerome and Origen, had at times given wide range to their imagination. And so anyone who was somewhat more skilled in contriving allegories was also regarded as a rather learned theologian. Augustine, too, was led astray by this conviction; and, especially in the instances of the Psalms, he disregards the historical sense and has recourse to allegories.[24] They were all convinced that, especially in the historical accounts of the

---

exegetical technique, he would sometimes revert to allegorical interpretations. Richard Muller explained the basic Reformation approach in this way: 'Both Luther and Calvin strengthen the shift to the letter (increased by the emphasis on textual and philological study), but they then proceeded to find various figures and levels of meaning embedded in the letter itself' " (*Reading Scripture with the Reformers* [Downers Grove, IL: IVP Academic, 2011], 152). George references Richard A. Muller's essay, "Biblical Interpretation in the Era of the Reformation: The View from the Middle Ages," in *Biblical Interpretation in the Era of the Reformation: Essays Presented to David C. Steinmetz in Honor of His Sixtieth Birthday* (Grand Rapids: Eerdmans, 1996), 12. Robert Kolb writes, "Although ever less present in [Luther's] exegetical lectures and preaching, allegory never disappeared from his interpretive toolbox" (*Martin Luther and the Enduring Word of God: The Wittenberg School and Its Scripture-Centered Proclamation* [Grand Rapids: Baker Academic, 2016], 158).

23. The editor of Luther's lectures on Genesis, Jaroslav Pelikan, here remarks: "As Luther says here, his early exegesis was filled with allegorical interpretation, of which his commentary on Judges of 1516 (Weimar, IV, 529–586) is a good illustration; there are some scholars who attribute it to John Agricola rather than to Luther" (*Lectures on Genesis*, 232n77). More recent studies are more confident that Luther stands behind the transcribed lectures (e.g., John A. Maxfield, *Luther's Lectures on Genesis and the Formation of Evangelical Identity*, Sixteenth Century Essays & Studies 80 [Kirksville, MO: Truman State University Press, 2008]).

24. Pelikan comments, "For an instance of Luther's use of Augustine's works on the Psalms cf. *Luther's Works*, 13, p. 95, note 32" (*Lectures on Genesis*, 232n78).

Old Testament, the allegories represented the spiritual meaning; but the historical account itself, or the literal senses, represented the carnal meaning. But I ask you, is this not a desecration of the sacred writings?[25]

Second, essential to making sense of Luther's apparently contradictory remarks on allegory is to observe that he understood the allegory that he practiced as distinct from that of the church fathers, which he so strongly criticized. This is a very significant point, and we will note four dimensions to it.

1. ALLEGORY IS SECONDARY TO THE HISTORICAL OR LITERAL SENSE

First, Luther saw *proper* allegory as secondary to the historical or literal sense of the biblical text, which was alone reliable for establishing doctrine and practice. At best, allegory adorns or embellishes a teacher's exposition of the Bible. Luther writes:

It is the historical sense alone which supplies the true and sound doctrine. After this has been treated and correctly understood, then one may also employ allegories as an adornment and flowers to embellish or illuminate the account. ... Therefore let those who want to make use of allegories base them on the historical account itself. The historical account is like logic in that it teaches what is certainly true; the allegory, on the other hand, is like rhetoric in that it ought to illustrate the historical account but has no value at all for giving proof.[26]

In keeping with this secondary and conditional nature of allegorical adornment, when Luther discusses permitted allegorical reflections, he cites Paul's teaching on prophecy in Romans 12:6. Thus, the Reformer implies that allegory must be constrained by an external standard, is not finally authoritative, and is potentially wrong or misleading.[27]

---

25. *LW* 1:232. See similarly *LW* 2:150–51.

26. *LW* 1:233.

27. *LW* 9:25. Luther writes, "Hence the rule of Paul should be observed here, that allegories should be kept in second place and be applied for the strengthening, adorning, and enriching

In his lectures on Genesis regarding Jacob wrestling the angel near the Jabbok River, Luther says:

> Augustine resorts to allegory. But bare allegories should not be sought in the Holy Scriptures. For unless they have a story and a certain fact as a foundation, they are nothing else but fables like those of Aesop. Secondly, even if we have a story, it is not the business of all men to form allegories with it. Origen was not too successful, and Jerome had even less success with them, for they did not have a perfect knowledge of the narratives, without which no one can handle allegories successfully. So before all else the historical sense must be dug out. This teaches, consoles, and confirms. Afterwards allegory embellishes and illustrates it as a witness. But the narrative is the author, so to say, or the head and foundation of the matter.[28]

2. ACCEPTABLE ALLEGORY IS MODELED IN SCRIPTURE

Luther believed the Scriptures themselves provide the best model for acceptable allegory. He affirms, "Ever since I began to adhere to the historical meaning, I myself have always had a strong dislike for allegories and did not make use of them unless the text itself indicated them or the interpretation could be drawn from the New Testament."[29] When a New Testament author picks up an Old Testament text in a typological or historical-redemptive fashion, Luther eagerly allows the apostles to lead the way. For example, in discussing how Paul employs marriage in Ephesians 5:32 as a mysterious representation of Christ and the church, Luther comments:

> This allegory is ingenious and full of comfort, for what more delightful statement can be made than that the church is the bride and

---

of the doctrine of faith, or, as he says in 1 Cor. 3:11ff., they should not be the foundation but be built on the foundation, not as hay, wood and stubble but as silver, gold, and gems. This is done when, according to the injunction of Rom. 12:6, prophecy is according to the analogy of faith, namely, that you first take up a definite statement set down somewhere in Scripture, explain it according to the literal sense, and then at the end connect to this an allegorical meaning which says the same thing. Not as though the allegorical meaning proved or supported the statement or doctrine; but it is proved or supported by the statement, just as a house does not hold up the foundation but is held up by the foundation" (LW 9:25).

28. *LW* 6:125.

29. *LW* 1:232–33.

Christ the bridegroom? It expresses that most happy association and bestowal of all the gifts which the bridegroom possesses, as well as the obliteration of the sins and all the misfortunes with which the poor bride is burdened. Therefore it is a most delightful saying when St. Paul states (2 Cor. 11:2): "I have espoused you to one husband that I may present you to Christ as a chaste virgin."[30]

3. ALLEGORY MUST BE ROOTED IN THE HISTORICAL OR LITERAL SENSE

Luther believed all allegorical interpretations should be rooted in the historical or literal sense of the text.[31] So, for example, in speaking of Paul's use of Genesis in Romans 5:14, he writes:

In Rom. 5:14 [Paul] states: "Adam was the first figure of Him that was to come." How? "For just as through Adam many have died, much more has the grace of God and the gift by grace, which is of one Man, Jesus Christ, abounded unto man." See how well this allegory ties in with the historical account as its basis. Similarly, in Gal. 4:24 Paul makes two testaments out of Sara and Hagar. Let those who want to devise allegories follow this lead and look for their basis in the historical account itself.[32]

Scholars debate what exactly Luther intends by the *sensus literalis* ("literal sense") or historical meaning of the text. Some writers have claimed that, for Luther and his contemporaries, this literal sense included a spiritual meaning as well.[33] A quick survey of current literature demonstrates that modern scholars reach contradictory assessments of what the church fathers and Reformers meant by the "literal sense," the "plain

---

30. *LW* 1:233.

31. Kolb writes, "Chiefly ... Luther's exposition of texts began with knowing the linguistic devices used by the author and the historical circumstances in which the author had been bringing God's message to his people (*Between Wittenberg and Geneva*, 15).

32. *LW* 1:234.

33. Herman J. Selderhuis, ed., *Psalms 1–72*, Reformation Commentary on Scripture, Old Testament 7, ed. Timothy George and Scott M. Manetsch (Downers Grove, IL: IVP Academic, 2015), xlvi–xlvii. Similarly, see also Craig A. Carter, *Interpreting Scripture with the Great Tradition*, 152; cf. Frances F. Young, "Alexandrian and Antiochene Exegesis," in *A History of Biblical Interpretation*, ed. Alan J. Hauser and Duane F. Watson (Grand Rapids: Eerdmans, 2003), 1:334–54.

sense," and the "historical sense."[34] In fact, usage by ancient, medieval, and Reformation-era writers is varied, and to assume that they meant the same things by these terms is hazardous.[35] Each author should be assessed in light of his explicit uses of the terms.

For his part, Luther seems to speak interchangeably of the inspired human author, the divine author, the literal sense, and the historical sense of the text.[36] Luther is so confident in the clarity of Scripture that he judges its literal sense as being beyond dispute. Luther affirms, "No clearer book has been written on earth than the Holy Scripture. It compares with other books as the sun with other lights."[37] Elsewhere he says, "The Holy Spirit is the simplest writer and advisor in heaven and on earth. That is why his words could have no more than the one simplest meaning which we call the written one, or the literal meaning of the tongue."[38]

For Luther, the literal sense appears to be the meaning intended by both the inspired human author and the Holy Spirit, and it can be discerned by reading the clear assertions of the written text. If we are looking for a more technical analogy to Luther's approach, we might compare it to a form of literary criticism that seeks what the implied author is saying to the implied readers. For Luther, the implied author is a Holy Spirit-inspired human who speaks with both relevance in his own day and

---

34. For disagreement about the term among Reformation-era scholars, see James Samuel Preus, *From Shadow to Promise: Old Testament Interpretation from Augustine to the Young Luther* (Cambridge: Harvard University Press, 1969), 133–49, 176. Note that, for Luther, there is both a literal-historical sense (*LW* 12:312–13) and a literal-prophetic sense (*LW* 12:363). See C. Clifton Black, *Reading Scripture with the Saints*, 118n12.

35. See Charles J. Scalise, "The 'Sensus Literalis': A Hermeneutical Key to Biblical Exegesis," *Scottish Journal of Theology* 42, no. 1 (1989): 45–65; Kathryn Greene-McKnight, "Literal Sense," in *Dictionary for Theological Interpretation of the Bible*, ed. Kevin J. Vanhoozer (Grand Rapids: Baker, 2005), 455–56. Karlfried Froelich asserts that, at least in some places, by "literal sense" Thomas Aquinas essentially refers to the human author's intended meaning ("Paul and the Late Middle Ages," essay XIII, in *Biblical Interpretation from the Church Fathers to the Reformation* [Burlington, VT: Ashgate, 2010], 12–13).

36. Note, for example, in Luther's lectures on Genesis where he mentions Moses interchangeably with "the Holy Spirit," the "literal sense," and the "historical sense." *LW* 2:132–33, 150–52, 287, 386.

37. *WA* 8:236 (translation by C. Clifton Black, *Reading Scripture with the Saints*, 126n22).

38. *LW* 39:178. In discussing Luther's interpretation of Psalm 51 in *The Seven Penitential Psalms* (1517; 1525), C. Clifton Black writes, "We find here an exegetical certitude in Luther's manner, whereby he cites a biblical verse and paraphrases what he takes to be its plain meaning without the slightest equivocation (e.g., *LW* 14:169–75)" (*Reading Scripture with the Saints*, 115).

prophetic insight. The implied readers are both the original audience of the inspired writer (or possibly characters within the narrative), as well as, with a secondary application, God's holy people throughout all time, especially those to whom Luther is expositing the text.

To gain a clearer sense of what the Reformer intends by the *sensus literalis*, which he distinguishes from allegorical adornment, let us consider Luther's discussion of the raven and doves that Noah released from the grounded ark. Luther writes,

> In our discussion of the historical account, we stated that these events took place for the comfort of Noah and his sons, to give them the assurance that the wrath of God had come to an end and that He was now reconciled. It was not through her own effort that the dove brought back the olive branch; this was a divine power and miracle, just as the serpent in Paradise did not speak by its own effort but through the influence of the devil, by whom it was possessed. Just as in that instance the serpent spoke under the influence of Satan and seduced mankind to sin, so in this instance the dove did not bring back the olive branch through her own effort and instinct but under God's influence, in order that Noah might derive sure comfort from this most delightful sight. For the fruit of the olive tree is not the food of a dove, which likes wheat, barley, or peas.[39]

So, we see here that Luther had a clear understanding of the literal sense of Genesis 8 as describing God's historical deliverance of and provision for Noah following the worldwide diluvial judgement.

4. ALLEGORY MUST BE ASSESSED TELEOLOGICALLY

Finally, we see that, for Luther, allegories must be assessed teleologically. In other words, what do they accomplish? What is their goal? Luther condemns the allegories of Jerome, Augustine, and Bernard because they speculate on philosophical or moral questions. For Luther, a good allegory must be in accord with the rule of faith (i.e., core Christian doctrine) and exposit the center of the Bible—showing how the law of God reveals

---

39. *LW* 2:157.

guilt, while the gospel of Christ brings life and comforts the conscience.[40] So, for example, in his teaching on the Genesis account of the dove and the raven (Gen 8:6–12), after briefly discussing the historical meaning or literal sense, Luther reflects upon the appearances of doves, ravens, and olive trees throughout Scripture as a basis for an allegory, with the raven representing the law and the doves representing the gospel.[41]

CONCLUSION

In this paper, we began by noting the recent hermeneutical trend to promote allegorical exegesis. Next, we looked to Luther as both a critic and practitioner of allegory. We attempted to give a nuanced understanding of Luther's approach to allegory with the hope that he might inform the current hermeneutical discussion. Yes, Luther does practice allegory, but he also repeatedly insists that the literal or historical sense of the text is primary and solely reliable for doctrine and practice. Also, though Luther exposits the text allegorically, he often comments that what he is doing is secondary in nature, might not be appropriate, should not be done too extensively, or should not be the focus of interpretation.[42] These sober qualifications are quite different from the glee with which some modern interpreters embrace Origen. Modern exegetes who are eager to enlist Origen in their storming of evangelicalism's hermeneutical Bastille are also advised not to rely on secondary summaries of Origen but to read the influential church father for themselves.

I have attempted to let Luther speak for himself (through extended quotations) throughout much of this paper. It is fitting, then, to give the Reformer the final word:

There is no need at all for dwelling here at greater length on this matter of allegory. Let this reminder suffice: that those who wish to

---

40. George H. Tavard observes, "Luther streamlined the Scriptures to such a point that they became practically identical with one doctrine [viz. justification by faith]" (*Holy Writ or Holy Church: The Crisis of the Protestant Reformation* [New York: Harper, 1959], 89, cited by C. Clifton Black, *Reading Scripture with the Saints*, 126n23).

41. *LW* 2:157–64.

42. *LW* 9:24–25. You can see this motif of hesitation in Luther's writings on allegory collected by Carl L. Beckwith, ed., *Martin Luther's Basic Exegetical Writings* (St. Louis: Concordia, 2017), 466–86.

make use of allegories, make use of these which the apostles point out and which have a sure basis in the words themselves or in the historical account. Otherwise it will happen that we build chaff and stubble on the foundation, and not gold (1 Cor. 3:12).[43]

---

43. *LW* 1:234.

3

—

LUTHER'S *TENTATIO* AS THE CENTER OF PAUL'S THEOLOGY

Channing L. Crisler

Interpreters have long searched for a so-called "center" to Paul's theology.[1] This illusive center is thought to shape and unify each strand of the apostle's thought.[2] After a century and more of such proposed centers, many scholars still probe the surface of the Pauline corpus in search of a Schweitzerian-sized "crater" large enough to articulate the transcendent

---

1. Any discussion about locating the center of Paul's theology raises several questions that are beyond the scope of this essay. Stan Porter summarizes many of these questions, noting, "Is the concern with the man himself or with his various manifestations as found within the letter? Which letters are to be of concern—those traditionally attributed to him or a more restricted corpus, or possibly only a single letter at a time? How narrow a topic can provide the basis for a Pauline theology, or an element of a Pauline theology? When one investigates such topics, does one take a thematic, existentialist, historical, salvation-historical approach, or something else?" Stanley E. Porter, "Is There a Center to Paul's Theology? An Introduction to the Study of Paul and His Theology," in *Paul and His Theology*, Pauline Studies 3, ed. Stanley E. Porter (Leiden: Brill, 2006), 6. A full response to such questions would require several more essays. However, to answer at least one of Porter's questions, I will stipulate from the outset that all thirteen letters of the Pauline corpus inform the discussion in this essay. While it is a minority position within the field of biblical studies today, I maintain that Paul is the author of each letter that bears his name (Παῦλος) in the respective letter openings. Simply put, the Pauline corpus does not contain so-called pseudonymous letters. For a defense of this position, see, e.g., E. Earle Ellis, *History and Interpretation in New Testament Perspective* (Atlanta: SBL, 2001), 17–29; Terry L. Wilder, "Pseudonymity, the New Testament, and the Pastoral Epistles," in *Entrusted with the Gospel: Paul's Theology in the Pastoral Epistles*, ed. Andreas J. Köstenberger and Terry L. Wilder (Nashville: B&H Academic, 2010), 28–52.

2. Various interpreters attempt to define the "center" with more precision. For example, H. W. Boers defines the "center," explaining, "The 'coherent center' of Paul's thought would be what links all the themes structurally. What holds everything together, syntactically and paradigmatically, is the grammar of his thought, constituted, in the sense of Greimas, by its syntactic and semantic components" (H. W. Boers, "The Foundations of Paul's Thought: A Methodological Investigation—The Problem of the Coherent Center of Paul's Thought," *Studia Theologica* 42 [1988]: 62).

features of the apostle's thought without falling into smaller and more historically conditioned subsidiary cavities.[3] The short list of proposals includes, "God, Christ or Christology, justification by faith, salvation history, reconciliation, apocalyptic, (mystical) participation in Christ, the cross, anthropology and salvation, resurrection and/or exaltation, ethics, and gospel."[4] A common tendency in so many of these explorations is to explain the center as a transcendent principle or action that provides coherence to all of Paul's thought regardless of the contingent nature of his letters.[5] This tendency includes those who have taken the long way around through various methods only to arrive at yet another suggested principle to serve as the center, such as existentialism, apocalypticism, or God's covenant faithfulness.[6]

---

3. Albert Schweitzer used the analogy of a crater on the moon's surface in discussing the center of Paul's theology. He favored Christ mysticism as the center over justification by faith, explaining, "The doctrine of righteousness by faith is therefore a subsidiary crater, which has formed within the rim of the main crater—the mystical doctrine of redemption through the being-in-Christ" (Albert Schweitzer, *The Mysticism of Paul the Apostle* [Baltimore: John Hopkins Press, 1998], 225). The analogy gained traction in subsequent studies. As N. T. Wright notes, Schweitzer's lunar image "haunts" discussions of Pauline theology still today. See N. T. Wright, *Paul and His Recent Interpreters* (Minneapolis: Fortress, 2015), xvii.

4. Porter, "Is There a Center to Paul's Theology?," 10. From a broader perspective, Joseph Plevnik suggests that Protestants have typically identified the center as justification by faith, while Catholic interpreters have placed Christ at the center. However, he also notes that, from the beginning of the twentieth century onward, several Protestant scholars have questioned the traditional position (Joseph Plevnik, "The Center of Pauline Theology," *CBQ* 51 [1989]: 461–78). Similarly, Don Howell suggests that most proposed centers have "their reference point in either soteriology or Christology" (Don N. Howell Jr., "The Center of Pauline Theology," *Bibliotheca Sacra* 151 [1994]: 50).

5. Like Schweitzer's crater, J. Christian Beker's distinction between "coherence" and "contingency" in Paul's thought has also shaped subsequent discussions. Beker explains, "I have argued throughout this study that the nature of Paul's theological thinking is characterized by two fundamental features: the contingent nature of his hermeneutic and his sure grasp of the coherent center of the gospel. The latter focuses on Christ as the proleptic fulfillment of the triumph of God, that is, the redemption of the created order, whereas the former manifests itself in the occasional and opportune character of the letters" (J. Christian Beker, *Paul the Apostle: Triumph of God in Life and Thought* [Philadelphia: Fortress, 1980], 351).

6. The leading proponents here are well known. They have had a seismic impact on Pauline theology in the twentieth and twenty-first centuries. However, their proposed centers are ultimately principled in nature. For instance, as he commences his analysis of Paul's theology, Bultmann suggests: "Every assertion about God is simultaneously an assertion about man and vice versa. For this reason and in this sense Paul's theology is, at the same time, anthropology." See Rudolf Bultmann, *Theology of the New Testament* (reprint; Waco: Baylor University Press, 2007), 1:190–91. With respect to apocalypticism, J. L. Martyn's comments on Gal 1:4 are representative for what he sees as the center of Paul's theology, though he does not use the term "center." He suggests that Paul's perception of the "human plight" is far

In this way, interpreters often treat Paul's theology and its center as a purely rational knowledge. It is a kind of "theo-logic" that operates on a set of principles, with one main principle that shapes and directs the whole. To borrow from Oswald Bayer's critique of theology in general, Paul's theology is often treated as more science (*scientia*) than wisdom (*sapientia*). Bayer explains the difference:

> Since the time of Aristotle, academic disciplines have been guided by necessary, basic principles, *principia*, and at its deepest level, by one single *principium*; according to the Aristotelian scientific system, that deepest principle is rational theology, theo-logic. Scientific endeavors carried out within the framework of this philosophical concept of God are part of a closed system. Wisdom, by contrast, in a non-Aristotelian sense, deals in the realm of experience.[7]

Bayer, who is reflecting upon the way Martin Luther challenged the Aristotelian-laden approach to theology, suggests that theology unfolds within time and through experience rather than only in a "closed system" of theory and practice.

With Bayer's critique in view, rather than treat Pauline theology and its center as a purely rational theology with a controlling principle, one alternative is to approach it as an "experiential wisdom," where scientific

---

more than human guilt. In Martyn's reading of Paul, humanity is "in fact, trapped, enslaved under the power of the present evil age." Based on that plight, Martyn concludes, "That is the background of God's invasive action in his sending of Christ, in his declaration of war, and in his striking the decisive and liberating blow against the power of the present evil age" (J. L. Martyn, *Galatians: A New Translation with Introduction and Commentary* [New Haven: Yale University Press, 1997], 105-6). Martyn's apocalyptic "plight" and "invasion" are still principled in nature. Finally, toward the close of his lengthy discussion on Paul's theology in his tome on Paul, N. T. Wright notes that he uses the category "covenantal" as a "heuristic label" in which he combines Paul's "law court language" and "being in Christ language." He explains, "There may be better labels, but 'covenantal' still has merit. It highlights, in particular, Paul's great emphasis: that everything, in the last analysis, comes back to the question of God. And among all the other things which one might say, and which Paul does say, about God, this stands out as one of the main clues to Paul's theology, and hence to the strengthening of his worldview and the energizing of his mission: that God is, and has been, faithful" (N. T. Wright, *Paul and the Faithfulness of God* [Minneapolis: Fortress, 2013], 2:1264). Wright's suggestion as well bears the stamp of a principled approach.

    7. Oswald Bayer, *Martin Luther's Theology: A Contemporary Interpretation* (Grand Rapids: Eerdmans, 2008), 30.

knowledge is not distinct from experience but included within it.[8] In this way, Luther, though browbeaten in many corners of Pauline studies over the past several decades, offers a fresh perspective for analyzing Pauline theology and its center.[9]

The main argument in what follows is that, by applying Luther's three "rules" for studying theology to the study of Paul's life and letters, the center of his theology can be understood as a recurring event of certainty in all that the gospel promises necessitated by various forms of suffering. Luther described the study of theology as an event wherein the interplay between prayer (*oratio*), meditation on Scripture (*meditatio*), and affliction (*tentatio*) resulted in an experience of certainty in the divine word.[10] While he did not conceive of these as three sequential steps, Luther did identify *tentatio* as the touchstone that led to a "wisdom beyond all wisdom."[11] In approaching Paul's theology within the same triadic matrix, one finds an interplay between what the apostle asked for in prayer, the gospel he meditated upon,

---

8. Bayer's critique is informed by Martin Luther's understanding of what constitutes theological knowledge. Bayer explains, "In response to the question posed to him about what type of knowledge is involved in theology, Luther opted for an understanding of theology according to which it is more wisdom (*sapientia*) than science (*scientia*)—already the early Luther spoke of theology as a *sapientia experimentalis* (an experiential wisdom), as a wisdom that comes by experience, and he stays with that understanding; *scientia* is not utterly distinct from *sapientia* but is included within it. Wisdom reflects on the relationship of what science can contribute to understanding the connection of the academic with the preacademic world of life" (Bayer, *Martin Luther's Theology*, 30).

9. The criticism directed toward Luther comes from many corners of Pauline studies. One flashpoint for the criticism is Krister Stendahl's seminal 1963 essay in which he accused Luther of reading his own angst about sin, guilt, and divine wrath into Paul. See Krister Stendahl, "The Apostle Paul and the Introspective Conscience of the West," *Harvard Theological Review* 56 (1963): 199–215. This kind of criticism of Luther is now axiomatic for many Pauline interpreters, though it is more often asserted than demonstrated from a careful reading of Luther himself. As Erik Heen notes in his retort to New Perspective proponents, "It must also be asked to what extent do the majority of NPP practitioners actually have a knowledge of Luther's complex dialectical theology or a feel for the variegated confessional tradition that goes by the rubric Lutheranism? It is possible, of course, to choose isolated statements from Luther and Melanchthon or the long period of Lutheran Orthodoxy that followed without much concern for situational context or issues of historical development, and construct a caricature of Lutheranism's understanding of law or justification" (Erik M. Heen, "A Lutheran Response to the New Perspective on Paul," *Lutheran Quarterly* 24 [2010]: 285).

10. Luther retained these three Latin terms (*oratio, meditatio,* and *tentatio*) in the preface to the Wittenberg edition of his German writings, where he briefly discussed his three rules for studying theology. In keeping with his presentation of the rules, I have likewise used the Latin terms throughout this essay. See *WA* 50:657–60; *LW* 34:283–88; *TAL* 4:478–88.

11. *TAL* 4:486.

and what he and his recipients suffered. Moreover, in his life and letters, *tentatio* functions as the touchstone for the coherence and contingency of his thought. This means that the center of Paul's theology is something like a recurring experience (event) of certainty in the promise of the gospel.

What I offer in this essay is preliminary in nature with the hope of further exploration in the future. An exhaustive discussion of the various issues that are raised in what follows would require monograph-length treatment. We will begin with a brief overview of Luther's three rules followed by an analysis of *oratio*, *meditatio*, and *tentatio* in Paul's life and letters.[12]

AN OVERVIEW OF LUTHER'S THREE "RULES" FOR THE STUDY OF THEOLOGY

In the preface to the 1539 Wittenberg edition of his German writings, Luther redirected the reader's attention from his own works to the sacred text.[13] He included three rules drawn from his reading of Psalm 119, which he believed pointed to a "correct way of studying theology."[14] These are not rules that establish a linear process for studying theology but, as Oswald Bayer describes it, they are "three moments within a single process."[15] He explains:

---

12. Before proceeding, I would like to express my heartfelt gratitude to *mein Doktorvater*, Mark A. Seifrid. I am still discovering the deep impact that his scholarship and faith in Jesus have had on me. I once asked Dr. Seifrid to explain to me his approach to exegesis. He began his explanation with eight unforgettable words, "Channing, the first thing I do is pray." I now realize that his first rule was one of the rules discussed in this essay, namely *oratio*. I also realize that those eight words captured the ethos of Mark Seifrid, an ethos I admire and strive to emulate.

13. Erik H. Herrmann notes that Luther resisted the notion of a published collection of his writings because he worried that it would detract from the biblical text as the "sole source for Christian edification and learning" (Erik H. Herrmann, "Preface to the Wittenberg Edition of Luther's German Writings 1539," in *The Annotated Luther*, vol. 4, *Pastoral Writings*, ed. Mary Jane Haemig [Minneapolis: Fortress, 2016], 476). Luther's reluctance to have his works published as a collection is clear throughout the preface. He finds some consolation in the belief that his works will soon be forgotten. He explains, "My consolation is that, in time, my books will lie forgotten in the dust anyhow, especially if I (by God's grace) have written anything good. *Non ero melior patribus meis.* He who comes second should indeed be the first one forgotten" (*TAL* 4:480–81).

14. *TAL* 4:482.

15. Oswald Bayer, "Lutheran Pietism, or Oratio, Meditatio, Tentatio in August Hermann Francke," *Lutheran Quarterly* (2011): 383. See also Ralf Stolina, "Gebet—Meditation—Anfechtung:

A theologian is one who, driven by *Anfechtung*, delves into Holy
Scripture prayerfully, is himself or herself interpreted by it in order
that he or she may then interpret it to others who are in the midst
of *Anfechtung*, so that they likewise—in prayer—may delve into
Holy Scripture and be interpreted by it.[16]

As Bayer notes, Luther's *tentatio* (*Anfechtung*) is the catalyst for the
entire process wherein interpreters become the interpreted so that they
can rightly interpret the Scriptures for those embroiled in their own *tentatio*. Moreover, while Luther's three rules, or moments, comprise a single
process in the study of theology, he discussed them separately, as I will here.

ORATIO

Luther begins by reflecting on *oratio*. He urges the reader to pray for an
understanding of the Scriptures in the same way that the psalmist did.[17]
Based on his examination of the psalmist's many requests throughout
Psalm 119, Luther concludes: "Although he well knew and daily heard and
read the text of Moses and other books besides, still he wants to lay hold
of the real teacher of the Scriptures himself, so that he may not seize upon
them pell-mell with his reason and become his own teacher."[18]

He then encourages the reader to imitate the psalmist's requests for
understanding God's word: "But kneel down in your little room and pray
to God with real humility and earnestness, that he through his dear Son
may give you his Holy Spirit, who will enlighten you, lead you, and give
you understanding."[19]

For Luther, God answers the plea for understanding the Scriptures
through the gift of the Holy Spirit. The understanding that Luther

---

Wegmarken einer theologia experimentalis," *Zeitschrift für Theologie und Kirche* 98 (2001):
81–100.

16. Bayer, "Lutheran Pietism," 383. Bayer elsewhere explains, "We are dealing with a single
rule—a single dynamic movement, or a process that is by no means linear, in which we can
distinguish three main factors, all of which are interconnected" (Oswald Bayer, *Theology the
Lutheran Way* [Minneapolis: Fortress, 2017], 42).

17. See, e.g., Pss 119:18, 26, 27, 29, 33, 34, 64, 66, 68, 71, 73, 102, 108, 124, 125, 135, 144, 146,
169, 171.

18. *TAL* 4:482–83.

19. *TAL* 4:482.

ultimately had in view was not purer contemplation of a principle or application of the text but a certainty of the word, which cannot be attained by pure reason or action. Bayer explains: "What this learning receives and attains beyond what it knows is the certainty of what it knows, a certainty that cannot be given by knowledge and science."[20] This is not to suggest that Luther jettisons the pivotal role that grammar, logic, and philosophy play in scriptural and theological understanding.[21] However, Luther's *oratio* underscores his belief in a kind of theological understanding beyond contemplation and action. This understanding is best described as an event. It is experiential wisdom of certainty in the divine word, which can only be supplied by the Spirit in conjunction with the petitioner's meditation on Scripture (*meditatio*) and affliction (*tentatio*).

MEDITATIO

This brings us to Luther's second rule for the study of theology, *meditatio*. In reflecting further on Psalm 119, Luther observes:

> Thus you see in this same psalm David constantly boasts that he will talk, meditate, speak, sing, hear, read, by day and night and always, about nothing except God's words and commandments.[22]

This kind of scriptural meditation is God's "external" answer to the "internal" request for understanding.[23] Luther did not conceive of *meditatio* as searching the inner self or even listening for the Spirit's voice inside of

---

20. Bayer, *Theology the Lutheran Way*, 49.

21. As Bayer explains, "What the theologian does not yet know and is still seeking is not knowledge and insights into texts. Therefore, it is not a matter of discovering what a text is saying with the aid of grammar, rhetoric, and dialectics (logic and philosophy in the wider sense) in order to be able to teach it in the school or academy. For that, of course, 'knowledge of the liberal arts' (*bonarum atrium cognitio*) is necessary, and Luther stresses its importance for the study of theology as much as the 'grace of the Spirit (*gratia Spiritus*)" (*Theology the Lutheran Way*, 48).

22. *TAL* 4:484.

23. Bayer notes, "With his second rule Luther takes what he had previously considered, especially in its inner aspect, and now turns it outwards. He feared that what he had said about prayer could be misunderstood in a spiritualistic and thus speculative way, despite all his emphasis on the connection between inner illumination and scripture. Luther therefore points out in a sharp if not abrupt way that the book of Holy Scripture, as it is written, should not be used 'in the heart alone but also outwardly' " (Bayer, *Theology the Lutheran Way*, 51).

one's self.[24] Instead, meditation is "interaction" with the word, where God gives the Spirit. However, this moment takes time and must be repeated. Luther warns against a disposition in which theologians think they have sufficiently meditated upon the sacred text:

> And take care that you do not grow weary or think that you have done enough when you have read, heard, and spoken them once or twice, and that you then have complete understanding. You will never be a particularly good theologian if you do that, for you will be like untimely fruit which falls to the ground before it is half ripe.[25]

According to Luther, the theologian must repeatedly return to meditate upon the Scriptures. This is neither an academic nor pietistic ritual. It is a repeated moment within an ongoing triadic experience (*oratio, meditatio, tentatio*), where God answers the request for certainty in the sacred text through the Spirit again and again.

TENTATIO

Finally, we come to *tentatio* (agonizing struggle).[26] As noted above, Luther referred to *tentatio* as the touchstone of the three rules:

---

24. In reflecting on Luther's *meditatio*, Bayer warns, "Those who want to search for the Holy Spirit deep inside themselves, in a realm too deep for words to express, will finds ghosts, not God." He continues, "They will only be amusing themselves with baseless thoughts. As Luther said, 'We all know from experience that our mind and thoughts are so uncertain, slippery and unstable, that if we want to ask a serious question or think about God without words and Scripture, we will be a hundred miles away from our thoughts before we even know it' " (*Theology the Lutheran Way*, 55).

25. *TAL* 4:484. In his *Large Catechism*, Luther gives a similar criticism of pastors who treat the catechism in such a shallow and flippant way. He quips, "Oh, these shameful gluttons and servants of their bellies are better suited to be swineherds and keepers of dogs than guardians of souls and pastors" (*BC* 379).

26. In the 1539 preface to his German works, Luther retains the Latin term *tentatio*. However, he also includes the German term *Anfechtung*, an idea that plays no small role in his theology. This is clear in the opening lines of his *De libertate Christiana*. Luther opines, "Many people view Christian faith as something easy, and quite a few people even count it as if it were related to virtues. They do this because they have not judged faith in light of any experience, nor have they ever tasted its great power. This is because a person who has not tasted the spirit in the midst of trials and misfortune cannot possibly write well about faith or understand what has been written about it" (*TAL* 1:487). On this point, see Bayer, *Theology the Lutheran Way*, 61–62.

This is the touchstone that teaches you not only to know and understand, but also to experience how right, how true, how sweet, how lovely, how mighty, how comforting God's word is, wisdom beyond all wisdom. Thus you see how David, in the psalm mentioned, complains so often about all kinds of enemies, arrogant princes or tyrants, false spirits and factions, whom he must tolerate because he meditates, that is, because he is occupied with God's word (as has been said) in all manner of ways.[27]

In Luther's reading of Psalm 119, the psalmist's many afflictions are the quintessential feature of his experience—an experience propelled by spiritual attack wrapped up with meditation upon God's word and requests for understanding. Luther perceived this agonizing struggle as a necessarily recurring moment.[28] In Luther's thought, the struggle is multifaceted and definitive for the entire Christian experience. Bayer notes that *tentatio*, like so much of Luther's thought, is tied to the first commandment:

Whoever meditates upon the first commandment is entangled thereby in the battle between the one Lord and the many lords. One cannot extricate oneself from this entanglement by holding to a speculative idea about the unity of God. It is not enough just to know about the unity and thus about the almighty nature of God; it is not enough for the spiritual eye to hold onto such realities as timelessly present; each person must in a more real way also experience such realities. But such experience takes time; it sets one forth on a journey that brings with it times of testing, that takes one farther than one wishes to go, even to the point that it insists on being experienced.[29]

This required and repeated experience does not demonstrate the believing individual's power and credibility. Instead, it demonstrates the power and credibility of God's word. Such an experience of Scripture,

---

27. *TAL* 4:486.

28. In this way, *tentatio*, or *Anfechtung*, is in Luther's thought "a one-word theological concept." See David P. Scaer, "The Concept of *Anfechtung* in Luther's Thought," *Concordia Theological Quarterly* 47 (1983): 15.

29. Bayer, *Martin Luther's Theology*, 36.

not merely contemplation and application of it, is indissolubly bound to agonizing struggle.[30]

Oratio, meditatio, and *tentatio* do not constitute a linear process. They comprise an interrelated, simultaneous, and recurring moment. One does not move from an experience of one "rule" to the next as if there is "progress" in all of this.[31] Therefore, when one speaks of one rule, one is speaking about all three. However, since *tentatio* is the "touchstone" for this entire experience, it has the most prominent role in the following discussion.

TENTATIO IN PAUL'S LIFE

At the close of his Letter to the Galatians, Paul makes one last request: "Finally, let no one cause trouble (κόπους) for me, for I bear in my body the marks of Jesus (τὰ στίγματα τοῦ Ἰησοῦ)" (Gal 6:17). These *stigmata,* whatever their precise nature, left a lasting mark in Paul's body.[32] They were an external reminder to Paul, and to those who saw him, that his life in Christ was constantly marked by suffering. However, suffering not only left a mark upon Paul's body. It also left an indelible impression upon his thought. What I would like to consider now is how the marks of suffering left on Paul's thought resemble Luther's three rules for what makes a theologian. In both the seminal and mundane moments of his life, Paul prayed, meditated on the gospel, and suffered. This recurring experience, abbreviated here as *tentatio,* did more than shape Paul's theology. It occupied

---

30. Bayer uses the description of "sensory" experience rather than mere consciousness. He explains, "Contrary to the misleading ideas of the modern theology of consciousness, the affects that we are talking about here, which include the senses, the emotions, the imagination, the memory, and the desires, are not primarily the effects of the believer or of the unbeliever, but the affects produced by the word of God. They are the effects of the *deus dicens,* who is not a mere mind devoid of feelings and desires, like the God of metaphysics, but he is a God who speaks through sensory means" (Bayer, *Theology the Lutheran Way,* 62–63).

31. As Athina Lexutt observes with resepct to Luther's *tentatio/Anfechtung,* "Anfechtung does not accommodate itself to the Zeitgeist, which delights only in progress and maintains a brazen attitude towards tradition, from whose wrinkles it scrapes away all the makeup so that everything one had attempted with great difficulty to conceal becomes visible" (Athina Lexutt, "In Praise of Anfechtung," *Lutheran Quarterly* 27 [2013]: 439).

32. As Peter Oakes notes, the τὰ στίγματα τοῦ Ἰησοῦ in Galatians 6:17 refer "presumably to scars and other forms of bodily damage acquired through persecution or the hazards of itinerant ministry" (*Galatians* [Grand Rapids: Baker, 2015], 193). Of course, as Paul indicates in Galatians 6:17 and elsewhere, these marks were more than scars. They represent far more about the pain of Paul's experience, which impacted his thought, self-perception, and his expectation for how other Christians would treat him. Cf. 2 Cor 11:22–29.

the central place of his theology for the duration of his life. Three salient points from Paul's life bear this out.

To begin, *tentatio* marks Paul's encounter with the risen Christ on the Damascus Road, an encounter that had an inestimable impact on his life and thought. Pauline interpreters have never reached a consensus on the precise theological impact of Paul's experience. Suggestions usually fit into either soteriological, christological, missiological, or doxological models.[33] What is sometimes underappreciated in this discussion is the role that suffering played as it relates to the event's initial and subsequent effect on Paul's theology.

Tentatio certainly characterizes Paul's initial encounter with the risen Christ. The whole episode in Acts is shot through with pain, as Paul suffered blindness, hunger, thirst, a failed attempt on his life once he arrived in Damascus, and a shameful escape in a basket lowered from the city wall.[34] Furthermore, the brief dialogue between Jesus and Paul, as well as between Ananias and Paul, indicates that the apostle was afflicted by the theological and life-altering implications of the divine revelation. After all, Jesus announced to Paul (via Ananias) that he had been divinely slated for suffering: "For I will show to him how much he must (δεῖ) suffer (παθεῖν) for my

---

33. Bruce Corley helpfully summarizes the four models for understanding the theological impact of the Damascus Road experience: (1) *"Soteriological*: Damascus revealed Christ as the end of the law (Rom 10:4); the crucified Messiah overcame the curse of the law by his resurrection and offered salvation apart from the law." (2) *"Christological*: Damascus revealed Jesus as the Messiah of Israel (Gal 1:12), whose death and resurrection inaugurated the 'Age to Come' and fulfilled the covenant promises of the Old Testament Scriptures." (3) *"Missiological*: Damascus revealed the divine intention (Rom 1:5) to incorporate the Gentiles into the people of God by faith and to claim Paul for a world mission." (4) *"Doxological*: Damascus revealed Jesus as the Lord of glory (2 Cor 4:6), whose radiance intimated the very presence of God and the eschatological glory to come." See Bruce Corley, "Interpreting Paul's Conversion—Then and Now," in *The Road from Damascus: The Impact of Paul's Conversion on His Life, Thought, and Ministry*, ed. Richard N. Longenecker (Grand Rapids: Eerdmans, 1997), 16. In addition to the theological impact, many scholars evaluate the Damascus Road experience from sociological or cultural anthropological perspectives. See the discussion by Bernd Kollmann, "Die Berufung und Bekehrung zum Heidenmissionar," in *Paulus Handbuch*, ed. Friedrich W. Horn (Tübingen: Mohr Siebeck, 2013), 80–91.

34. See Acts 9:9, 23, 25; 22:11–13; 2 Cor 11:33. With respect to doubts about the historicity of Acts for assessing Paul's life, I think the late F. F. Bruce's observation still rings true: "The Paul of Acts is the historical Paul as he was seen and depicted by a sympathetic and accurate but independent observer, whose narrative provides a convincing framework for the major epistles at least and may be used with confidence to supplement Paul's own evidence" (F. F. Bruce, *Paul: Apostle of the Heart Set Free* [Grand Rapids: Eerdmans, 2000], 17). See also N. T. Wright, *Paul: A Biography* (San Francisco: HarperOne, 2018), xi–xii.

name" (Acts 9:16; cf. Phil 1:29). Within this agonizing struggle, Paul prayed. The reference to his prayer is embedded in Jesus' instructions to Ananias:

> And the Lord said to him, "Rise and go to the street which is called Straight, and seek in the house of Judas for a man from Tarsus named Saul, for behold, he is praying (προσεύχεται) and he saw a man named Ananias having entered and having laid hands on him in order that he might see again." (Acts 9:11–12)

Although we are not privy to the content of his prayer in this moment, based on Ananias' encounter with Paul, it follows that he prayed for an end to his blindness in both a physical and spiritual sense.[35] Jesus granted the latter request through Ananias' instruction to Paul and the gift of the Holy Spirit:

> And the Lord said to him, "Go, because he is my chosen vessel to bear my name before the Gentiles, and kings, and the sons of Israel." ... Then Ananias went out and entered the house and having laid hands on him he said, "Saul brother, the Lord has sent me, Jesus the one who appeared to you in the way in which you were going, in order that you might see again and you might be filled with the Holy Spirit." ... "And now what are you about to do? Rise and be baptized and wash away your sins calling upon his name." (Acts 9:15–17; 22:16)

What we find then with the Damascus Road event, at least as it is described in Acts, is that Paul's experience with Jesus begins with agonizing struggle, reflection upon revelation, and an answered prayer highlighted by the gift of the Spirit.[36] In other words, it is a moment marked by

---

35. On the spiritual nature of Paul's blindness, Dennis Hamm observes: "The blindness/sight motif has a double valence throughout; even in Acts 9, Luke signals to the reader that Paul has his eyes opened spiritually even while he is physically blind." Such spiritual sight implies a prior spiritual blindness. See Dennis Hamm, "Paul's Blindness and Its Healing: Clues to Symbolic Intent (Acts 9, 22, and 26)," *Biblica* 71 (1990): 71.

36. Unfortunately, Paul's letters do not provide a detailed account of the Damascus Road experience. They do contain a few passing references to the episode (see, e.g., 1 Cor 15:8–11; Gal 1:15). Nevertheless, the absence of a full-orbed description by Paul does not necessarily mitigate the ongoing impact of the experience on his theological reflection. As Richard Longenecker notes, "As a result of his conversion, Paul's self-identity and thinking were dramatically changed. Christologically, he saw Jesus in an entirely new way, affirming as true all that the early church had claimed him to be: Israel's Messiah, the Son of God, and humanity's redemptive Lord. Also on the basis of his conversion—coupled with his own reflections

all three of Luther's "rules" for what makes a theologian, including the way in which God answers a cry for help and understanding through the gift of the Spirit in an external word.[37] If Paul's theological understanding begins in earnest with this moment, it begins with the interplay between *oratio*, *meditatio*, and *tentatio*.[38] The result of this interplay is certainty about the promise of a crucified and risen Christ, as demonstrated in Paul's immediate (εὐθέως, Acts 9:20) proclamation at Damascus.

Tentatio marks other seminal moments in Paul's life as well. For example, the enigmatic "thorn in the flesh" is both a seminal and chronic experience marked by *tentatio*. His struggle with the thorn had a flashpoint, but it subsequently became a part of his everyday life. The juxtaposition is clear in Paul's brief description of the experience to the Corinthians:

> Therefore, in order that I might not exalt myself, a thorn (σκόλοψ) was given to me in the flesh, a messenger of Satan, in order that he might torment me, in order that I might not exalt myself. For this I requested (παρεκάλεσα) of the Lord three times that it might depart from me. And he has said (εἴρηκέν) to me, "My grace is sufficient for you, for power is perfected in weakness." Therefore, most gladly, I will rather boast in my weaknesses, in order that the power of Christ might rest upon me. Therefore, I take pleasure in weaknesses, in insults, in pressures, in persecutions, in distresses, for Christ; for whenever I am weak, then I am strong. (2 Cor 12:7b–10)

Paul's agonizing struggle elicited a cry for help, which God answered by granting him an understanding of his pain rather than removing it. The divine answer results in Paul's certainty that God's grace and power toward

---

on that experience and the needs of his Gentile mission—Paul came to transpose some of the language of those early affirmations and to develop his own distinctive christological proclamation" (Richard N. Longecker, "Realized Hope, New Commitment, and Developed Proclamation," in *The Road from Damascus: The Impact of Paul's Conversion on His Life, Thought, and Ministry*, ed. Richard N. Longenecker [Grand Rapids: Eerdmans, 1997], 40).

37. In this instance, the "external word" comes via Ananias' instructions (see Acts 9:15–18; 22:14–16). A similar experience occurs between Peter and Cornelius. Ultimately, the divine answer to Cornelius' prayer comes through Peter's preaching (see Acts 10:2, 34–43).

38. It is difficult to gauge how slowly or rapidly Paul's thinking developed in the aftermath of the experience. What is clear is that the change in his thought began immediately and intensely. On this point, see Martin Hengel and Anna Maria Schwemer, *Paul Between Damascus and Antioch: The Unknown Years* (Louisville: Westminster John Knox, 1997), 105.

him was paradoxically hidden in the weakness of his pain rather than in healing and strength. The certainty did not derive from pure contemplation or action but through the interplay of *oratio*, *meditatio*, and *tentatio*.

The Damascus Road encounter and thorn in the flesh are seminal moments that resulted in an experiential wisdom of the gospel. However, Paul indicates that such experiential wisdom marked by *tentatio* characterized his everyday life.[39] As he describes it to the Corinthians, "I die daily" (1 Cor 15:31a).[40] Consequently, Paul's prayers and reflection on the truth of the gospel constantly occurred in a context of agonizing struggle. In Paul's life, his desire to know (γνῶναι) the crucified and risen Christ could only unfold in "the fellowship of his sufferings (τὴν κοινωίαν τῶν παθημάτων αὐτοῦ)" (Phil 3:10) that took place on a daily basis.[41]

TENTATIO IN PAUL'S LETTERS

Like his life, Paul's letters contain an interplay between *oratio*, *meditatio*, and *tentatio* that resulted in certainty about the promise of the gospel for both himself and his recipients. One of the classic issues here is the perceived tension between the coherence of Paul's theological thought and the historical contingencies that he addressed. However, when we view the center of Paul's theology as an experience, rather than a principle or action, this tension actually becomes advantageous. It softens the tension between the diversity of historical circumstances and variety of theological motifs that Paul employs by highlighting the common occurrence of *tentatio*, which unifies the coherence and contingency of his thought.

TENTATIO

It is with *tentatio* in Paul's letters that we begin because it is indeed the "touchstone" for the entire experience. The historical particularities that Paul addressed and the manner in which he addressed them certainly vary from letter to letter. However, from a wider theological perspective, the *Sitz im Leben* of each letter is agonizing struggle foregrounded by eschatological

---

39. See also Rom 9:2; 1 Cor 15:30; 2 Cor 4:10–11; 6:10; 11:28.

40. Similarly, in 2 Cor 4:11, "For we who are living are always (ἀεί) being handed over to death because of Jesus, in order that also the life of Jesus might be revealed in our mortal flesh." See also Rom 8:36 with its citation of Ps 43:23 LXX.

41. See also Rom 8:17.

expectation. The struggle Paul and his recipients experienced stems from a multitude of interrelated sources, including sin, opponents/false teachers, Satan, the evil age, cosmic powers, ecclesiastical unrest, death, and the opposition between the Spirit and the flesh.

Paul portrays sin as a power that harms both believers and unbelievers. Sin (ἁμαρτία) is also an action, often in violation of the Mosaic law, in which believers and unbelievers alike can be complicit. Paul commits a great deal of space in his letters to the struggle with sin in the cosmos and church.[42] He also exerts literary energy to combat false teachers/opponents who, because of their attempts to undermine his apostolic authority and change the truth of the gospel that he preached, adversely affected him and his recipients.[43] Paul must also address the various afflictions caused by Satan, such as travel hindrances, temptation, sowing a lack of forgiveness and disunity in the church, false teaching via human agency, and god-like rule over the present age exceeded only by God himself.[44] In close connection to the affliction perpetrated by Satan, Paul warns his recipients about the evil age in which they live and cosmic forces marshalled against them, with whom God's people must battle.[45] With respect to ecclesiastical unrest, the afflictions include theodicy-like questions regarding Israel's unbelief, friction between the "weak" and "strong" in faith, and a lack of love for one another.[46] Additionally, Paul portrays death as an enemy which, despite its proleptic defeat in Christ, afflicts him and his recipients. Death threatens to separate Christians from one another and looms over their lives.[47] While death looms, the opposition between the Spirit and the flesh is so intense that it drives

---

42. See, e.g., Rom 3:9; 6:1–23; 7:1–25; 8:10; Gal 3:22; Eph 2:1–3; 1 Tim 5:22; 2 Tim 3:6. For a discussion of sin in Paul's letters, see James D. G. Dunn, *The Theology of Paul the Apostle* (Grand Rapids: Eerdmans, 1998), 79–162; Michael Wolter, *Paul: An Outline of His Theology* (Waco: Baylor University Press, 2015), 357–61.

43. See, e.g., Rom 16:17–18; 1 Cor 15:12; 2 Cor 11:5; 12:11; Gal 1:6–9; 5:7–12; Phil 1:12–17; 3:2–4; Col 2:20–23; 1 Thess 2:14–16; 2 Thess 2:1–2; 1 Tim 1:3–11; Titus 1:10–12. For a discussion of Paul's opponents from various perspectives, see, e.g., Stanley E. Porter, ed., *Paul and His Opponents* (Leiden: Brill, 2005).

44. Rom 16:20; 2 Cor 2:11; 4:4; 11:14; 12:7; 1 Thess 2:18; 1 Tim 3:6–7.

45. Rom 8:38–39; Gal 1:4; Eph 5:16; 6:12.

46. Rom 9:1–23; 14:1–15:3; 1 Cor 3:1–17; 6:1–8; 8:1–13.

47. Rom 8:34–39; 1 Cor 15:50–58; 2 Cor 5:1–10; Phil 3:21.

one to lament and to crucify ungodly desires.[48] Finally, the foreground for all of the *tentatio* in Paul's letters is the parousia and/or final judgment.[49] Various earthly afflictions do not divert his attention from the eschatological horizon.[50] Rather, it is the primary place from which he reflects upon them. Suffering paradoxically raises concerns about the standing of Paul and his recipients before God while at the same time generating hope in that standing.[51]

MEDITATIO

This brings us to *meditatio*. Paul reflected on the gospel to address various contingencies in his letters. However, one unifying element in these reflections is that they address the suffering of Paul and his recipients. Therefore, reflection on the gospel in Paul's letters, regardless of historical particularities, is consistently propelled by suffering. This kind of *meditatio* within Paul's letters works on a few different levels. On the one hand, Paul reflected upon Israel's Scriptures, in concert with his own revelation from Jesus and early Christian tradition, to address the pain of his recipients.[52] Paul considered these interrelated sources as an external word from God where God gave hope to afflicted communities of faith. For example, as part of his effort to encourage the "strong" in Rome to help the "weak," after placing a line from Psalm 68 LXX on the lips of the crucified Jesus, Paul writes, "For as much as was written beforehand, it was written for our instruction, in order that through the endurance and encouragement of the scriptures we might have hope" (Rom 15:4). On the other hand, Paul believes that his own letters are an external word from

---

48. Rom 7:13–25; 8:13; Gal 5:16–26.

49. I choose the term "foreground" rather than "background" because the expectation of the parousia and final judgment is the most prominent feature in his discussion of the *tentatio* even when he does not make overt references to it.

50. Almost every letter makes an overt reference to either the return of Jesus or final judgment See, e.g., Rom 5:6–10; 14:10; 1 Cor 3:10–15; 4:4–5; 6:9–11; 9:27; 11:32; 2 Cor 5:10; Gal 5:5, 19–21; 6:1–5; Eph 5:6–7; Phil 3:17–21; Col 1:21–23, 28; 3:1–4, 6, 24; 1 Thess 1:10; 2:19; 3:11–13; 5:7–11; 2 Thess 1:3–10; 2:13–14; 1 Tim 6:13–16; 2 Tim 1:12; 4:1–5; Titus 1:2; 3:7. The one exception is Philemon, which contains no overt references to the parousia or final judgment.

51. Rom 5:1–5; 1 Cor 9:27; 2 Cor 13:4.

52. Rom 15:4; 1 Cor 15:3–4; Gal 1:11–12.

God for his afflicted recipients.[53] For example, at the close of his response to the Corinthians' questions about marriage, Paul notes, "And I think that I also have the Spirit of God" (1 Cor 7:40). This understanding was shared by early Christian readers of Paul's letters who also considered them to be a divine word.[54]

ORATIO

Finally, *oratio* is the third piece of the experience that stands at the center of Paul's theology in his letters. It is also the most difficult to examine. That is because we only have fragments of Paul's actual prayers, or prayer reports, and interpreters often neglect the theological insight it affords us with Paul in comparison to the attention that is paid to other elements of his thought.[55] In any case, Paul clearly prayed on a frequent basis and admonished his recipients to do the same. Paul did not treat prayer as a spiritual discipline but as an absolute necessity given the rupture between the ages in which both he and his recipients found themselves.[56] The suffering experienced in that rupture drove Paul and his recipients to ask for understanding and reassurance. We have already seen this on display in Paul's thrice repeated "thorn in the flesh" prayer, where he received theological insight within his pain and as a response to his request. Paul prayed that similar insight would be granted to his recipients.[57] It is not insight detached from his teaching, but it is ultimately an experience of understanding and certainty regarding what God had revealed to him and what he thereby taught others.

---

53. As Martyn suggests in his comments on Paul's doxological statement in Galatians 1:5, "It is there, Paul thinks, that God will cause Paul's epistolary words to become the word of God" (Martyn, *Galatians*, 91).

54. See, e.g., the comments about Paul's letters in 2 Pet 3:14–16.

55. As Patrick Miller observes, "No single practice more clearly defines a religion than the act of praying" (Patrick D. Miller, *They Cried to the Lord: The Form and Theology of Biblical Prayer* [Minneapolis: Fortress, 1994], 1).

56. Even Paul's much cited imperative, "Pray without ceasing," (1 Thess 5:17) is set within an eschatological context. See 1 Thess 1:10; 2:19; 3:11–13; 4:13–17; 5:1–11.

57. See, e.g., the prayer report in Eph 1:15–23, where Paul indicates that he asked God to grant the Ephesians an understanding of the "wealth" ($\pi\lambda\omega\tilde{\tau}\omega\varsigma$) they had in the crucified, risen, and exalted Jesus. See also the assurance in 2 Tim 2:7.

CONCLUSION

According to Luther, God makes theologians through what they suffer. Nothing elicits cries for understanding and reflection upon the word of God like the crucible of pain in which we move and have our being. This triadic experience does not merely result in theological formation. It *is* theological formation. That is because the theologian—at least the theologian of the cross—does not stand above the fray while reflecting upon the ways of God; the theologian stands within it.

Something similar occurs with Paul's theology. In his life and in his letters, Paul always reflected prayerfully upon the hope of the gospel while bearing the stigmata of Jesus, being joyfully afflicted by a God-given messenger of Satan, and daily enduring a catalogue of other agonizing struggles. Given this inescapable context, Paul and all his recipients, regardless of their specific situations, needed to experience clarification and certainty about their standing before God presently and eschatologically. After all, it was because of God that they were daily dying like sheep for the slaughter (Rom 8:36). That experience of certainty could only occur through prayerfully hearing the promise of the gospel with all its implications and relevance in any and every agonizing struggle. Rather than a mere principle or action directing his theology regardless of the experience, it is this experience of *tentatio* that tests, refines, and clarifies the external promise that is constantly challenged by pain. It is an experiential wisdom, which Mark Seifrid captures in his analysis of Paul's thorn in the flesh:

> Christ did not remove the thorn from Paul. Yet Christ did not remain silent or give him a dismissive No! He gave Paul an answer that arrived, not simply from the heights of the divine throne, but from the depths of human suffering and need. Christ spoke to Paul as the one who himself was "crucified in weakness" but "lives by the power of God." His answer contains within itself the wonder of his own suffering and deliverance. His word to Paul is inseparable from his person: "My grace is sufficient for you, for power is perfected in weakness."[58]

---

58. Mark A. Seifrid, *The Second Letter to the Corinthians* (Grand Rapids: Eerdmans, 2014), 448–49.

This is the kind of agonizing experience that gave Paul certainty in the gospel's promise, and it is the kind of experience that could very well stand at the center of his theology. It is an experience in which the crucified and risen Christ daily elicited Paul's cries for deliverance (*oratio*) brought on by death with him (*tentatio*) while answering those cries through a reassuring word that there was life with him as well (*meditatio*).

4

—

MARTIN LUTHER'S PEDAGOGICAL EXPOSITION OF THE LETTER TO TITUS

Robert Kolb

As he prepared his translation of the New Testament for publication in 1522, Martin Luther introduced the Epistle to Titus as "a short epistle but a model of Christian teaching, in which is comprehended in a masterful way all that is necessary for a Christian to know and live."[1] Five years later, in December of 1527, he chose this epistle as the topic for the lectures he delivered to students who had remained in Wittenberg when the university had officially shifted its teaching to Jena because of an outbreak of the plague. Notes from his most important amanuensis, Georg Rörer (1492–1557)—whose faithful service in recording Luther's lectures and sermons earned him an electorally-appointed position as the professor's scribe and editor[2]—allow us to listen in on these lectures, which provide insights into Luther's pedagogical agenda and method.

Luther's superior in the Order of Augustinian Hermits, Johannes von Staupitz (1469/70–1524), had slated this young brother for his own teaching post in Wittenberg as part of Staupitz's plan for reform through the preaching of his brothers. Once he had earned his doctorate in 1513, Luther abandoned lectures on Peter Lombard's (ca. 1100–ca. 1160) *Sententiae*, the staple of medieval theological education, for treatment of biblical books.

---

1. *WADB* 7:284–85; *LW* 35:389.

2. *Georg Rörer (1492–1557), Der Chronist der Wittenberg Reformation*, ed. Stefan Michel and Christian Spehr (Leipzig: Evangelische Verlagsanstalt, 2012).

Analyses of what remains of these lectures have largely concentrated on their doctrinal content and exegetical method. Both content and method provide vantage points for assessing his pedagogical approach to the students who were preparing for pastoral ministry or teaching. Luther's paradigmatic redefinition of the nature of the Christian religion abandoned the medieval ritualistic approach to God, which was centered on human effort and the performance of the mass. He found in Scripture that God approaches human creatures in his word. This redefinition of the heart of being a Christian transformed the understanding of the priest or pastor of a local congregation.[3] Therefore, Luther's pedagogical approach to the biblical text played a significant role in his carrying out his calling as *Doctor in Biblia*.

LECTURING ON TITUS:
BREAD FOR THE PLAGUE

The plague broke out in 1527. It drove most professors to Jena, leaving only a small contingent behind in Wittenberg. Luther decided to provide himself and this remnant something to occupy themselves so that they would not be "idle, eating our bread without earning it."[4] His choice fell upon four New Testament epistles seldom included in the Wittenberg curricular offerings. He began with 1 John. This epistle had given him plenteous opportunity to dwell on christological proclamation and God's faithfulness in redeeming and restoring his people through Christ's death and resurrection.[5] That left him free to address the ministerial task before the remnant who constituted his audience when he turned to Titus in mid-November. Once again, he found this epistle to be "a kind of epitome and summary of other, wordier epistles."[6]

Through literary-theological analysis of its structure and method, Luther found that Paul's writing was designed to teach (presenting biblical doctrine) and to admonish (urging Christian living). "By his teaching he sets down what is to be believed by faith, and by his exhortation he sets

---

3. Robert Kolb, *Martin Luther and the Enduring Word of God: The Wittenberg School and Its Scripture-Centered Proclamation* (Grand Rapids: Baker Academic, 2016), 1–6, 35–42.

4. WA 25:6.4–5; LW 29:3.

5. WA 20:499–801; LW 30:219–327.

6. WA 25:6.7–8; LW 29:3.

forth what is to be done."[7] This distinction does not simply repeat Luther's
distinction of law and gospel, since what is to be believed by faith includes
both God's plan for human living, the law, and the message of deliverance
from sin and the restoration of righteousness, his preferred definition
of gospel. In this scheme, teaching conveys God's truth, and exhortation
applies it to life. A comment on Titus 1:5–9 makes that clear: the passage
is "paranetic and exhortatory" instruction on moral actions.[8] In Titus
2:15, "declare these things," Luther explained what had to be taught regarding both faith and love—instruction regarding both Christ as gift and the
good works that this gift produces. He defined exhortation by stating, "One
must constantly repeat, inculcate, and listen to" what has been taught to
move hearers to Christian living.[9] The professor concluded the lectures by
observing that the Letter to Titus is "brief but is filled with good instruction and admonitions," adding a not untypical exaggeration, "so that there
is almost nothing in the church that is not treated here."[10] The church
should remain faithful to this "summary of being Christian," which presents "Christ given for us" and love, trust in Christ and new obedience, and
gospel and law as instruction for the God-pleasing life.[11] The *argumentum*
prepared students for following the instructor's plan to analyze a biblical
book in the lectures to come.

This brief epistle offered an ideal way to fill the gap until the return of
colleagues and students from Jena. It also lent itself effectively to the task
of cultivating pastors who would anchor their ministries in the faithful biblical preaching and consolatory pastoral care that defined the Wittenberg
vision of the servants of God's word. John Maxfield notes that "Luther
attempted to form in his students a new identity." Maxfield continues,
"Luther's Genesis lectures shed light on how he used scripture to instill in his
students a worldview that reflected the ideals of the Lutheran Reformation
and that, therefore, contributed to the break between Evangelicals and
those who remained within the papal church."[12] In expositing the Epistle

7. WA 25:6.10–17; LW 29:3.
8. WA 25:16.5–6; LW 29:16.
9. WA 25:54.21–55.5; LW 29:68–69.
10. WA 25:69.10–11; LW 29:89.
11. WA 25:69.10–13; LW 29:89.
12. Maxfield, *Luther's Lectures on Genesis*, 2; cf. 216–21.

to Titus, Luther was performing this task as well. He did not ignore the topics that formed the heart of his theology—justification by faith through forgiveness conveyed by God's word in spoken, written, and sacramental forms—but he concentrated more on using the text—particularly Paul's description of the calling of ministers of God's word, concentrated in Titus 1—to form the self-image of students in this calling.

LUTHER'S EXEGETICAL METHOD

Luther's lectures on Titus followed his usual exegetical method. This method employed frequent use of passages from throughout Scripture to place individual words into the larger biblical context. His concern for both language and historical context led him to treat such issues that he regarded as necessary for understanding the text and putting it to use. Students were reading the Latin text, but Luther presumed that they knew Greek and Hebrew. He concentrated on definitions of words, sometimes using German equivalents to clarify meaning;[13] he often explained shades of meaning of Greek or Hebrew words (always rendered by Rörer in Latin letters),[14] once treating the meaning of סגלה (segulah) to explain God's purifying the church for himself as personal property.[15] Luther reminded the students that they needed to read the Latin text that they were using with their Hebrew and Greek in mind, for the biblical writers often used Hebraisms and Greek idioms that seemed awkward in Latin or German.[16]

Philip Melanchthon (1497-1560) gave Wittenberg students excellent training in rhetoric. Luther also drew on his own university study of Quintilian (ca. AD 35-ca. 96), Demosthenes (384-322 BC), and Cicero (106-43 BC) to alert students to rhetorical devices in the text. Such comments included more casual observations of the implicit meaning of "trust in God" behind the label "reliable, infallible," or the "gibe" implicit in "in the faith" (3:15) against those who had given Paul trouble.[17] Luther also explained expressions with technical rhetorical vocabulary, e.g.,

---

13. E.g., WA 25:14.17; 20.22–30; 33.30; LW 29:14, 30, 57.

14. E.g., WA 25:21.31–32; 25.35–26.8; 42.35–43.3; 55.28–31; 60.1–33; 61.27–62.10; LW 29:23, 29, 69–70, 74–77, 78–79.

15. WA 25:54.1–2; LW 29:67.

16. WA 25:28.15–19; LW 29:33.

17. WA 25:69.3; LW 29:89.

"*antonomasia*" (the use of a name, title, or descriptive phrase in place of a proper noun),[18] "*tapinosis*" (language designed to insult or diminish the importance of another person),[19] and "*praeoccupatio*" (an argument against an anticipated objection).[20]

Luther's university education had equipped him to cite ancient authors such as Pliny (ca. AD 24-79), Suetonius (ca. AD 70-ca. 122),[21] Virgil (70-19 BC),[22] and Aristotle (385-323 BC), as well as patristic sources, e.g., Jerome (ca. AD 347-420),[23] and the medieval book of the lives of the saints, the *Legenda aurea*.[24] From the beginning of his exegetical activity, Luther had used works by biblical humanists, including Johannes Reuchlin (1455-1522), Jacques Lefèvre d'Étaples (ca. 1450-ca. 1537), and Desiderius Erasmus (ca. 1467-1536). Erasmus also aided Luther in explaining the Epistle to Titus.[25]

Luther's belief that God works in the midst of human history dictated that he pay attention to historical settings and led him to use historical examples to interpret texts. Students were to recognize that Paul wrote this letter toward the end of his life, helping to set in personal context the apostle's disappointment at criticism from his foes.[26] Luther explained something of the ancient practice of slavery in commenting on Titus 2:9, applying Paul's admonition to faithful service to the servants of his own day, of whose carelessness and laziness he often complained.[27] Examples from ecclesiastical and secular history also served his application of certain texts. A rehearsal of the unfortunate imposition of celibacy upon the clergy at Nicaea in 325 provided support for pastors being the "husband of one wife" (1:6)[28] as the professor continued his deconstruction of false elements of medieval pious practice and teaching. Cassiodorus's (c. 485-c. 583)

---

18. WA 25:33.29-30; *LW* 29:39.

19. WA 25:36.11-13; *LW* 29:43.

20. WA 25:68.19-20; *LW* 29:88.

21. WA 25:12.31-33; *LW* 29:12.

22. WA 25:54.3-5; *LW* 29:67.

23. WA 25:25.27-29; *LW* 29:29.

24. WA 25:62.1-2; *LW* 29:79. This seems to refer to a story about the apostle Peter in the *Aurea Legenda*.

25. WA 25:45.14-17; 58.29-31; *LW* 29:56, 74.

26. WA 25:10.4-14; *LW* 29:8.

27. WA 25:48.15-51.16; *LW* 29:60-64; cf. Large Catechism, *BSELK* 1008/1009; *BC* 416.

28. WA 25:18.15-19.6; *LW* 29:19-20.

report of Spyridon's (270-348) assertion of Christian freedom against a person who defined being Christian by observance of rules for Lenten fasting illustrated proper witness against works-righteousness.[29] Emperor Frederick II (1194-1250) exemplified the absence of *epieikeia* in rulers.[30] Jan Hus's (ca. 1370-1415) concentration on proclaiming Christ embodied the confessor of the truth of God's word against error and a rejection of allegory for proper textual interpretation.[31] Luther found his own elector, Frederick the Wise (1463-1525), an excellent example of sober judgment (1:8).[32] Memories of the Peasants' Revolt of 1524-1525 gave occasion to criticize nobles who, during Emperor Maximilian's (1459-1519) time, had ignored the need for public order until the revolt, "when they really took a bath but still refused to repent."[33]

Luther grounded his study of the text in its historical setting, for he believed that God spoke through the prophets and apostles at specific times in specific places. He brought to that focus a strong command of classical and medieval rhetorical analysis, which he believed added to the students' ability to penetrate the text. But he intended they do so in order to be able to apply God's commands for their people's daily life (law) in light of all that Christ had accomplished for them in his death and resurrection. He delivered this message through straightforward analysis of the historical and rhetorical aspects of the text in a catechetical manner. In his lectures on Titus he employed narratives, one of his frequently used methods in preaching and in some other exegetical lectures, and little typology.[34] He focused on the cultivation of the pastoral skills on the basis of this text.

TITUS AS THE MODEL PASTOR

The first chapter of Titus presented Luther with an excellent basis for imparting to his students his model for the person of the pastor, his conduct of his office, and his most important tasks. Luther's instruction

---

29. WA 25:36.19-29; LW 29:43; cf. Cassiodorus, *Historia tripartita*, I:10.

30. WA 25:59.21-23; LW 29:75.

31. WA 25:28.21-23; 62.35-63.2; LW 29:33, 80; cf. Philip N. Haberkern, *Patron Saint and Prophet: Jan Hus in the Bohemian and German Reformation* (Oxford: Oxford University Press, 2016), 150-210.

32. WA 25:26.7-9; LW 29:29-30.

33. WA 25:60.32-36; LW 29:77.

34. Kolb, *Martin Luther and the Enduring Word of God*, esp. 153-67.

methodically followed the epistle's text, but his comments make clear what he wanted his students to become as he pursued his goal of fashioning evangelical preachers of God's word and caretakers of their congregations. The preacher is a "servant of God," not of the law or of other people. Luther made a point of reminding the students that although all believers exercise the obligation of sharing God's word with others, they would receive an office, a formal position, as a public minister of the gospel. God's commission to teach publicly gave Paul assurance as an apostle; they, too, could be certain of Christ's support through their public calling.[35] Anabaptist preachers had begun to enter Saxon territory in 1526.[36] Because they were working outside the established order of the church, Luther regarded them as subversive. Therefore, he assured his students that their orderly call to public ministry would give them confidence as they fulfilled their duties. All Christians are priests and therefore are to be teaching, praying, and sacrificing the sacrifice of love and service for others (Rom 12:5; Heb 13:1–3). But Paul's command that Titus appoint elders for the congregations on Crete revealed that not all should publicly teach and exhort.[37] Commenting on the bishop as the manager of God's household (1:7), Luther noted that those appointed to be ministers of the word take care of God's family, "preaching the gospel and administering the sacraments, instructing the uneducated, exhorting those who have been educated, rebuking those who misbehave through the moderating use of the Word and prayer and the sacraments."[38] Luther believed that all the baptized are called to be priests of God, with direct access to him in prayer and with the commission to apply God's word to others in calling them to repentance and forgiving their sins. But the public discharge of the tasks of leadership and public teaching fell to those with special calls to the calling of pastor.[39]

God has given the pastoral office to the church especially for the proclamation of his word. The apostle himself served as a model for proclaiming

---

35. WA 25:7.21–30; LW 29:5.

36. John S. Oyer, *Lutheran Reformers against Anabaptists: Luther, Melanchthon and Menius and the Anabaptists of Central Germany* (The Hague: Nijhoff, 1964), 46–69.

37. WA 25:16.17–28; LW 29:16.

38. WA 25:21.8–14; LW 29:22–23.

39. Robert Kolb and Charles P. Arand, *The Genius of Luther's Theology: A Wittenberg Way of Thinking for the Contemporary Church* (Grand Rapids: Baker Academic, 2008), 175–220.

Christ and an illustration of the difference between earlier proclaimers of God's message, from Moses through the prophets and apostles, because he preached Christ, "the greater glory" (2 Cor 3:7–18).[40] The proclamation of Christ and his benefits for the cultivation of a life centered on Jesus' death and resurrection defined the task of the pastor. Paul served as one appointed to provide Christ's ministry and message to God's people, and Titus was to follow suit as his true son, to whom the apostle had passed on his new birth in Christ. Luther's students were to follow Luther in like manner.[41] Decrying the medieval model of the parish priest, whose chief duty was the conduct of ritual with works parallel to those commanded by Moses, Luther condemned "ceremonies such as those of the Pharisees, rosaries, vows, masses, vigils, monastic works of the papists, abandonment of material goods by the Anabaptists"—"the outward show of chanting through the night, fasting, torturing the body," as Luther had experienced in the monastery. On the contrary, "where God's Word is diligently used, there is pure worship. Souls are aroused to faith, love toward God and neighbor is taught. This is our, the Christian, religion, to believe in Christ and to be moved to compassion for the poor and the weak ... and if the cross approaches, that is the complete Christian religion."[42] Luther's own experience over the previous decade, beginning with his excommunication and condemnation as an imperial outlaw in 1521, had placed Christian living in the context of the eschatological battle, in which Satan and God engage in battle on the field of God's people, as church and as individuals. The cross had become for him a mark of the church.[43]

SERMONS

In his *German Mass* of 1526, Luther had defined the sermon as "the most important part of the divine service."[44] To prepare to preach well, pastors must steep themselves in the study of Scripture. In explaining how bishops were to "hold firm" (1:9), Luther admonished his students never to lay the Bible aside but to read it diligently "and stick to it for others,"

---

40. WA 25:8.1–14; LW 29:5.

41. WA 25:14.17–15.22; LW 29:14–15.

42. WA 25:10.31–11.16; LW 29:11–12.

43. As he wrote a decade later, WA 50:513.1–16; 641.20–643.5; LW 41:12, 164–66.

44. WA 19:78.26–27; LW 53:68.

but also "constantly meditate on it for [themselves]," as Paul had admonished Timothy (1 Tim 4:13-15). They were to pour themselves totally into the Scripture. Failure to do so causes pastors to rust and fall into neglect of God's word and contempt for it. "Even if you know Holy Scripture, it must nevertheless be read again and again, because this Word has the power to set you ablaze each time. I have been preaching the gospel for five years,[45] but I experience a new flame repeatedly."[46]

The regular study of Scripture lay the foundation for pastors to proclaim God's word and combat its foes. In treating Titus 3:5, Luther emphasized that students were to center their preaching on Christ, for, as he had noted at Titus 1:14, "Our faith depends solely on Christ. He alone is righteous; I am not. For his righteousness stands for me in the face of God's judgment and against God's wrath."[47] He urged students to meditate on passages such as Titus 3:5, repeatedly reading them in order to prepare their application to the lives of their people, both the uninstructed and those whom he labeled "young theologians" (probably his students), so that they not be diverted from the historical sense of the text into the kind of allegories that had so devastated the theologies of Jerome and Origen (ca. 185-ca. 254).[48] This reinforced Luther's observation on Titus 2:15, encouraging exhortation and reproof: "If one pays attention when opening the book, he will not leave it without its bearing fruit. It refreshes a person, purging evil thoughts and introducing good thoughts." When evil thoughts return, one should open the book again, for Scripture is called "a book of patience." "The nature of this Word is to cleanse the heart and set it afire." Therefore, Luther urged prayer along with reading the biblical text to fend off Satan's attacks and those of the world.[49]

In addition, Luther warned students against delving into "sophistic disputes about useless and uncertain myths" and "unhealthy and doubtful" questions, mere "opinions," in the manner of the "Schwärmer,"[50] "who

---

45. Possibly an indication that Luther believed that the core of his theology had come together for him around 1522.

46. WA 25:27.5-8; LW 29:30-31.

47. WA 25:35.1-3; LW 29:41.

48. WA 25:62.20-63.11; LW 29:80.

49. WA 25:55.13-19; LW 29:69.

50. On Luther's invention of this term and his use of it, see Amy Nelson Burnett, "Luther and the *Schwärmer*," in *The Oxford Handbook to Martin Luther's Theology*, ed. Robert Kolb, Irene

know nothing about what they are discussing" (1 Tim 1:7). In this way the students would be prepared to teach and to counter false teachings effectively, opposing unhealthy teachings with what is "correct, stable, and reliable."[51] As in the days of Jan Hus, Satan was continuing to raise up those who wished to pervert God's word, Luther cautioned, preparing his hearers for the conflicts that they would face. For "the faithful shepherd not only feeds his flock but also protects it" by calling attention to heresies and errors, such as the "Sacramentarians" with whom Luther was contending at that time, above all Andreas Karlstadt (ca. 1480–1541), Huldrych Zwingli (1484–1531), and Johannes Oecolampadius (1482–1531).[52] They could expect to encounter "home-grown Satans," who would reject the proper teaching of God's word and who could not be persuaded of the truth but continued their "empty talk" (1:10).[53]

CHARACTER

Luther also had definite ideas about the person and personality of his students as they entered the service of congregations. The Epistle to Titus presented a rich vein of resources for cultivating this image of a faithful shepherd of God's people. Luther paid careful attention to the nuances conveyed by the adjectives of the candidates for ministry that Titus was to foster for the church on Crete. "Blameless" did not refer to the kind of perfection that Jerome's interpretation had envisioned but signified that the pastor should have no public guilt that would cause offense. This reflects Luther's awareness that those who are honest with themselves struggle with temptation as had the high priests, who also exhibited weakness (Heb 5:2).[54] Paul's prescription that pastors should be the husband of one wife gave occasion for an intense polemic against clerical celibacy, which in

Dingel, and Ľubomír Batka (Oxford: Oxford University Press, 2014), 511–24.

51. WA 25:27.9–28.14; LW 29:31–32.

52. See further Amy Nelson Burnett, *Debating the Sacraments: Print and Authority in the Early Reformation* (Oxford: Oxford University Press, 2019).

53. WA 25:28.17–31.6; LW 29:33–36.

54. WA 25:17.19–27; LW 29:17–18.

1527 continued to be a significant issue and the prime cause of the imprisonment of priests under Roman episcopal control.[55]

Paul's condemnation of profligacy in Titus 1:6 prompted him to tell students to avoid *asotia*, noting that the Greeks tended toward drunkenness and sexual carousing, like the sons of Eli (2 Sam 2:12–17) and many children of the nobility in their own day. Luther seldom passed up a chance to criticize the nobility, especially princely courtiers. He labeled the young noblemen who resisted the imposition of order upon their lives "intractable" and "incorrigible."[56] Luther viewed greed as the most widespread form of idolatry;[57] Paul's admonition against seeking "filthy lucre" in Titus 1:7 gave Luther reason to criticize priests of the old order who charged for conducting masses, another effort at the deconstruction of medieval practice.[58]

The professor interpreted the Latin *percutere* ("to strike or pierce") as the violence of harassing consciences and imposing laws upon believers that burden their consciences without biblical grounds, a habit he ascribed to papal followers.[59] This violence of "words and behavior" "is a great vice of preachers ... who rail against the faults and persons of their hearers. They strive for the favor of the mob." The mob, Luther observed, likes to hear such preaching, especially when the magistrates are being attacked. Although Luther also insisted on the necessity of calling local nobles and town councils to repentance from the pulpit when they perpetrated social injustice,[60] he here condemned unseemly attacks upon them in a sermon. He warned against seditious preaching, noting that the common people also needed to be reprimanded, and cautioned against public criticism before the proper order prescribed by Jesus in Matthew 18:15–17 had been followed, since only the Holy Spirit can truly convict (John 16:8). Bishops are called to comfort the weak and to heal the contrite in heart, with admonitions conducted in a spirit of gentleness, as Paul dictated (Gal 6:1).[61]

---

55. WA 25:17.28–20.14; LW 29:17.18–21; cf. Marjorie Elizabeth Plummer, *From Priest's Whore to Pastor's Wife, Clerical Marriage and the Process of Reform in the Early German Reformation* (Farnham: Ashgate, 2012), 123–29, 134–35.

56. WA 25:15–33; LW 29:21–22.

57. BSELK 932/933; BC 387.

58. WA 25:25.20–21; LW 29:28–29.

59. WA 25:21.22–29; LW 29:23.

60. Robert Kolb, "Luther on Peasants and Princes," *Lutheran Quarterly* 23 (2009): 125–46.

61. WA 25:24.20–25.9; LW 29:27–28.

The Greek word *authades* ("arrogant") referred to clinging to honors and being pleased with oneself, Luther contended. Such arrogance is not in accord with the mind of Christ commended by Paul in Philippians 2:5–11, for "he emptied himself" (Luther presumed the entire passage would come to his students' thinking with the mention of a phrase). Faithful ministers of God's word share their gifts of learning with others without calling attention to their learnedness.[62] Luther linked arrogance to irascibility, a vice bishops were also to avoid. "He should be gentle and meek that he may be able to bear their weaknesses and all the diseases of their souls … and have the attitude of a father or a mother." For Peter had forbade domineering over those entrusted to a pastor (1 Pet 5:3; 2 Cor 4:5).[63] Luther commented quite briefly that Paul's admonition against drunkenness (Titus 1:7) condemns an arrogance that tyrannizes the congregation; he added that one may drink wine but must remain sober and not be given over to the wine.[64] In Titus 1:8 Paul's admonition to exercise sober judgment mandated that pastors be modest and moderate in judgment, both in food and drink but also in the way they treated people and interacted with them, resisting an excitable spirit and an impulsive heart, acting only after listening and reflecting.[65]

Bishops in apostolic times were often wealthy and could afford generous hospitality at an economic level his students could not expect to enjoy, but they were to receive both good and evil people hospitably. As pastors, they were to favor the good and promote piety, the study of Scripture, peace, harmony, and friendship among neighbors, as well as other good causes. They were to urge town council members and princes to support orphans and widows, strike down evildoers, and help the good.[66]

Luther interpreted Paul's admonition to be "just" as the pastor's instruction to decide cases of adjudication without partiality, resisting misleading feelings of affection for one party in the matter. Bishops dare not let money play a role in their decision-making—Luther's reaction against the pecuniary pressures faced by medieval clergy. He rejected the medieval

62. WA 25:21.30–22.28; LW 29:23–25.
63. WA 25:23.2–15; LW 29:25.
64. WA 25:24.13–20; LW 29:27.
65. WA 25:25.35–26.6; LW 29:29.
66. WA 25:22–34; LW 29:29.

concentration on holy objects, such as relics, in defining what "holy" meant for ministers of God's word: it meant that they belong to Christ, not to Satan, dedicating themselves to teaching, living, praying, and meditating in a godly manner, not cursing or engaging in other profane thoughts, talk, actions, and habits. The apostle also commanded moderation in food, drink, and sexual relationships, in word and deed (1 Cor 9:27).[67]

THE MINISTERS OF GOD, THE WORD
OF GOD, THE PEOPLE OF GOD

Luther's theology developed between the poles of biblical authority, faithfully interpreted for God's people by their shepherds, and pastoral care, the apt application of God's word to the lives of their hearers. The professor reminded his hearers that, like the bishops Titus was to commission, they should "be the kind of bishop who keeps watch over his flock."[68] The personality that Paul described in chapter one laid the necessary foundation for the pastor's "principal activity," teaching, which, for Luther, referred to every mode of communicating God's word. Teaching presumed a pastor's "integrity, seriousness, ability to use proper words, and blamelessness" (2:7). Luther explained Paul's words. "Integrity" meant "preserving and being responsible for" God's word in its true form, not adulterating it by mixing it with other teachings or squandering it. The admonition to "seriousness" forbade "tickling the ears of hearers with jokes" (2 Tim 4:3), as had some medieval preachers by retelling a body of amusing stories in Easter sermons. Their teaching had to be clear and unassailable on the basis of the Scriptural text.[69]

Proper teaching centered for Luther, as noted above, on the proclamation of Christ and the forgiveness of sins apprehended through faith, as he had emphasized at numerous places in his recently concluded lectures on 1 John. When the text of Titus warranted, Luther repeated this central message and deduced from it the characteristics of the righteous actions that followed from trusting God's pronouncement of the righteousness of believers through Christ's death and resurrection. His comments on

---

67. WA 25:26.12–27; LW 29:30.
68. WA 25:19.22; LW 29:20.
69. WA 25:47.19–48.14; LW 29:59–69.

Titus 1:1–2 set in place his presupposition regarding the entire Christian life, that its basis is grounded in knowing the truth of God's action and trusting his message that "Christ was handed over into death for our sins and raised to restore our righteousness" (Rom 4:25). Trust in God alone and his work creates the holiness and purity of believers, not their works. "Nothing leads to righteousness except [this] faith and knowledge."[70] Repeatedly Luther used the text of Titus to condemn papal reliance on works for contributing to deliverance from sin.[71] Christ delivered his people not only from sin but also from death, the wages of sin (Rom 6:23). That produces hope in believers (Titus 1:1–2), even in the midst of the ongoing struggle against sin. "Hope means to expect life in the midst of death and righteousness in the midst of sins" (1:2). Luther emphasized the reliability and faithfulness of God and his promise, following the epistle's text (1:2–3).[72]

In lecturing on Titus, Luther spoke about forgiveness and justification, but, as throughout his lecturing and preaching, he put other synonyms for God's saving work in Christ to use when the text dictated this.[73] Luther elaborated occasionally on the language of purification or cleansing from the filth of sinfulness. Faith cleanses from sin because it trusts in God's promise and produces the purity of a life of love for others.[74] Luther used the medieval pairing of Christ as *donum* or *sacramentum*, gift or that which delivers from sin, and *exemplum*, the model for the life of faith, in these lectures to interpret what it means that God's grace has come into the world. Therefore, he easily moved from trust in Christ to Christian living, noting that believers experience the conflict between flesh and spirit, as Luther himself frequently admitted of himself, but they have confidence that God aids them in showing love to the neighbor, rendering obedience to rulers, and dealing uprightly with others.[75]

---

70. *WA* 25:8.15–9.25; *LW* 29:6–7.

71. *WA* 25:10.31–11.7; *LW* 29:9.

72. *WA* 25:11.15–13.24; *LW* 29:9–13.

73. Ian D. K. Siggins, *Martin Luther's Doctrine of Christ* (New Haven: Yale University Press, 1970), 154–56.

74. E.g., *WA* 25:37.26–38.32; 54.1–17; *LW* 29:45–46, 67–68.

75. *WA* 25:51.17–52.13; *LW* 29:64–65. Cf. Norman Nagel, "*Sacramentum et Exemplum* in Luther's Understanding of Christ," in *Luther for an Ecumenical Age*, ed. Carl S. Meyer (St. Louis: Concordia, 1967), 172–99.

Commenting on Titus 1:1, where Luther defined the Christian life as believing in Christ and having compassion for the poor and weak, he continued by defining the godliness of Christian living as the parental feeling toward children, which he had begun to experience the previous year.[76] He repeated his illustration of the good tree of trust in Christ producing the good fruit of believers' works.[77] His own understanding of Christian living based the new obedience of faith on the Christian's callings in the three walks of life envisioned by medieval social theory—*ecclesia, politia, oeconomia*—carried out in accord with God's commands. The second chapter of the Epistle to Titus provided a most suitable text for treating the different situations of human life in this structure of God's call to serve in all three spheres of daily life. He followed the epistle's outline of human life with extensive treatment of topics he would soon cover in similar fashion in his *Large Catechism*: family life,[78] the calling of servants so vital for household and economic activities,[79] and political duties, both of rulers and subjects.[80]

Luther's lectures on the Epistle to Titus echo his treatment of the central themes of his thinking, as reflected, for example, in his commentaries on Galatians or Genesis. Lecturing on Titus, Luther revealed his key concerns for what his students did with their Wittenberg education and his method for cultivating the person whom he was sending into the ministry of God's word. He sought to mold a minister whose personal character reflected God's commands for human life and whose abilities enabled him to bring hearers to repentance and give them the consolation of the gospel of Jesus Christ.

---

76. *WA* 25:22.13–21; *LW* 29:10. Cf. Birgit Stolt, "Martin Luther on God as Father," *Lutheran Quarterly* 8 (1994): 385–95.

77. E.g., *WA* 25:41.19–42.15; *LW* 29:50.

78. *WA* 25; *LW* 29; cf. *BSELK* 896/897; *BC* 366.

79. *WA* 25; *LW* 29; cf. *BSELK* 898/899; *BC* 366.

80. *WA* 25; *LW* 29; cf. *BSELK* 894/895–896/897; *BC* 365.

5

—

GOD'S WORD, BAPTISM, AND REGENERATION

Timo Laato

Generally, when baptism is discussed, doctrinal problems and many misunderstandings arise.[1] When discussing it with Anabaptist movements, the discussion centers on what baptism is not: it is not a means of grace; it is not a sacrament; it does not convey forgiveness of sins; it does not regenerate; it does not save; in vain do many people trust in it and not God's mercy; etc. One would think that the Baptist churches should, in light of their name, concentrate on speaking especially about baptism and the marvelous heavenly gifts conveyed by it. In practice the opposite is often the case. They seldom emphasize those aspects of baptism. At most they teach that baptism is the first act of obedience to God performed by the believer. That is all.

On the other hand, in the proclamation of state churches of Western Christendom, the problem is often the undisputed fact that many baptized persons do not live according to the requirements of their baptism. Must one still consider them to be regenerate? Are they still all God's children? Will they finally reach heaven? Does baptism imprint on them some kind of indelible stamp or character? And what about if they sometime later in life become "true believers," as the saying goes? What really happens within them at that point? Are they perhaps born again a second (or third, or fourth, or fifth) time? How does one reconcile their own experience or

---

1. This article has been translated from the Finnish original by Risto Relander. After translation, the essay was revised by the author (Timo Laato). See "Jumalan sana, kaste ja uudestisyntyminen," in *Kirkon parhaaksi 30 vuotta*, ed. T. Eskola ja J. Rankinen, Iustitia 35 (Helsinki: 2018), 164–207.

testimony of their conversion with the official teaching of the church? Consequently, when it comes to discussions of baptism, state churches have just as many problems as the Anabaptists.

Matti Väisänen, bishop emeritus of the Luther Foundation in Finland, has written extensively on baptism. He has published books on it comprising over two thousand pages. Although there is a lot of repetition in them and his presentation of this topic has not always been very polished or succinct, he has really toiled and labored with the doctrine of baptism. In the preface of his latest monograph he maintains that it "does not surely exhaust the entire treasure chest of baptism" and that others will sooner or later "come along to complete, and if necessary to correct, what I have written on baptism."[2] The most discussion has been caused by Väisänen's severe criticism of orthodox Lutheranism (which is in fact also directed against Luther and the Lutheran Confessions) as well as the scriptural content of his arguments. The fact that Väisänen has been a bishop of a Lutheran, confessional Mission Diocese has aroused even more amazement and astonishment. In that capacity he has ordained many a pastor into the holy ministry and required of them all that they pledge themselves to the Lutheran Confessions. In the course of years, the Mission Diocese overseen by him has published and distributed his books in Finland and also elsewhere in the world. This has created an extraordinary situation, a kind of doctrinal impasse, whence it is difficult to find one's way out.

As I understand it, Väisänen has by and large succeeded in defending the right of infant baptism. Regarding that aspect there is no great reason to pursue a dialogue with him. However, more careful consideration and investigation of grounds is needed, insofar as he rejects important emphases of orthodox Lutheranism. The key issue here is the question of the regenerating power of God's word. So as to get a synopsis of the matter, we must first briefly present Väisänen's teaching. Later on, we can take up different details of his teaching. We do not, of course, have the opportunity to present an all-encompassing summary of his books. After the general presentation we shall examine his teaching critically, with special concern given to the regenerating power of God's word.

---

2. M. Väisänen, *Baptism, Faith, and Salvation: In the Bible and Lutheran Confessions* (Helsinki: The Evangelical Lutheran Mission Diocese of Finland, 2017), 6.

I will briefly mention here that in this study the concept "regeneration" is taken to mean the generation of faith, or spiritual birth. A "born again" person is one who believes in the forgiveness of sins by God's grace, for Christ's sake, and who will receive life everlasting.[3]

THE CURRENT DISCUSSION OF REGENERATION

Väisänen restricts regeneration to baptism only. He specifically denies and rejects the idea that God's word could regenerate. That kind of teaching would, according to him, lead to a peculiar "theology of the two ways of salvation." If regeneration took place also in some way other than baptism, there would be no sense in baptizing anyone, since they would already have been born again before their regeneration! As a necessary corrective, Väisänen states that God's word indeed has regenerating power, but only in baptism, not outside of it. Thus he dissociates himself from orthodox Lutheranism, which teaches the "theology of two ways of salvation" rejected by him. Furthermore, he emphasizes that he has found support for his views from Luther and also from the Lutheran Confessions that supposedly teach otherwise than Lutheran orthodoxy.[4]

Now and again, Väisänen appeals to our use of language, where (natural) "birth" denotes something that takes place once and for all and is not anything repeatable. Likewise, spiritual birth also takes place once and for all. Consequently, it comes to pass in baptism only, never in any other way. A scriptural example is Jesus' incarnation, his "regeneration" into a man.[5] In the "process of His 'regeneration,' the Son of God was conceived by the Holy Spirit through the Word" and was born as a man. In a similar manner, "our regeneration as children of God is preceded by conception through the Word of God," but regeneration takes place only in baptism.[6] Beside the concept of regeneration, Väisänen creates a new concept, "reconception."

---

3. The concept "regeneration" can also mean renovation following the generation of faith or both of them. Later on I shall refer to the analysis of the Lutheran Confessions as to the different meanings.

4. Väisänen, *Baptism, Faith, and Salvation*, especially 30–113.

5. Väisänen, *Baptism, Faith, and Salvation*, especially 30–50.

6. Väisänen, *Baptism, Faith, and Salvation*, 34.

What he means is that "God conceives, i.e. initiates, a new man" through his word, but only in baptism "God gives birth to a new man."[7]

Furthermore, Väisänen has noticed those passages in the New Testament "where regeneration, the new birth, through believing the Word (of the Gospel) is mentioned and nothing is said of baptism"[8] (especially 1 Cor 4:15; Gal 4:19; 1 Pet 1:23; Jas 1:18[9]). He points out that these passages speak about either "reconception" (1 Cor 4:15), staying as God's child (Gal 4:19), or regeneration in baptism when viewed in their context (1 Pet 2:23; Jas 1:18). Therefore, they do not say anything about the power of the gospel word to regenerate.[10]

In addition, Väisänen examines many passages in the Acts which speak of believing the word before baptism (e.g., 2:41; 8:12, 36; 16:14; 18:8). These texts he explains by speaking of "the two-fold character of faith" and makes a careful distinction between two faiths: faith before baptism and after baptism.[11] The former is a still-unsaved person's assent to be saved, the latter "the faith of the saved."[12] The faith before baptism is "conceived by the Holy Spirit through the Word." It is "taking hold of the Gospel of Christ" and "hungering and thirsting for righteousness," but without assurance of salvation. Not until baptism is faith received "as the gift of the Holy Spirit." Such Spirit-given saving faith includes "living from the Gospel of Christ" and "righteousness, joy, and peace," and also assurance of salvation.[13] From this logically follows that the pre-baptism faith engendered by the gospel or Christian proclamation in the Acts was not yet saving faith.

Now and again Väisänen refers to John 3:5. He considers it one of the principal passages when trying to convince his readers of regeneration taking place in baptism only and nowhere else. Being "born of the water and of the Spirit" speaks anticipatorily and specifically of the Christian baptism.[14]

---

7. Väisänen, *Baptism, Faith, and Salvation*, 84.
8. Väisänen, *Baptism, Faith, and Salvation*, 37.
9. Väisänen, *Baptism, Faith, and Salvation*, 38–46.
10. Väisänen, *Baptism, Faith, and Salvation*, 38–46.
11. Väisänen, *Baptism, Faith, and Salvation*, 90–99.
12. Väisänen, *Baptism, Faith, and Salvation*, 94.
13. Väisänen, *Baptism, Faith, and Salvation*, 98.
14. Väisänen, *Baptism, Faith, and Salvation*, 246 (index of Scripture passages referred to).

From these (and many other details), Väisänen considers it proven that regeneration in the New Testament is only applied to baptism. It is a unique and singular event. Because justification takes place in baptism, it too is a unique and singular event. It can never be repeated as such. "By contrast, a person's *participation* in it can be disrupted, even several times. Justification does not vanish, but our participation in it can be severed."[15]

My brief summary of Väisänen's book (and books) will suffice. Later on many of his explanations and their details shall be examined in greater depth.

REGENERATION IN LUTHER'S THEOLOGY, THE LUTHERAN CONFESSIONS, AND THE BIBLE

In the evaluation of Väisänen's teaching we shall primarily proceed from the general to the particular. Consequently, the two main principles of the Reformation are to be discussed first, and then the Lutheran conception of the relationship between the word and the sacraments. From the overview it will be easier to focus on the many details without losing sight of the big picture. Furthermore, all doctrine and teaching must be founded on Scripture. Therefore, we must also study the Scriptures.

THE DOCTRINE OF LUTHER AND THE LUTHERAN CONFESSIONS

God's word and God's Word

The main principles of the Reformation are the authority of Scripture and the message of salvation. They belong together and must never be separated from each other. Furthermore, they are both intimately connected with Christ's person. God's Son is the Word become flesh. Therefore, he is the whole Scripture. He has merited the forgiveness of sins for the world on the cross. Consequently, he is himself our righteousness. Put another way, he saves us through faith, which he works and engenders in us by the power of his word. *Solus Christus* ("Christ alone") entails both *sola Scriptura* ("the Bible alone") and *sola fide* ("through faith alone"). As a result, Christ is "all in all," and there is no glory left to us. This is just what the Reformation was all about!

---

15. Väisänen, *Baptism, Faith, and Salvation*, 67.

The word combined with the baptismal water is basically nothing else than the Word become flesh, Christ, the omnipotent God. Naturally, he has already in himself, on the basis of his omnipotence, the power to regenerate. Denying that power indicates an ominous, Arian distortion in doctrine, as Christ's true divinity is denied and at the same time an impression of orthodoxy of a kind is attempted. Because God's word and God's Word are always inseparably connected, there is no difference between them. One cannot belittle and disparage the word without belittling and disparaging the Word. Therefore, in all the means of grace, it is just the word—i.e., the Word—that is the main thing. They do not convey grace without it and him, but would stay empty as to content, becoming mere ceremonies.

In Reformed theology, that is, in Zwingli's and Calvin's thinking, the main principles of the Reformation utterly disappeared in completely other kinds of solutions. Scripture was not as such considered to be God's powerful word, but God speaks through it only when the Holy Spirit makes it God's word. Thus Scripture does not in itself have the power to regenerate anyone. For that, a heavenly influence from outside the word is needed. Then something happens. Correspondingly, the salvation earned by Christ does not really pertain to the whole humankind, but to those alone who have been predestined to eternal life; they shall receive grace during the time of grace. It was not even intended for others. Consequently, the word of the gospel does not apply to everyone, nor does it engender faith in others than the elect, a group carefully limited, who have been predestined to salvation. Thus the Holy Spirit "initiates" the saving power of Scripture, as it were, from outside, conditioned by predestination. Only then does Scripture become powerful to regenerate certain, carefully selected hearers.

The teaching that denies the regenerating power of God's word originates, therefore, in sources utterly foreign to scriptural Lutheranism. It derives from Reformed theology of the likes of Zwingli and Calvin. Väisänen has formerly represented the so-called Fifth Awakening in Finland. He has led the movement from the beginning to his retirement. Typical of that movement has been the denial of baptismal regeneration, but on the other hand, accepting regeneration through the word. Now the swing of the pendulum has surprisingly reached the other extreme: one has come to reject regeneration through the word but accept baptismal regeneration.

As a result, today's Väisänen is a mirror image of yesterday's Väisänen. The Fifth Awakening is called Neopietism, which does not always draw its teaching from scriptural Lutheranism, but from evangelicalism influential all over the world. There is a lot of good in evangelicalism, but it is strongly swayed by Reformed theology. Väisänen's view, which absolutely rules out the regenerating power of God's word, stems from this historical background. In an early stage, he began to modify his doctrine of baptism in a more Lutheran direction. At the same time, he started to modify his doctrine of the word in a more Reformed direction. Thus an ominous distortion developed. According to it, God's word has no regenerating power. Consequently, it ushers in an exceedingly peculiar theology, which is in deep conflict with the other main principle of the Reformation and the whole of orthodox Lutheranism (see below).

The Relationship between the Word and the Sacraments

As we have seen, Väisänen thinks very straightforwardly and one-sidedly that God's word cannot regenerate because regeneration takes place in baptism only. In this sense, he plays baptism against the word. It is a matter of "either/or," not "both/and." As a means of grace, baptism gives something that the word, as a means of grace, is not able to give. Then one must ask whence the word has its regenerating power in baptism, if it does not have that power before and outside of it. Luther, as we know, asks in the Small Catechism, "How can water do such great things?" He answers:

> Clearly the water does not do it, but the Word of God, which is with and alongside the water, and faith, which trusts this Word of God in the water. For without the Word of God the water is plain water and not a baptism, but with the Word of God it is a baptism, that is, a grace-filled water of life and a "bath of the new birth in the Holy Spirit."[16]

Thus the regenerating power of baptism is in God's word, which does not first receive this power when it is combined with the water but has this power in itself before and outside of baptism. Does Luther mean that the special gift of baptism becomes null and void if God's word regenerates?

---

16. *The Small Catechism* 4.3, quoting Titus 3:5; BC 360.

How does he, in that case, precisely understand the relationship between the word and baptism, or more generally, between the word and the sacraments?

The sole content of all the means of grace (the word of the gospel, baptism, the holy communion, and absolution) is Christ himself and his grace. Because he is God's Word, the means of grace have God's word as their central and effective factor. The sacraments (baptism and the holy communion, and sometimes also absolution) are the "visible word" because in them the word is combined with a visible element (that is, water, bread and wine, the lips of the confessor). In this way they all belong together and, as means of grace, convey one and the same grace. It is not, however, denied that baptism is especially the sacrament of regeneration, the holy communion the sacrament of the Lord's body and blood, and absolution the sacrament of the oral forgiveness of sins.

God's word is thus demonstrably "all in all." We need it either in written or heard or visible form. Only it saves. God's word has the power to regenerate its hearers. Therefore it directs them to baptism, where regeneration takes place through the "visible word." Likewise, God's word feeds and nourishes Christians who prayerfully read it. Therefore it leads them to holy communion, where the feeding and nourishing take place through the "visible word." Furthermore, God's word testifies to everyone that sins have already been forgiven. Therefore it directs them to absolution, where the forgiveness of sins takes place not so much through the "visible word," but through the word that is heard. Because God's saving word is present in all the means of grace either in written or heard or visible form, they all together, and also each by itself, bring salvation. The significance or content of none of the means of grace will be nullified because of Christ being present in them all. And where Christ is, there is also his entire grace. No less will suffice for the sinner.

In accordance with this, Melanchthon speaks in the Lutheran Confessions, in the Apology, of the sacraments—that is, baptism, the holy communion, and also absolution—as "rites" and teaches about them:

> Just as the Word enters through the ear in order to strike the heart, so also the rite enters through the eye in order to move the heart. The word and the rite have the same effect. Augustine put it well

when he said that the sacrament is a "visible word," because the rite is received by the eyes and is, as it were, a picture of the Word, signifying the same thing as the Word. Therefore both have the same effect.[17]

In the same vein, Luther writes in the Lutheran Confessions, in the Smalcald Articles:

We now want to return to the gospel, which gives guidance and help against sin in more than one way, because God is extravagantly rich in his grace: first, through the spoken word, in which the forgiveness of sins is preached to the whole world (which is the proper function of the gospel); second, through baptism; third, through the holy Sacrament of the Altar; fourth, through the power of the keys and also through the mutual conversation and consolation of brothers and sisters.[18]

Therefore, it is futile and downright wrong to accuse orthodox Lutheranism of teaching "two ways of salvation" and to condemn as false the notion that both God's word and baptism save. If one necessarily wants to think so, then orthodox Lutheranism could very well be accused of teaching "three or four ways of salvation," for according to it, absolution and the holy communion also save. Then we must also accuse Luther, for he teaches similarly. However, it is not of course a matter of two, three, or four salvations, but one and the same salvation, which all the means of grace convey to us. It is completely arbitrary to play the means of grace, given to us by God for blessing, against one another. Rather, he is "superabundantly rich in his grace," which is given to us in different ways, so that no one has to doubt the truth and certainty of the gospel word.

The Incarnation of God's Son and the Sacraments

Furthermore, Luther points out that the miracle of the incarnation of Christ (who is God's Word) is the "incarnation of the word" in the sacraments. He speaks especially of the holy communion, but the same naturally

---

17. *The Apology of the Augsburg Confession* 13.5, BC 219–20.
18. *The Smalcald Articles* 3.4, BC 319.

applies also to baptism. In his book *On the Babylonian Captivity of the Church* he says,

> Thus, what is true in regard to Christ is also true in regard to the sacrament. In order for the divine nature to dwell in him bodily [Col 2:9], it is not necessary for the human nature to be transubstantiated and the divine nature contained under the accidents of the human nature. Both natures are simply there in their entirety, and it is truly said: "This man is God; this God is man." Even though philosophy cannot grasp this, faith grasps it nonetheless. And the authority of God's Word is greater than the capacity of our intellect to grasp it. In like manner, it is not necessary in the sacrament that the bread and wine be transubstantiated and that Christ be contained under their accidents in order that the real body and real blood may be present. But both remain there at the same time, and it is truly said: "This bread is my body; this wine is my blood," and vice versa.[19]

In accordance with this, the same unfathomable "Christmas miracle" takes place in baptism and the holy communion: the Word becomes flesh. He becomes the visible Word to help and save us. Therefore, a baptized person can really be glad of the grace of regeneration and step to the altar to partake of the body and blood of his heavenly Benefactor for forgiveness of sins. Thus, the miracle of Christmas is repeated through the whole church year, again and again. The selfsame Word, who is present in the gospel and himself is that very gospel, is visibly present also in the sacraments. Hence one will find him in the pulpit, beside the baptismal font, and at the altar. In that manner, God's grace encounters the sinner in the miracle of Christmas, in the word and the sacraments. This gospel, good news, engenders and strengthens faith.

Väisänen sees the incarnation of God's Word as a model for the sinner's regeneration.[20] Accordingly, he does not connect it, like Luther, with the sacraments, which effect the regeneration. As a result, the focus moves, as in false Pietism, onto man's own experience and the internal change

---

19. *The Babylonian Captivity of the Church*, LW 36:35.
20. Väisänen, *Baptism, Faith, and Salvation*, 30–35.

taking place in him. The theological shift entails that the assurance of salvation is no longer clearly and solely grounded on the means of grace. Besides, the miracle of the incarnation of God's Son consists in the conception of God's Son and not only his birth later on. Väisänen, when speaking of regeneration and making an artificial distinction between reconception and regeneration, does not actually mean that "true salvation" is conveyed by reconception, but by regeneration alone. Consequently, his emphasis on the alleged correspondence of the "regeneration" of God's Son with ours breaks down right from the outset. As such, God's Son certainly does not need any re-generation; he simply was born as a human being. We, by contrast, need to be born again, for we are sinners and godless by nature. Let this be said so that the miracle of Christmas in connection with the sacraments does not degenerate into some indefinite, obscure teaching, from which it is not evident what is meant.

There is no reason to call God's vivifying and regenerating word, which is tantamount to God's eternal Word become flesh, the "dry word," as Väisänen does when speaking of baptism as the "soaking wet word."[21] This kind of language does not do justice to the holy word, that is, Scripture, nor to the Word become flesh, that is, God's Son. The celebration of Christmas does not mean a celebration of some "dry word," but on the contrary, the celebration of the Word, through whom the seas and the waters, the land and the continents, and the heights and the depths have been created, and who stooped into a manger and later onto the cross so as to be the Savior of the whole of humankind. Without this Word, and this word, we have nothing, neither baptism nor the holy communion. Let our speech and expressions in holy awe bring forth the divine truths. "Dry" is our own reasoning, our attempts to understand and explain, our theological ramblings. Also we ourselves are "dry," or rather dead, because of sin, but God's Word has risen from the dead, and his word is "living and powerful" (Heb 4:12) forever. He makes our dry bones live again (Ezek 37).

---

21. Väisänen, *Baptism, Faith, and Salvation*, 217. Here he refers to A. Simojoki's "amusing" expression.

Luther's Teaching on Baptism in His Church Postil:
The Three Gospel Sermons on Ascension Day

So far, the central theological emphases of the Reformation regarding the word and the sacraments in general have been presented in a summary. Our focus lies next on Luther's written sermons and the more detailed analysis of his main thoughts there. First, let's consider an extract from his *Church Postil* with three sermons on Ascension Day. The text is Mark 16:14–20.

The Reformer teaches perfectly clearly (and differently from Väisänen) that a person comes to true faith already through the proclamation of the gospel, and that is precisely why he then wants to come to Christian baptism, in which his faith is strengthened by a "visible sign." When reading the following extracts from the sermon, please note they do not speak of two kinds of faith: "a faith that is not so real" (which the gospel purportedly generates before baptism) and "true faith" (which is engendered in baptism). That sort of explanation would nullify the scriptural teaching that God's word regenerates. Further notice how baptism, exactly as being the "visible word," corroborates that which has taken place through the word when the gospel was proclaimed. Thus, both of these means of grace are in agreement, the word being everywhere the factor that effects everything. But let us now hear Luther; the following extracts are from the Gospel postil on Ascension Day.

> "If someone asks and wants to know how to be saved, then this should be the chief point or chief doctrine: believing and being baptized." ... Here Christ announces and explains exactly what the chief doctrine of the Gospel is to be; He bases it only on faith and baptism, and He concludes that we are saved because of it, when we have Christ through faith in baptism.

> "Believing" essentially means regarding as true and depending with your whole heart on what the Gospel and all the articles of faith say about Christ. ... So that our faith would grasp and hold this all the more firmly, He gives us Baptism to testify with this visible sign that God accepts us and assuredly gives us what is proclaimed and offered to us through the Gospel.[22]

---

22. "Gospel for the Ascension of Christ," in *Church Postil*, LW 77:278–79.

Later on, Luther emphatically rejects the misconception that true faith engendered by the gospel could leave baptism aside or completely reject it. On the contrary, God's word, which regenerates, directs its hearer to baptism, in which regeneration then takes place through the "visible word" (as above in brief has been shown and proven from Luther's teaching):

> It does not follow from [Matthew 28:19–20] that we can for that reason omit Baptism or that it is enough if someone asserts that he has faith and does not need Baptism. Whoever becomes a Christian and believes will surely also be glad to accept this sign so that he both has this divine testimony and confirmation of his salvation and can find strength and comfort from it in his whole life. He will also publicly confess before all the world that both parts belong to a Christian, as Paul says, believing with the heart before God and by himself and confessing with the mouth before the world (Romans 10[:10]). Yet it can happen that a person can believe even though he is not baptized, and, on the other hand, some receive Baptism and yet do not truly believe.[23]

Furthermore, Luther unmistakably emphasizes that true faith, engendered by the gospel, saves a person, even if he should die before baptism, provided that he wants to receive baptism as a "visible sign" and does not put it off without good reason:

> For that reason we must understand that in this text Baptism is commanded and confirmed as something we should not despise but use, as has been said. Nevertheless, we should not stretch it so very tightly that someone who was unable to come to Baptism would be condemned because of it.
>
> In summary, these four statements come from this text:

(I)   Some believe and are baptized, which is the general command of Christ and the rule that we are to teach and observe.

(II) Some believe and are not baptized.

---

23. "Gospel for the Ascension of Christ," in *Church Postil*, LW 77:285.

(III) Some do not believe and yet are baptized.

(IV) Some do not believe and also are not baptized.

The text itself gives this distinction. It has always been unanimously observed that if someone believed and yet died unbaptized, he would not be condemned for that reason. It could perhaps
happen that someone believes and (even though he desires Baptism)
is overtaken by death. It is unnecessary to say more about this now.[24]

In his second Gospel sermon on Ascension Day, Luther has already
stated the matter briefly:

> God has always accompanied his Word with an outward sign to
> make it the more effective to us, that we might be strengthened in
> heart and never doubt his Word, not waver. ... Thus has he done here,
> adding to this promise of his—"He that believeth and is baptized
> shall be saved"—an outward sign, namely baptism, and also the sac-
> rament of the bread and the wine, which was especially instituted
> for use in times of temptation, and when death draws near, that by
> it we might strengthen our faith, and remind God of his promise,
> and hold him to it.
>
> A man can believe even though he be not baptized; for baptism
> is nothing more than an outward sign that is to remind us of the
> divine promise. If we can have it, it is well; let us receive it, for
> no one should despise it. If, however, we cannot receive it, or it is
> denied us, we will not be condemned if we only believe the Gospel.
> For where the Gospel is, there is also baptism and all that a Christian
> needs. Condemnation follows no sin except the sin of unbelief.[25]

Also, in his first Gospel sermon on Ascension Day, Luther teaches the same
even more briefly and compactly:

---

24. "Gospel for the Ascension of Christ," in *Church Postil*, LW 77:285

25. *Luther's Church Postil: Gospels; Pentecost or Missionary Sermons*, trans. John Nicholas
Lenker (Minneapolis: Lutherans in All Lands, 1907), 3:203–4. This sermon is from the postil
edited by Stephan Roth; see WA 10.1,2:269–70; WA 10,3:133–47, here pp. 141–42. On Roth's edi-
tions of postils and Luther's estimation of them, see Benjamin T. G. Mayes, "Introduction to
the Luther-Cruciger *Church Postil* (1540–1544)," *LW* 75:xvii–xxii.

Now, God has so ordained that our faith should be manifested before the heathen; hence, whosoever is a Christian and has received baptism, is in danger of his life among the heathen and the unbelievers. It is necessary that we receive baptism if we are Christians; or, if that is beyond our reach, that we say, at least: I sincerely desire to be baptized.

Moreover, the sign of baptism is given us also to show that God himself will help us, and that we should be certain of his grace, and that everyone be able to say: Hereunto did God give me a sign, that I should be assured of my salvation, which he has promised me in the Gospel. For he has given us the Word, that is, the written document; and beside the Word, baptism, that is the seal. So faith, which apprehends the Word, may be strengthened by the sign and seal.[26]

The cited passages show undoubtedly that Väisänen does not do justice to the teaching of the Reformer. He downright distorts the clear and lucid thoughts of the Reformation.

Luther's Teaching on Baptism in the Church Postil:
The Gospel Sermon on Trinity Sunday

We will have a few more extracts from Luther's *Church Postil*, from the Gospel sermon on Trinity Sunday. The text is John 3:1–15, the conversation Jesus had with Nicodemus. Väisänen has many a time referred especially to verse 5 (as we have shown above) and emphasized that regeneration "of water and of the Spirit" makes baptism the only means of grace effecting regeneration and that baptism therefore becomes absolutely necessary for salvation. Again he repeats his claim that God's word thus cannot regenerate.[27]

By contrast, Luther, when speaking of regeneration "of water and of the Spirit," constantly emphasizes not only baptism but rather "preaching and baptism." His much more comprehensive and profound teaching should not be bypassed and once more either wittingly or unwittingly

---

26. *Luther's Church Postil*, 3:189. This sermon is also from the postil edited by Stephan Roth; see *WA* 10.1,2:268; *WA* 12:555–65, here pp. 560–61.

27. Väisänen, *Baptism, Faith, and Salvation*, especially 180–81, 214.

misinterpreted. It is worthwhile to take note of the fact that he also refers to what he has in an earlier setting more extensively taught about the matter. Evidently he means the three sermons on Ascension Day, which we have above examined. Thus, all these different sermons are in agreement and express the same truth. We quote from the sermon on Trinity Sunday:

> Note, first, how [Christ] leads and directs Nicodemus to the external office in His Church, which is preaching and Baptism, because He says, "Man must be born anew from water and Spirit." ... He wants to point him to this, and in so doing He confirms John's preaching and Baptism. This office should continue and be regarded as something arranged by God through which we are born anew. ...
>
> Thus He shows that there is no other work or means through which man is born anew and comes into God's kingdom than this, which is the preaching office and Baptism and the Holy Spirit bound to them, who works through this office on man's heart. He is not talking about the Spirit who is hidden and cannot be known—as He is for Himself personally in His divine essence alone and without means—but the Spirit who reveals Himself in the external office which we hear and see, namely, in the preaching office of the external office which we hear and see, namely, the preaching office of the Gospel and of the Sacraments. ... Rather, He has arranged it so that the Holy Spirit is to be available for people's ears and eyes in Word and Sacrament, and will work through this external office, so that people will know that what happens has truly happened through the Holy Spirit.
>
> Therefore, these words "unless someone is born anew from water and Spirit" [John 3:5] say just as much as if He said, "A person must be born anew through this preaching of the Gospel and the office of Baptism, in which the Holy Spirit works," etc. Through the Word He enlightens the heart and shows God's wrath against sin and, in turn, God's grace promised for the sake of His Son, Christ, through which hearts are kindled, begin to believe, turn to God, take comfort in His grace, appeal to Him, etc. In order to arouse and strengthen faith, He also gives Baptism as a sure sign along with the Word, that He washes away and blots out our sins, constantly grants

us the grace He promised in order to keep us steadfast, and gives us the Holy Spirit, etc. More will be said about this at another time.[28]

Here, Luther teaches, in accordance with his earlier sermon, that the gospel works true faith and precisely therefore it directs the believer to baptism, in which God, through a visible and sure "sign," abundantly dispenses his grace and rich gifts. In the following he teaches, in harmony with his earlier sermon, that one should not without good reason put off baptism, for we need God's grace being preached, read, heard, and seen.

> From this you can further see that Baptism is not something unnecessary, as the Anabaptist sect slanders. ... That is why it does not work to despise it or to delay it for a long time, for that would be wantonly despising and abandoning God's arrangement. Obviously, there will be no Holy Spirit there.
>
> However, I say this about the common arrangement and rule which ought to be observed wherever and whenever we can have Baptism. Where there is danger or a situation in which someone cannot come to [Baptism], then, as in similar cases of emergency, it must be enough to desire Baptism and to bring and offer up people to Christ based on the Word. There is nothing further to be said about that now.[29]

All this said, Luther's teaching is evident: God's word regenerates the one who hears and apprehends the gospel through faith, and precisely therefore the word directs him to baptism, in which regeneration takes place through the "visible" word.

The Lutheran Confessions and Their Teaching on Regeneration

From Luther's texts we proceed to the Lutheran Confessions. We have already quoted the Apology, in which the similar effects of the word and the sacraments are underscored. The passage bears repeating:

> Just as the Word enters through the ear in order to strike the heart, so also the rite enters through the eye in order to move the heart. The

---

28. "Gospel for Trinity Sunday," in *Church Postil*, LW 78:37, 38.
29. "Gospel for Trinity Sunday," in *Church Postil*, LW 78:39, 40.

word and the rite have the same effect. Augustine put it well when he said that the sacrament is a "visible word," because the rite is received by the eyes and is, as it were, a picture of the Word, signifying the same thing as the Word. Therefore both have the same effect.[30]

The passage shows a genuine Lutheran emphasis, according to which the sacrament effects and signifies "the same thing as the word," though in a "visible" manner. Thus, God's word regenerates; so does baptism, in which regeneration takes place in a "visible" manner. Correspondingly, God's word feeds and nourishes; so does the holy communion, in which consuming takes place in a "visible" manner. Further, God's word forgives sins; so does absolution, in which acquittal takes place through a voice heard entering the ear.

In the Formula of Concord, the concept of regeneration is carefully defined:

> For the word *regeneratio* (that is, "rebirth") is in the first instance used to include both the forgiveness of sins because of Christ alone and the resultant renewal, which the Holy Spirit effects in those who are justified through faith. This word is also used in the limited sense, "pro remissione peccatorum et adoptione in filios Dei" (that is, it refers only to the forgiveness of sins and our adoption as children of God). It is very often used in the Apology in the latter sense, where it is written, "Iustificatio est regeneratio" (that is, justification before God is rebirth).[31]

Väisänen asserts that in the Lutheran Confessions, justification, like regeneration, is a unique and singular event taking place in baptism and nowhere else (see above). This kind of assertion (without any further arguments) does not convince: from the Confessions it is evident that justification is not limited to one occasion. And even if we should postulate that justification takes place only once, Melanchthon without a doubt mainly speaks of it as being an effect of believing the gospel. In that case, it is through the regenerating power of God's word that justification or

---

30. *The Apology of the Augsburg Confession* 13.5, BC 219–20.
31. *The Formula of Concord*, Solid Declaration 3.19, BC 565.

regeneration takes place and not solely through baptism. To illustrate the matter, one example will suffice. Melanchthon writes in the Apology about how "faith in Christ justifies" as follows:

> What can possibly be said more simply and clearly about the conversion of the ungodly or about the manner of regeneration? Let them bring forward a single commentary on the *Sentences* out of such a vast array of writers that has indicated how regeneration takes place. When they speak about the disposition [*habitus*] of love, they imagine that people merit [the Holy Spirit] through works— just as the present-day Anabaptists teach—and do not teach that it is received through the Word. However, God cannot be dealt with and cannot be grasped in any other way than through the Word. Accordingly, justification takes place through the Word, just as St. Paul notes [Rom 1:16]: the gospel "is the power of God for salvation to everyone who has faith." Likewise [Rom 10:17], "Faith comes from what is heard." At this point we could even take up the argument that faith justifies, because if justification takes place only through the Word and the Word is grasped only by faith, it follows that faith justifies. But there are other and more important arguments. We have discussed these things so far in order to show how regeneration takes place and in order that it might be understood what kind of faith we are talking about.[32]

Väisänen does not examine and explain the teaching of the Lutheran Confessions very extensively. More carefully, he studies in particular the following passage in the Smalcald Articles:

> For both those who believe prior to baptism and those who become believers in baptism have everything through the external Word that comes first. For example, adults who have reached the age of reason must have previously heard, "The one who believes and is baptized will be saved" [Mark 16:16], even though they were at first without faith and only after ten years received the Spirit and baptism.[33]

---

32. *The Apology of the Augsburg Confession* 4.65–68, BC 131.
33. *The Smalcald Articles* 3.8, BC 322.

Väisänen tells us one should make a nice distinction between two kinds of faith: "There is a theological difference between the verb 'to believe' and the noun-based expressions 'to be in faith' or 'to come to faith.' " The former expression does not, according to him, denote saving faith, but a faith preceding saving faith (before baptism), whereas the latter phrase designates genuine, true faith (after baptism). Thus, this passage would not prove that God's word is able to regenerate.[34]

Not to put too fine a point on it, Väisänen's explanations are nothing short of nonsense. He quite haphazardly reads his own arbitrary distinction into the text. He must somehow try to make Lutheran doctrine harmonize with his teaching. In the light of Luther's entire theology, the passage in the Smalcald Articles is perfectly clear. According to him, the "preceding, outward" word of the gospel creates genuine faith even before baptism, and precisely therefore directs the one who believes the gospel to baptism, in which faith is strengthened through a "visible sign." It is impossible that the verb "to believe," occurring twice in the passage, should mean two different things. In the Latin text, the same verb (*credere*) is used in both cases, and it cannot have two different meanings in one and the same sentence. The Smalcald Articles do not make anywhere the kind of distinction Väisänen does. It is utterly foreign to Luther. He teaches scripturally and does not succumb to pedantry and hair-splitting.

Elsewhere, the Lutheran Confessions, entirely in accordance with the Reformer, teach that God's word has regenerating power. For example, in the Formula of Concord it is stated as follows:

> The pure teachers of the Augsburg Confession have taught and contended that human beings were so corrupted through the fall of our first parents that in spiritual matters concerning our conversion and the salvation of our soul they are by nature blind, and that when God's Word is preached they do not and cannot understand it. Instead, they regard it as foolishness and cannot use it to bring themselves nearer to God. On the contrary, they are and remain God's enemy until by his grace alone, without any contribution of their own, they

---

34. Väisänen, *Baptism, Faith, and Salvation*, 214.

are converted, made believers, reborn, and renewed by the power
of the Holy Spirit through the Word as it is preached and heard.[35]

In the Augsburg Confession itself it is stated in the famous passage regarding the obtaining of faith:

> To obtain such faith God instituted the office of preaching, giving
> the gospel and the sacraments. Through these, as through means,
> he gives the Holy Spirit who produces faith, where and when he
> wills, in those who hear the gospel. It teaches that we have a gra-
> cious God, not through our merit but through Christ's merit, when
> we so believe.[36]

In the Apology we find the following:

> Accordingly, justification takes place through the Word, just as
> St. Paul notes [Rom. 1:16]: the gospel "is the power of God for sal-
> vation to everyone who has faith." Likewise [Rom. 10:17], "Faith
> comes from what is heard." At this point we could even take up the
> argument that faith justifies, because if justification takes place only
> through the Word and the Word is grasped only by faith, it follows
> that faith justifies. But there are other and more important argu-
> ments. We have discussed these things so far in order to show how
> regeneration takes place and in order that it might be understood
> what kind of faith we are talking about.[37]

Further, the Apology says also the following:

> Therefore we conclude with this phrase that we are justified before
> God, reconciled to him, and reborn by a faith that penitently grasps
> the promise of grace, truly enlivens the fearful mind, and is con-
> vinced that God is reconciled and propitious to us because of Christ.[38]

---

35. *The Formula of Concord*, Solid Declaration 2.5, BC 544.

36. *The Augsburg Confession* 5.1–3, BC 40.

37. *The Apology of the Augsburg Confession* 4.67–68, BC 131.

38. *The Apology of the Augsburg Confession* 4.386. This text is from the first edition of the
Apology (known as the "Quarto Edition"). Melanchthon heavily revised this passage in the
second edition of the Apology (known as the "Octavo Edition"). See Theodore G. Tappert's

In the Large Catechism, Luther explains the third article as follows:

> He has a unique community in the world, which is the mother that
> begets and bears every Christian through the Word of God, which
> the Holy Spirit reveals and proclaims, through which he illumi-
> nates and inflames hearts so that they grasp and accept it, cling to
> it, and persevere in it.[39]

A little later on, Luther continues:

> Therefore we believe in him who daily brings us into this commu-
> nity through the Word, and imparts, increases, and strengthens
> faith through the same Word and the forgiveness of sins. Then
> when his work has been finished and we abide in it, having died
> to the world and all misfortune, he will finally make us perfectly
> and eternally holy. Now we wait in faith for this to be accomplished
> through the Word.[40]

There are a lot of passages like these in the Lutheran Confessions. We will
not go on adducing them anymore; the matter itself will have been proven.
One does not need more proofs but rather willingness to read and study
them and understand them in their simplicity.[41]

To sum up all that has been presented thus far, Väisänen's teaching is
in stark disagreement with Luther and the Lutheran Confessions. In the
following, his teaching will be examined in the light of Scripture.

---

edition of the *Book of Concord* (Philadelphia: Fortress, 1959), 166, BC 172n232. On the two edi-
tions of the Apology, see "Editors' Introduction to the Apology of the Augsburg Confession,"
108-9.

39. *The Large Catechism* 2.42, BC 436.

40. *The Large Catechism* 2.62, BC 439.

41. My thanks are due especially to D. Puolimatka, who has expertly collected dozens
of passages from the Lutheran Confessions dealing with the relationship between the word
and regeneration.

The Language of Scripture

The language of Scripture does not in every respect correspond to our usual modes of speaking. It has its own peculiar idiom. Understanding it is necessary to avoid misunderstandings. Luther aptly speaks of the "grammar of the Holy Spirit." The model for this language is not earthly linguistics, but heavenly speech, which sometimes deviates from our normal way of expressing ourselves.[42]

Väisänen argues for his views very much on the basis of general linguistic laws. To begin with, let us briefly see how he proceeds in his argumentation. He emphasizes that a person is born again in baptism only. Regeneration is a unique and singular event. Again and again Väisänen points out that linguistic analogy (correspondence) with our own idiom must be safeguarded. We are not born into this world more than once, he reminds us. Consequently, with regard to the spiritual life, too, we are born once only, and that takes place in baptism. If one who has been baptized falls from grace, he becomes spiritually dead (being, however, still God's child in a judicial sense, albeit a lost one). Should he later return to the grace given in baptism, he awakes spiritually—in other words, he rises from spiritual death and is saved.[43]

The problem with this construct is that the writer's own presumption concerning linguistic correspondence begins to guide his Bible exposition and theological thinking: because we are born into our world once only, we are not born into our spiritual life more than once; we are only born again in baptism. However, the expressions used by the New Testament (truthfully describing the reality) do not function this way; its rich and manifold idiom directs us to a totally different understanding.

To illustrate the matter, let us take the familiar teaching of Romans 6 relating to the crucifixion, death, burial, and resurrection together with Christ taking place in baptism. In this instance, too, we are dealing with a crucifixion, death, burial, and resurrection that, according to our way of

---

42. See, for example, Oswald Bayer, *Theology the Lutheran Way*, ed. and trans. by J. G. Silcock and M. C. Mattes (Grand Rapids: Cambridge, 1994), 80–82.

43. Väisänen, *Baptism, Faith, and Salvation*, 102–4.

speaking, takes place once. Still, it is obvious as regards spiritual life that Paul urges believers to crucify their old man daily, to die from sin again and again, and to rise together with Christ and live with him. Of course, this has all once taken place by the grace of God in baptism. It does not, however, follow that it is a matter of one singular event taking place once and for all. According to Romans 6, the final death from sin and resurrection to new life does not take place until the last day. It would be wrong to "flatten" the teaching of Scripture and mold or force it so that it should nicely fit our linguistic requirements. Thus, Väisänen's oft-repeated demand for "linguistic analogy" as to baptismal regeneration does not correspond to the language of Scripture.[44]

In accordance with this, in the Small Catechism Luther teaches the old man's daily dying and the new man's daily rising up. In addition, he repeatedly connects baptismal regeneration and the spiritual rising again. There is no real difference between the expressions. In both of them we are dealing with heavenly life beginning and continuing in the Christian. For example, in the famous Heidelberg Disputation, Luther points out: "To be born anew, one must consequently first die and then be raised up with the Son of Man."[45] In his *Babylonian Captivity of the Church* he teaches likewise: "This death and resurrection we call the new creation, regeneration, and spiritual birth."[46]

---

44. In his email to me (dated February 26, 2018), R. Kolb writes sharply that Väisänen's recurring appeal to linguistic analogy between natural birth and spiritual regeneration "breaks down because of the mystery of the continuation of sin and evil in the lives of the faithful." He adds later: "Natural birth is not followed by anything comparable to the return of sin and the need to again mortify the flesh and be raised up to walk in Christ's footsteps, as Paul explains happens in Romans 6 and 7 and in Colossians 2 and 3."

45. *The Heidelberg Disputation*, LW 31:55.

46. *The Babylonian Captivity of the Church*, LW 36:68. Accordingly, Luther writes in his *Holy and Blessed Sacrament of Baptism*: "The significance of baptism is a blessed dying unto sin and a resurrection in the grace of God, so that the old man, conceived and born in sin, is there drowned, and a new man, born in grace, comes forth and rises. ... Just as a child is drawn out of his mother's womb and is born, and through this fleshly birth is a sinful person and a child of wrath, so one is drawn out of baptism and is born spiritually. Through this spiritual birth he is a child of grace and a justified person. Therefore sins are drowned in baptism, and in place of sin, righteousness comes forth" (LW 35:30). Also: "Similarly the lifting up out of the baptismal water is quickly done, but the thing it signifies—the spiritual birth, the increase of grace and righteousness—even though it begins in baptism, lasts until death, indeed, until the Last Day. Only then will that be finished which the lifting up out of baptism signifies. Then shall we arise from death, from sins and from all evil, pure in body and soul, and then

Väisänen's presumption about "linguistic analogy" is threatening to force some of his explanations away from the natural meaning of Scripture texts. He obviously runs the risk of explaining the verses that admonish us to awaken and rise from the sleep of sin as pertaining to backsliders. In the background there remains the idea that the one who has been born again in baptism but then has died spiritually is in need of this kind of admonition. Indeed he does; but that same proclamation of awakening from sleep is necessary for all Christians. They, too, have daily to rise from sin, according to Romans 6.

In this connection, Väisänen points out that Scripture uses terms other than regeneration regarding "the return of a backslider into communion with Christ." He mentions awakening from slumber, rising from the dead, coming back to life, and the lost being found.[47] As grounds for his interpretation he refers to Romans 13:11, where the listeners are admonished to "awake out of sleep: for now is our salvation nearer than when we believed" (KJV). It is not, of course, an admonition given only to backsliders. On the contrary, it is written to all Christians. They, too, need a sermon of repentance, although they have already been born again in baptism—died to sin and raised up to new life with Christ. Let it be repeated once more that in Romans 6, rising from the dead likewise applies to *all* Christians, and that daily.

Quite evidently, Väisänen's wish to force the language of Scripture into the narrow tracks of his own language and theology resembles an attempt at a rational explanation, a sort of ratiocination: he does not let the text speak and define what it is about, but from outside brings in a pattern of thinking foreign to it and by force makes the interpretation required by that the only correct meaning. In the following we shall have to come back to the distortion in his starting point.

---

shall we live eternally. Then shall we be truly lifted up out of baptism and be completely born, and we shall put on the true baptismal garment of immortal life in heaven" (LW 35:31).

47. Väisänen, *Baptism, Faith, and Salvation*, 103.

The Times of the Old Testament and the Baptism of John

Regeneration is not something that only takes place in the time of the New Testament. Naturally, also in the times of the Old Testament the people became believers. They put all their hope and trust in the Lord, the Almighty God. Out of his mercy they were forgiven their scarlet sins. His creative word vivified them when they had turned away from him to the brink of self-destruction. David, who like others was "conceived in sin," was given a new, "clean heart" (Ps 51:5, 10). And not only him, but the whole of Israel came to experience that same renewal (Ezek 11:19; 36:26). It would be superfluous to enumerate any more examples of that kind. It is crystal clear that, in the time of the Old Testament, God's word effected regeneration and what that entails.

Someone might object that baptism was instituted to be the sacrament of the new covenant. Therefore, what happened during the old covenant has really no importance here. However, this is not the case. The fact that God's word effected (in the manner described above) during the time of the Old Testament what regeneration expresses and means loses its importance only if someone presumes to teach that God's word since those days has *lost* its power. Only then could someone try to affirm somewhat reasonably that baptism alone regenerates; otherwise not. Thus Väisänen is actually confronted with all the damning evidence in the Old Testament, which is against his views.

John the Baptist acts between the Old and the New Testament as a connecting link, as it were. His activity of baptizing did not go on very long and ended in the past. Thus it no longer has direct practical value. Nonetheless, it is necessary to say something about its use and effect. To begin with, we take into consideration Jesus' conversation with Nicodemus (John 3:1–22), which we have spoken about in connection with a sermon of Luther.

Väisänen presupposes without further ado that regeneration "of water and of the Spirit" (John 3:5) exclusively denotes the Christian baptism.[48] His deduction without a doubt holds true as far as the passage is applied to Christian readers of John's Gospel; they will read the text in the light of their familiar frame of reference. Therefore, they will surely find allusions to Christian baptism in chapter 3 as well as allusions to the Lord's Supper

---

48. Väisänen, *Baptism, Faith, and Salvation*, 30–32, 36, 69–72.

in chapter 6. On the other hand, Jesus presupposes that Nicodemus, as a "master of Israel," should himself be able to answer his own question as to how regeneration takes place (3:10). If Jesus here speaks of Christian baptism (which was instituted long after the conversation), his demand seems quite unreasonable. How was Nicodemus to have known something about it beforehand? It seems more natural to think that the expression "of water and of the Spirit" meant something that he could understand there and then. Only in that case could one expect a clear answer from him as to how regeneration takes place.

It is not possible to present here a comprehensive overview of the matter, which would take the several different interpretations into consideration. In our brief study, we must let much less suffice. I shall only present my own understanding with its arguments. It deviates somewhat from several (if not all) common explanations. In any case, it is clear that John 3:5 does not simply and solely speak of the power of Christian baptism to regenerate, if and when in the whole conversation regeneration is regarded as a present possibility "here and now" (and not sometime in the distant future in connection with the Christian church).

The talk about "water and the Spirit" should be understood on the basis of what has up to then been told in John's Gospel. In the first chapter, John the Baptist has proclaimed that he baptizes "with water" (1:26, 31), and the Messiah, who would come after him, would baptize "with the Holy Spirit" (1:33). He by no means asserts a contrast between two baptisms, but rather their intimate connection, for "that he should be made manifest to Israel, therefore am I come baptizing with water" (1:31). The same connection is evident from chapter 3 right after the extensive conversation of Nicodemus and Jesus (3:22–30). "He must increase, but I must decrease" (3:30).

Further, the central focus of John the Baptist's proclamation of repentance was the demand for regeneration. He presented it to all hearers, but especially the Pharisees, or that "generation of vipers" (Matt 3:7). "And think not to say within yourselves, we have Abraham to our father: for I say unto you, that God is able of these stones to raise up children unto Abraham" (Matt 3:9). To that selective Jewish piety movement Nicodemus also belonged (John 3:1). A corresponding debate as to who are truly the children of Abraham is found later on in John's Gospel (8:31–59). It culminates in the assertion that the Jews are of their "father the devil" (8:44), or, as it were, a "generation of that old serpent." Their natural or fleshly origin does not change the situation.

In his conversation with Nicodemus, Jesus appeals to his predecessor's (John the Baptist's) teaching. Nicodemus should understand that he is not God's child on the basis of his ancestry. He must be born again. For that to happen, he needs to be baptized "with water and of the Spirit"—that is, to repent by receiving John's baptism in the Jordan without being ashamed of communion with Jesus and the efficacious presence of the Spirit active in him. Both belong together (in the Greek, one and the same preposition governs both words, thus "of water and the Spirit").[49] In other words, John 3:5 points out to the Pharisee Nicodemus the central message of John the Baptist, which culminates in all that Jesus himself represents. The miracle of regeneration is not effected by religious exercises, the minute fulfillment of the law of Moses, the sacrificial rites performed in the temple, or simply Jewish ancestry. "That which is born of the flesh is flesh" (John 3:6). Instead of human pedigree, what is needed is the "baptizing with the Holy Spirit," which is Jesus' life mission. And that baptism requires, in that era of salvation history, submitting to John's baptism. John the Baptist goes before, preparing the way for the one who comes after him and brings the long-awaited, prophesied completion. In communion with Jesus finally also John 3:6 prevails: "That which is born of the Spirit, is spirit." In this way, the regeneration takes place that is a prerequisite of entering the kingdom of God.[50]

It follows from the above that the sermon on Trinity Sunday in Luther's *Church Postil* dealing with Jesus' conversation with Nicodemus hits the meaning at least in broad outline. Luther writes that Jesus confirms the

---

49. See, for example, W. C. Weinrich, *John 1:1—7:1* (St. Louis: Concordia Publishing House, 2015), ad loc. Also, in 1 John 5:6, one and the same preposition (διά) governs two nouns, "blood" and "water." We have there two events, which both belong together: "water" refers to Jesus' baptism (in other words, to the beginning of his public activity), and "blood" refers to Jesus' death on the cross (in other words, to the finish of his public activity). Weinrich justifiably points out that the use of a single common preposition connects the expressions closely to each other (418-20). Cf. my interpretation of John 3:5.

50. Compare my interpretation with the interpretation of, for example, H. N. Ridderbos (*The Gospel of John: A Theological Commentary*, trans. by J. Vriend [Grand Rapids: Cambridge, 1997], 124-29). He does not, however, take into consideration the similarities between John 3:5-6 and the proclamation of John the Baptist. Therefore, his conclusions do not reach so far as mine. One often appeals to several passages of the Old Testament (especially Isa 44:1-5 and Ezek 36:25-27) as a background to John's Gospel. We do not have the opportunity to go into them here. As I see it, it is important to explain John 3:5-6 also in its own immediate context.

preaching and baptism of John: they "are to be in force and operation forever, and are appointed by God for the purpose of the new birth."[51] Additionally, if one emphasizes that John the Baptist's proclamation was directed to him who "baptizes with the Holy Spirit," then the explanation that I have briefly delineated in the light of John's Gospel seems reasonable. I shall again point out that the Christian reader naturally understands the whole conversation between Jesus and Nicodemus from his own familiar frame of reference and therefore sees it as a text indicating churchly baptism. Without doubt he draws a correct conclusion, for in the following it is stated that John must decrease (and thus also the baptism he administers) and recede more and more into the background, so that Jesus remains as a heavenly bridegroom, alone with his bride (John 3:29-30).

All in all, one cannot use John 3:5 to prove that only Christian baptism regenerates. Jesus' conversation with Nicodemus shows that regeneration could very well have taken place in that moment (before the institution of Christian baptism). It is effected by God's "living and powerful" word (Heb 4:12), either as such or combined with visible means of grace in the time of the Old as well as New Testament. Otherwise the common factor in the old and the new covenant ceases to exist.

Regeneration in the New Testament—General Observations

The New Testament teaches unequivocally that baptism is "the washing of regeneration" (Titus 3:5); there is no doubt about that. Let us keep this clear in our minds. When teaching that baptism is the washing of regeneration, need one or must one necessarily draw the conclusion out of it that God's word does not regenerate? That is the question. In scriptural, confessional Lutheranism, one has never arrived at the kind of one-sidedness that Väisänen represents with his teaching. It is now our intention to examine more closely the claims and arguments that are propounded by him.

When Väisänen denies the regenerating power of God's word, he must somehow explain away—or explain in some other way—those Bible passages that indicate regeneration or faith being kindled by the word. Consequently, to prove his views he has to (1) make a distinction between two kinds of faith, so that the faith wrought by the gospel can be reckoned

51. *Luther's Church Postil*, 3:432; see also *LW* 78:37.

as "a faith not really true"; (2) create a completely new concept, "recon-ception," aside from the traditional concept of "regeneration," so that the texts referring to the regenerating power of the gospel can be interpreted as alluding to "reconception"; (3) interpret all the verses speaking of regen-eration by the word in some other way and claim that they speak of nothing else than baptism; and (4) assert that regeneration is a unique occurrence on the analogy of natural birth, although in scriptural idiom the logic of our language does not apply, and therefore Scripture speaks of many seem-ingly unique occurrences as repeating themselves often, even daily, in the believer's life (like the crucifixion, death, burial, and resurrection taking place in baptism according to Romans 6).[52]

The last point is already dealt with above, so we will not return to it. In the following we shall explore the rest of the arguments.

God's Word Regenerates—1 Peter 1:23 and James 1:18

Both 1 Peter 1:23 and James 1:18 speak of God's word which regenerates. Christians have been "born again, not of corruptible seed, but of incorrupt-ible, through the living and abiding word of God." That is, God has "given birth to" them or "brought them forth" "with the word of truth" (Jas 1:18).

Väisänen emphasizes that both passages actually speak of baptism because there are several indirect allusions to it in the context. Thus he concludes that baptism must be thought of as being somehow included in the word by which regeneration takes place.[53] Consequently, his conclu-sions are diametrically opposed to what the text itself says. Even if one might suppose that baptism is justifiably included in the word, it does not follow that the clear, literal meaning of the text can be outright denied.

Since both passages remind the recipients of the letters how they became believers, there is nothing strange in the fact that baptism will be referred to or at least indirectly alluded to. The main emphasis, at any rate, lies on the apostolic word which was being preached. The idea is that hear-ers were converted through the word; they were born again. Thereafter they wanted to be baptized, having been exhorted by that very word. In this way, the word and baptism belong together. Grace is being testified

52. See above my more detailed account of the arguments adduced by Väisänen.

53. Väisänen, Baptism, Faith, and Salvation, 39–44.

to as a reality both heard and seen. In my opinion, there is no reason to do violence to the obvious meaning of the texts under consideration and claim that 1 Peter 1:23 and James 1:18 only speak of baptism.

Moreover, it is quite apparent from the context of 1 Peter 1:23 what is meant. In verse 25 it is said that the word that has regenerated the recipients of the letter is "the word that was *preached* to you." Put another way, it is gospel proclamation that is being dealt with, not only the administration of baptism. Väisänen does cite this verse, but not in its entirety: he leaves out the last sentence (obviously on purpose because it does not agree with his overall views).[54]

On the basis of the above, Luther teaches perfectly correctly about 1 Peter 1:23. He asks:

> How does this take place? In the following way: God lets the Word, the Gospel, go forth. He causes the seed to fall into the hearts of men. Now where it takes root in the heart, the Holy Spirit is present and creates a new man. There an entirely new man comes into being, other thoughts, other words and works. Thus you are completely changed.[55]

Here Luther does not utter a single word about baptism. Later on, he explicitly emphasizes the word even more: "It is surely a divine power. Indeed, it is God Himself." Then he adds, looking far ahead, the "the seed is our Lord God Himself."[56] Therefore, of course, the word regenerates. It is tantamount to the Word made flesh. Denying this is demonstrably a sign of an Arian distortion in theology (see above).

James 1:18 also clarifies the significance of the word. The phrase "the word of truth" is a familiar expression in the New Testament. It appears several times in Paul's letters. He writes to the Ephesians, "in whom you also trusted, after that you heard the word of truth, the gospel of your salvation: in whom also after that you believed, you were sealed with that Holy Spirit of promise" (Eph 1:13). It is important to notice yet again the

---

54. Väisänen, *Baptism, Faith, and Salvation*, 42–43. For this he has been sharply criticized especially by M. Bergman; see his review of Väisänen's book: "Matti Väisänen: *Pelastuksesta osalliseksi. Raamattuargumentaation tarkastelua ja systemaattisteologisten ongelmien pohdiskelua*" [Examination of scriptural argumentation and discussion of problems relating to systematic theology], *Luterilainen* 5 (2017): 184–85.

55. *Sermons on the First Epistle of St. Peter*, LW 30:44.

56. *Sermons on the First Epistle of St. Peter*, LW 30:45.

reference to the *hearing* of the word. Likewise, Paul writes to the Colossians: "For the hope which is laid up for you in heaven, whereof you heard before in the word of the truth of the gospel, which is come unto you, as it is in the whole world; and brings forth fruit and grows, as it does also in you, since the day you heard of it, and understood the grace of God in truth" (Col 1:5–6). *Hearing* the word is here mentioned twice. Further, in his second letter to Timothy, Paul exhorts his young co-worker: "Study to show yourself approved unto God, a workman who needs not to be ashamed, rightly dividing the word of truth" (2:15). Lutheranism has traditionally understood the word of truth to mean preaching that properly distinguishes the law and the gospel. In any case, it is clearly a matter of proclamation according to the truth.[57] In the second letter to the Corinthians Paul speaks of himself and how he has proved himself to be a minister of God "by the word of truth," and immediately continues, "by the power of God" (2 Cor 6:7). These expressions are obviously closely connected with each other. The word of truth is the gospel that Paul preached, which precisely as such is "the power of God unto salvation to everyone who believes" (Rom 1:16). The gospel preaching thus has the power to generate living faith, which is the same as regeneration.[58]

All the above examples prove, in agreement with one another, that the concept "the word of truth" designates apostolic proclamation. It has the power to regenerate. Of that James 1:18 speaks in the first place. One should understand the verse in no other way. Gospel preaching and faith in it are then followed by baptism, which strengthens the regeneration that has taken place through the word.

God's Word Regenerates—1 Corinthians 4:15

In the first letter to the Corinthians, Paul introduces himself as the father of the church members who has "begotten" or "given birth to" (ἐγέννησα) them through the gospel (4:15). He had, however, baptized hardly any one of

---

57. For example, Melanchthon refers to 2 Tim 2:15 in the Apology: "And it is necessary to divide these things aright, as Paul says, 2 Tim. 2:15. We must see what Scripture ascribes to the Law and what to the promises. ... For the law and the promises need to be 'rightly distinguished' with care. We must see what Scripture attributes to the law and what it attributes to the promises" (Apology 4.188, BC 150).

58. See more about this in M. A. Seifrid, *The Second Letter to the Corinthians* (Grand Rapids: Eerdmans, 2014), 280.

them (1:14–16). He had left that (much more simple task) to his co-workers. Therefore, "begetting" or "giving birth to" through the gospel undeniably refers to apostolic proclamation, which, to be sure, led to baptism when received in faith. There is no need to separate gospel preaching and baptism here. In the Acts they always go together, and they are not dealt with separately from each other, still less as opposites to each other (more on this below). In any case, it is again evident that regeneration takes place through the word. It may be assumed that 1 Corinthians 3:6 speaks of the same distinction in principle between preaching and baptizing, albeit indirectly. Paul states there that he "planted" (or preached the gospel to the unconverted), and Apollos (and others) "watered" (or baptized the converted).

Väisänen considers talk about Paul being the one who spiritually gave birth to or delivered the Corinthian church members as completely "perverse" (or "sexually deviant").[59] He comes to that conclusion because modern-day use of language guides his interpretations into quite wrong directions (cf. earlier on his claim about regeneration being a unique occurrence like natural birth). In Luther's words, "the grammar of the Holy Spirit" does not always bend to our fleshly presuppositions and preferences. For example, in the early Christian creed it was confessed that the Son is "begotten of the Father" or "born of the Father" (see, e.g., Ps 2:7; Acts 13:33; Heb 1:5; 5:5), i.e., his only Son (ὁ Μονογενὴς Υἱός). It is inappropriate and offensive to regard the latter kind of expression as "perverse." It is holy language, and it is not meant to be understood according to our fleshly mind. Besides, Väisänen himself teaches correspondingly that, in baptism, God, who is the heavenly Father and the Almighty Lord, causes a person who is baptized to be born again, or that God "gives birth" to the baptized. He does not in that connection assert that teaching along those lines is "perverse" (see above his views on, e.g., 1 Pet 1:23 and Jas 1:18).

Väisänen translates 1 Corinthians 4:15 in the way that exclusively speaks of "begetting": "For in Christ Jesus I have begotten you through the gospel" (KJV). He then claims that the passage, for the very same reason, does not

---

59. In the Finnish original, Väisänen speaks of a "perverse" expression (see his book *Pelastuksesta osalliseksi. Mitä Raamattu ja Tunnustuskirjat opettavat pääsystä Kristuksen yhteyteen* [Helsinki, 2017], 39). In the English translation his text has been altered and that kind of speech has been omitted (see *Baptism, Faith, and Salvation*, 38–39).

at all speak of regeneration (it did not take place until their baptism).[60] Instead, Paul speaks here of "the *seed of the Word* proclaimed, the seed he had sown" in his hearers' hearts. Thus he only "conceived them through the Word of God, and the Corinthians were regenerated as a result in Holy Baptism."[61] It follows that Väisänen in fact creates a new concept, "reconception," beside the concept "regeneration," and in addition distinguishes between them in the above manner. In accordance with his distinction, he emphasizes that "reconception" takes place through the word and "regeneration" through baptism. His aim in doing so is, of course, to completely deny and reject the regenerating power of the word.

Actually, the artificial distinction between "reconception" and "regeneration" makes the "reconception" taking place through the word a more significant occurrence than the "regeneration" taking place in baptism because "reconception" is the beginning of new life while "regeneration" is only the result of and a consequence of it. That conclusion is hardly what Väisänen had in mind when he came to make his distinction: he set out to prove that one cannot put the word on a par with baptism, but that only baptism marks the beginning of true spiritual life. Now, however, his attempt to explain the matter turns it upside down! Moreover, Väisänen teaches, as we have seen, that the incarnation of God's Son is a model for the regeneration of the sinner. Here he again goes astray in his interpretation because the incarnation of God's Son did not begin when he was born, but at the moment of conception. Thus, Väisänen undermines his own interpretations. His arguments meet a complete dead end.[62] If and when there is no way out, it is worth one's while to return to the plain and simple teaching of Scripture.

In principle, 1 Corinthians 4:15 can be translated in both ways: "I have begotten you," and "I have given birth to you." The Greek verb used denotes both "beget, become a father" and "give birth to, become a mother." However, it is not justifiable to think that "the part played by the father" (begetting) should somehow be more insignificant or even half-finished until "the part played by the mother" (giving birth) is completed. The main

---

60. Väisänen, *Baptism, Faith, and Salvation*, 38–39.

61. Väisänen, *Baptism, Faith, and Salvation*, 38–39.

62. In his email to me (dated February 26, 2018), R. Kolb writes that Väisänen's "idea of reconception is unclear or nonsense or both."

emphasis is on the fact that the man becomes a father and the woman becomes a mother. They are both parents to their child, the father by way of begetting and the mother by way of giving birth. In Greek it is one and the same verb. As to the man, it does not designate a sort of "preparatory stadium of parenthood," and as to the woman, a "mature stadium of parenthood." Väisänen's distinction is artificial. We have already shown at what kind of contradictions he arrives by following his interpretation.

Against the background I have outlined, the manner in which Scripture speaks of regeneration crystallizes into an entirely understandable whole. It does not really matter that much whether we translate 1 Corinthians 4:15 "I have begotten you" or "I have given birth to you," namely "in Christ Jesus through the gospel." The meaning is, in any case, that Paul has, by preaching of the gospel, become a father or a mother—in other words, a parent—to the Corinthians. The gospel preached by him, or "the message of the cross," is "the power of God" (1:18), and believing it, his hearers have not, for the time being, stayed in the limbo of "reconception," but have already gotten to fully enjoy the gifts of heaven. Therefore, Paul calls himself their father and not, for example—if I am allowed to use a modern term—a "sperm donor." Because the New Testament repeatedly speaks of regeneration in a way that the subject is a male person (the heavenly Father or a male incumbent of the apostolic ministry representing him), one can speak about Paul as being the "mother" or "the one giving birth" to the Corinthians without the meaning being violated (or turning into something "perverse"). Väisänen claims that the regeneration through the word "would make baptism null and void" or even "superfluous." However, this is not the case. On the contrary, the apostolic proclamation directs one to baptism, the fountain of new life. Baptism confirms that which the message of the cross has secured.

Let us repeat for the sake of clarity that, correspondingly, in the beginning of his first letter, Peter praises the heavenly Father, "who according to his abundant mercy has begotten (or given birth to) us again (ἀναγεννήσας) unto a living hope by the resurrection of Jesus Christ from the dead" (1 Pet 1:3), and therefore "you call on him as Father" (1:17). Also, here the whole exposition would go astray and arrive at all kinds of folly if one started to talk about some sort of begetting by the heavenly Father that would not be equal to regeneration. The same Greek verb "to beget, to give birth to" is often used in the first letter of John (e.g., 2:29; 3:9; 4:7; 5:1, 4, 18). These verses are ordinarily translated so that they mean regeneration ("born of God," in spite of the fact that 3:9 speaks of God's "seed," in the Greek the same word as "sperm"). Not even Väisänen has attempted to translate these and other similar passages with expressions referring to begetting, but he sticks to the "traditional" translation.[63]

Thus, 1 Corinthians 4:15 shows that Scripture speaks of becoming a believer through the word as regeneration, for example, when evangelizing non-Christians on the mission field. That does not nullify baptism but rather directs to it.

God's Word Regenerates—Galatians 4:19

In the letter to the Galatians, Paul shows that he (as a spiritual father!) must once more travail in birth, wanting to give birth anew to his dear children, who had already been born again, so that "Christ be formed" in them and they might become God's children like their heavenly Brother (4:19). Also, now we notice that it is not foreign to the idiom of Scripture to combine a very feminine experience ("travailing in birth") with a masculine word. Neither is it here a case of some "perverse" phenomenon—as Väisänen puts it in connection with 1 Corinthians 4:15 (see above)—but an expression used by holy Scripture, respectively, "the grammar of the Holy Spirit."

Väisänen thinks that "Paul's concern is not over their [the Galatians'] becoming children of God but rather over their remaining children of God; not over their regeneration but their spiritual growth." Furthermore, he claims that the apostle is in pain "in order that they [the Galatians] might grow as children of God." They were—as it seems—"forgetting the Gospel unto salvation and drifting toward confidence in their own deeds."[64]

Now and again, I stand in amazement before the vividness of Väisänen's imagination when he argues for his views. His arguments seem so far-fetched, particularly in this case. If and when Paul speaks about "travailing in birth," he would allegedly not mean giving birth, but bringing believers up, as if he spoke about "travailing in bringing up" or "having bringing-up

---

63. Väisänen, Baptism, Faith, and Salvation, 35–46 (especially 43).

64. Väisänen, Baptism, Faith, and Salvation, 44–45.

pains." Thus, Galatians 4:19 would not mean that the Galatians must be born again, but that they must keep growing. I do not doubt that Väisänen has propounded his arguments in full earnest. However, it is difficult for the reader to take them at face value. Whom does he think he will convince with them? Later on, in the same chapter of the Letter to the Galatians, "bearing" is held by Paul to be equal to "travailing" (verse 27). And that is what it is all about.[65]

Moreover, it seems very much far-fetched to claim that the Galatians were "forgetting the Gospel unto salvation and drifting toward confidence in their own deeds." In actual fact, they had already completely rejected the gospel. Having strayed and having been led astray, they had turned back to the law, trusting their own works. They no longer lived—not all of them, anyway—in faith, getting hold of grace. Galatians 5:4 states the matter clear as crystal, without any equivocation: "Christ has become of no effect unto you, whosoever of you are justified by the law; you are fallen from grace." It is thus a case of extreme emergency. The Galatians (many of them) had discarded the Christian faith. Therefore, they had to be regenerated anew. That was not how it should have been; those who had once been born as their Father's children were not meant to abandon their high position and return back to nothingness. Nevertheless, that is what happened. By writing his letter, Paul brings the Galatians back to true faith—that is, through the word he writes (preaches), he regenerates them again to be God's children and heirs of heaven. Undoubtedly, Galatians 4:19 calls the backslider to return to his baptismal grace, regeneration. So also Luther explains this passage:

> As though he were to say: "Through the Gospel I truly became your father. But those corrupters and distorters came and established a new image in your heart, not that of Christ but that of Moses, so that your confidence no longer rests on Christ but on the works of the Law." ... "In short, I am in travail with you; that is, I am laboring anxiously again to call you back to your original faith, which you lost when you were deceived by the cleverness of the false apostles and fell back into the Law and works. Therefore a new and difficult

---

65. On this, see especially the thorough review of Väisänen's book by H. Ahlskog, *Biblicum* 81, no. 3 (2017): 139–40 (in Swedish).

labor has been laid upon me, to lead you back from the Law to faith in Christ." This is what he calls "being in travail."[66]

Thus, Galatians 4:19 shows that when speaking of becoming a believer through the word—for example, when proclaiming the gospel to those baptized but then fallen away from baptismal grace—Scripture calls it regeneration. That does not nullify baptism but directs one back to living out from it.

Faith and Baptism in the Acts

What is more, Väisänen explains the many passages in the book of Acts in which believing before baptism is mentioned (e.g., 2:41; 8:12, 36; 16:14; 18:8) by supposing that they do not speak of saving faith, but of faith that precedes being saved. He teaches "two" faiths (or "the two-fold process of salvation"), albeit in principle he, too, recognizes that "according to the Bible, faith is one (Eph. 4:5)."[67] His presupposition is simply based on the idea that God's word does not regenerate, and therefore it is not able to engender saving faith—except in baptism. From this follows that those passages in the Acts have to be explained away or explained in some other way than is common.

Väisänen's idea about the double faith or two kinds of faith is in actual fact completely arbitrary. In Greek, the word meaning "faith" is one and the same word. Therefore, the talk is about one and the same faith. It is not justifiable to claim that the same verb in the same context means now "faith that does not yet save," now "faith that already saves." When we are reading the Acts, that sort of sophistry and hair-splitting is not needed. No one should teach the Holy Spirit rhetoric. He is quite able to express his meaning precisely and properly (Luther). We do not face any theological problem when we are told about the faith of the hearers even before baptism on the basis of the preached word: they received the word they heard—and then, naturally, they were baptized. It seems entirely purposeless to give an unequal status to the effect of the word and of baptism or even play them against each other. It appears much more reasonable to consider them one organic whole, where the word engenders true saving

---

66. *Lectures on Galatians* (1531; 1535), *LW* 26:430, 431.
67. Väisänen, *Baptism, Faith, and Salvation*, 92, 97; more extensively, see 90–99.

faith, which precisely as such apprehends the salvation given in baptism. God's goodness and mercy do not encounter the sinner in only one way. He dispenses his plentiful grace in manifold ways. To that purpose, the book of Acts shows that the salvation, the life everlasting, is effected by the preached gospel as well as baptism.

The claim about regeneration taking place exclusively in baptism falls also in those cases in which the one who is baptized does not in fact believe. A telling illustration is provided in the story of Simon the Sorcerer, whose conversion was superficial and dishonest (see Acts 8:18–24). Under such circumstances, the person is not born again, for regeneration is not something automatic. The long history of the church, changing situations in mission fields, and experiences of the work among immigrants abound in similar or corresponding narratives. Consequently, it is not an exceptional case (notwithstanding its grotesque features). To be sure, only the one who has been born again will be saved. When will that be? In the light of Scripture, it takes place at the moment one believes the gospel: God's word about the forgiveness of sins for the sake of Christ's atoning work.

Väisänen attempts to justify his view regarding the two kinds of faith by accounting for it in more detail. He describes man's state before and after baptism. When someone believes before baptism, he lacks saving faith. However, (1) he has a faith that the Holy Spirit "conceives" through the word; (2) he even takes hold of the gospel of Christ; furthermore, (3) he hungers and thirsts for righteousness. Despite all this, he is not saved. After his baptism, the Christian is saved. Along with his saving faith, he, among other things, (1) has the Holy Spirit within him; (2) lives from the gospel of Christ; and (3) experiences righteousness, joy, and peace in the Holy Spirit.[68]

Quite obviously, the distinction made by Väisänen and the explanations he offers badly confuse law and gospel. How does faith that is effected by the Holy Spirit through the word not save? How is the sinner who apprehends Christ's gospel not saved? The Sermon on the Mount declares that the one who hungers and thirsts after righteousness is blessed, actually "beatific" (Matt 5:6). Surely, this is saving faith and nothing less. Väisänen, however, defines it as something quite contrary, that is, a faith that does not save. Here he fails grievously. What is more, the Holy Spirit's presence

---

68. Väisänen, *Baptism, Faith, and Salvation*, 98.

in the believer, living from the gospel of Christ, and experiences of righteousness, peace, and joy are rather consequences of saving faith, not really
saving faith itself. If one has to reach those and similar emotional or mental
states in order to be saved, timid souls are driven to complete despair or at
least to terrible insecurity. The gospel is distorted to law. Is it in this way
that the gospel is preached? Do we need this sort of theology so that we are
able to explain away the passages in the Acts speaking of faith on the basis
of the gospel which is proclaimed and heard? To further muddle the issue
and confuse his readers, Väisänen applies Paul's notion of being "saved
by hope" to the non-saving faith of the unbaptized.[69] The quotation stems
directly from the Letter to the Romans (8:24) and speaks, as we know, of
the *baptized* before the day of the resurrection.

Judging by everything he says, Väisänen does not in the end talk about
two kinds of faith only, but he is forced to conclude that there are actually
three kinds of faith. He has to deal with the special case of those who have
fallen from baptismal grace. According to him, they are still God's children
and, in that sense, already justified. However, without faith they are not
saved. Of what kind, then, is the faith they receive when they return to
baptismal grace and participation in justification, and how should one conceive of this faith with regard to the two kinds of faith? That is explained
nowhere. The reader is left with the impression of an entirely incompre-
hensible mishmash of concepts. By contrast, the simple talk about unam-
biguous faith in the Acts does not leave anything to guesswork or give any
cause for a complicated and outright confused theology.[70]

Other Scripture Passages on the Creation of Faith

Scripture speaks also in many other passages of the creation of faith or
regeneration through the power of the word preached and heard. In the
citations from the Lutheran Confessions we have already met with two
texts from the Letter to the Romans: the gospel is "the power of God for the
salvation of everyone who believes" (1:16), and "faith comes by hearing, and
hearing by the word of God" (10:17). Väisänen interprets the latter passage

---

69. Väisänen, *Baptism, Faith, and Salvation*, 94.

70. As regards Väisänen's confused theology, see more closely *Baptism, Faith, and Salvation*,
86–99.

as a statement mainly pertaining to the preaching of the law,[71] in spite of the fact that the context speaks of the power of the gospel to engender faith. Moreover, the law never works faith, but knowledge of sin and remorse.

In the Gospel of John, Jesus says about his own words that "they are Spirit, and they are life" (6:63), just as he himself, as the Word made flesh, is "the resurrection, and the life" (11:25). The new creation and regeneration are effected by the power of his word. His disciples are already "clean through the word" that he has spoken to them (15:3). Furthermore, in his high priestly prayer, he prays for them and "also for those who will believe in me through their word" (17:20).

Väisänen wishes to remind us that when "Jesus speaks about salvation taking place through the Word, we have to remember that the baptism of the New Covenant did not yet exist at that moment."[72] His observation, in itself valid, does not, however, undermine the fact that regeneration and salvation demonstrably take place through the word. Only if it is indisputably proven that after the institution of baptism the power of the word preached by Christ and the apostles authorized by him *ceased* and could no longer regenerate has the situation changed decisively (see above the power of God's word during the times of the Old Testament).

As it is, everyone can continue reading their Bible and find still more passages dealing with the power of the word to engender faith and trust in the Lord. All of them speak unequivocally against Väisänen's teaching. By accentuating baptism, he has been driven to extremes, and his views do not in that regard correspond to the truth.

SUMMARY

To sum up, we can state that Väisänen's teaching is in sharp disagreement not only with the Lutheran Confessions but also with the Holy Scriptures. His interpretations often seem contrived and far-fetched. They leave much to be desired. As I see it, Väisänen is driven to impossibilities since he in fact is forced to explain away all the passages that speak of the regenerating power of God's word. If he should allow even one exception, his own standpoint would fall, and that creates an almost panic-like necessity, in

---

71. Väisänen, *Baptism, Faith, and Salvation*, 87–88.
72. Väisänen, *Baptism, Faith, and Salvation*, 209.

view of which he sets to work. The result in that regard is, in my opinion, a complete fiasco.

THE CATECHISM PUBLISHED BY THE MISSION DIOCESE AND ITS EDITORIAL WORK

Finally, we can note that the ominous breaking-down process of scriptural and orthodox Lutheran theology is seen in the catechism published by the Mission Diocese.[73] There we find Question 251, regarding the sacrament of baptism: "Is it possible for an unbaptized person to be saved?" The answer runs as follows:

> Only unbelief merits condemnation. Those rejecting baptismal grace in their unbelief will be condemned. There cannot be faith in the heart of one who despises baptism and rejects it contrary to his better judgment. Of those, however, who believe the Gospel, yet die before they have opportunity to be baptized, there remains good Christian hope.[74]

The original text reads: "It is only unbelief that condemns. Faith cannot exist in the heart of a person who despises and rejects Baptism against better knowledge. But those who believe the Gospel, yet die before they have opportunity to be baptized are not condemned." Then there is a mention of the malefactor on the cross, who was saved without baptism, through faith only.[75] That reference has been left out of the Finnish translation. Likewise, a reference to 1 Peter 1:23, inserted in a later edition,[76] has also been left out.

It is crystal clear that the original text of the catechism presents perfectly faithfully what Luther has written about the matter in his *Church Postil* (see above the third Gospel sermon on Ascension Day), "It has always been unanimously observed that if someone believed and yet died unbaptized, he would not be condemned for that reason. It could perhaps happen

---

73. *Martti Lutherin Vähä katekismus lyhyesti selitettynä* (Porvoo: Suomen evankelisluterilainen lähetyshiippakunta, 2017). Originally published in the United States under the title *Luther's Small Catechism with Explanation*, trans. by S. Siikavirta and R. Soramies.

74. *Martti Lutherin Vähä katekismus lyhyesti selitettynä*, 176.

75. *Luther's Small Catechism with Explanation, 1991 Edition* (St. Louis: Concordia Publishing House, 1991), ad loc.

76. *Luther's Small Catechism with Explanation, 2017 Edition* (St. Louis: Concordia Publishing House, 2017), ad loc.

that someone believes and (even though he desires Baptism) is overtaken by death."[77] In the catechism published by the Mission Diocese, this Lutheran teaching has disappeared because it is no more confessed that God's word (cf. "those who believe the Gospel") has regenerating power. It is quite gratifying that, according to the translation, there remains hope, and good hope at that; however, it does not ultimately bring any blessed comfort, for example, to such converts from the Muslim faith whom fanatic adherents of Islam have managed to kill before their baptism. They, as holy martyrs, do not of course need any such consolation—they are already with their Lord in everlasting joy—but to their Christian relatives and friends, the teaching of the Finnish catechism is, in the final analysis, dismal reading.

EPILOGUE

In his book on baptism, bishop emeritus Väisänen points out uncommonly often that God's word cannot regenerate. Hence, he there denies practically everything I have written above. For that reason, he comes into serious conflict with the second main principle of the Reformation, the doctrine on the Bible. Luther untiringly taught that God's word is all in all. He, if anyone, continually emphasized that without it there is nothing, not even baptism, absolution, or the holy communion. His talk about "the word and the sacraments" is based on the fact that God's word has his eternal power. Denying (or in some way weakening) that aspect is tantamount to silencing the heartbeat of Lutheranism.[78]

The newest book of bishop Väisänen on baptism has been published to mark the anniversary of the Reformation.[79] One cannot help asking

---

77. "Gospel for the Ascension of Christ," in *Church Postil*, LW 77:285.

78. When rejecting orthodox Lutheranism, Väisänen gives us to understand that he himself faithfully follows Luther's theology. This seems surprising to me because, when I was discussing his previous book on baptism with him in *Länsi-Suomen Herännäislehti* in 2014, he consistently bypassed each and every one of my citations from Luther and the Lutheran Confessions! He did not comment on them in the least, for they speak clearly of the regenerating power of God's word. Now, not mentioning our previous discussion at all, he bluntly asserts that he is following Luther. See my article "Kastekeskustelu jatkuu. Piispa emeritus Matti Väisäselle" [Discussion on Baptism Continues: To Bishop emeritus Matti Väisänen], *Länsi-Suomen Herännäislehti* 10 (2014): 11–12.

79. Väisänen, *Baptism, Faith, and Salvation*, 5–7. The book has been published by the Finnish Evangelical Lutheran Mission Diocese and printed by the publishing house SLEY-Media. The distribution has received financial support by Todistajaseura, an Evangelical Lutheran society (literally "Society of Witnesses," or "Testifiers").

whether it was really the way the 500th jubilee of the Lutheran tradition was meant to be celebrated. A highly questionable book, being in deep disagreement with the second main principle of the Reformation and Lutheran Confession, is published, thereby creating confusion and division among the shepherds and among many congregations. While the Finnish Evangelical Lutheran Mission Diocese has often, with good reason, criticized the decisions made by the Finnish state church, they might in all fairness examine themselves also. When saying this, the blessings that their work up to now has brought are not to be denied or belittled. Rather the hope remains that their congregations will be preserved and continued in the future as biblical, Lutheran—and awakening.

Many liberal theologians have, during the past centuries, constantly tried to convince us that they are following Luther, unlike orthodox Lutheranism, which, according to them, has given up his teachings, now on this matter, now on that. At the present, it is asserted in the name of confessional Lutheranism that not Luther, but Lutheran orthodoxy affirmed the regenerating power of the word. I do not at all believe that anyone who has really read Luther can fall into that trap. One of the main principles of the Reformation speaks of the authority and regenerating power of Scripture. Thus it appears utterly senseless to claim that the teaching about the regenerating power of Scripture, which has always been upheld in a central role in true, genuine Lutheranism, must be relegated to the scrap heap of a decayed, Philippistic Lutheranism.[80]

Väisänen's teaching on baptism comes astonishingly near the conception of absolution held by the so-called Old Laestadians in Finland. They have pointed out that one cannot receive the forgiveness of sins in a way other than in private confession (when a member of their own group pronounces it). If one could receive forgiveness through some other means of grace, or for instance when saying the Lord's Prayer, confession and absolution would "become devoid of any meaning." Now a teaching exactly corresponding to that is being presented in connection with the doctrine on

---

80. Väisänen, *Baptism, Faith, and Salvation*, especially 229–31 (see also 115–208). Väisänen's distinction between "reconception" and "regeneration" and his teaching on two kinds of faith (see above) actually presuppose that human beings before their conversion are able to cooperate on the basis of those abilities God has produced in them. That, if anything, is Philippistic Lutheranism!

baptism. Strangely, it is asserted that if God's word had regenerating power, baptism would "become devoid of any meaning." I wonder whether someone will next come up with the idea that if God's word had the power to nourish the soul of the one reading it, the holy communion would "become devoid of any meaning." We should desist from pursuing that sort of senseless theology. The pure Lutheran doctrine of the word and the sacraments maintains that the word is the common denominator or the connecting factor in all the means of grace while every means of grace has its own special character: baptism is the washing of regeneration, absolution is the cure for an anxious, distressed soul weighed down by the knowledge of sin, and the holy communion is the eating and drinking of Christ's body and blood. Put differently, that which the word creates and causes in itself, as such takes place in a visible and audible manner in the sacraments. To quote from the Lutheran Confessions (as adduced above): "The word and the rite have the same effect. Augustine put it well when he said that the sacrament is a 'visible word,' because the rite is received by the eyes and is, as it were, a picture of the Word, signifying the same thing as the Word. Therefore both have the same effect."[81]

The danger of erroneous teaching is, beside outright delusion and deception, that because of it also true teachers and preachers and Christians generally are frightened, as it were, and begin to shy away from certain biblical themes and phrases. They try to avoid giving the impression that they concur with those who teach falsely. Therefore I state with all seriousness that in Confessional Lutheranism, one must not shrink from clear proclamation about the new birth taking place in baptism: in baptism we have truly been born again. Yet, the right doctrine should not make us draw the horrific conclusion that God's word does not also regenerate. Instead, we proclaim, with Scripture, Luther, the Lutheran Confessions, and orthodox Lutheranism, the *whole* truth, not some ill-conceived and half-baked

---

81. *The Apology of the Augsburg Confession* 13.5, BC 219–20. In his email to me (dated February 26, 2018), R. Kolb makes an overall assessment of Väisänen's baptismal theology: It "makes me wonder how he could wander so far from biblical and Lutheran teaching on what seems to me to be both a core doctrinal principle and a fairly simple one at that! [...] It is a serious demonstration of a lack of understanding of how sixteenth-century Lutherans thought to single out any form of the means of grace as having a gospel kind of power that is different from the others. Indeed, each has its own uses, but they all share the nature of being God's instrument and power to salvation."

theology. Then we shall by God's grace preserve the precious heritage of faith for future generations: God's word, that is, Scripture, and his "visible" word, that is, the sacraments.[82]

---

82. In his master's thesis *Fredrik Gabriel Hedberg's Understanding of Regeneration* (Concordia Theological Seminary, 2020), O. Granlund deals with the question of regeneration. There he comments on the recent discussion between Väisänen and me. He tries to solve the tension with a reference to Matt 28:18–20. He maintains, on the basis of that passage, that regeneration "is brought about neither through Baptism alone nor the preached Word alone, but through both 'baptizing' and 'teaching' " (p. 108). However, this kind of thinking is found neither in the Bible nor in the Lutheran Confessions. Instead, they argue that regeneration is brought about in baptism and that also the preached and heard word brings about the regeneration (as Granlund himself affirms in his thesis). By maintaining on account of Matt 28:18–20 that regeneration is brought about neither through baptism alone nor the preached word alone, but through "both baptizing and teaching," we run the risk of losing a definite time and place for the regeneration, particularly since "to obey everything I have commanded you" is included in that teaching. When does the regeneration finally take place? Who has learnt everything that Jesus has commanded? Who is able to obey it all?

6

—

LUTHER ON THE SCRIPTURES IN GALATIANS—AND ITS READERS

A. Andrew Das

Thumbing through the pages of Martin Luther's Galatians commentaries, the Reformer's love for the wisdom of Ecclesiastes becomes apparent, and yet Luther leaves unsaid the author's most famous line: "There is nothing new under the sun." Were Luther to step out of a time machine into a modern class on Paul, he would soon encounter what is called the "new perspective." Not long thereafter, he would note with interest the cataloging of quotations, allusions, and even the fainter echoes of Scripture in the pages of Paul. Modern specialists apparently share the same love for the Old Testament Scriptures that he did, even if their preference is, strangely, to label them the Hebrew Bible or the Jewish Scriptures—as if they could be divorced from their rightful fulfillment in the New Testament. Then Luther would find himself doing a double-take and asking about that alleged "new perspective." Upon the instructor's further explanation, Luther would recognize the "new perspective" as really an old perspective, a perspective he had encountered early in his career. Luther's reactions, albeit imagined, suggest that the Reformer may be a helpful voice in the modern discussions of the apostle Paul.[1]

---

1. Mark Seifrid has, over the course of his career, treasured the wisdom of the Reformer over modern Pauline theorists; e.g., Mark A. Seifrid, "Paul, Luther, and Justification in Gal 2:15-21," *Westminster Theological Journal* 65 (2003): 215-30; Seifrid, "Blind Alleys in the Controversy over the Paul of History," *Tyndale Bulletin* 45 (1994): 73-95.

LUTHER AND THE ORIGINAL
"NEW PERSPECTIVE"

James D. G. Dunn is the most renowned proponent of the Pauline "new perspective." While appreciating much of Luther's theology and affirming the
Reformation's teaching on justification, nevertheless, Dunn faulted Luther
for not recognizing that the apostle Paul was not primarily concerned with
reclaiming justification by faith in Christ. The apostle was not faulting the
Jews of his day for earning their way to heaven by a path of works righteousness.[2] No, Paul was confronting a Jewish Christian overestimation
of the ethnic, ceremonial aspects of the law as still relevant for those in
Christ. For these Jewish Christians, it was not enough to believe in Christ;
one must also observe circumcision, food laws, and Sabbath. Was this a
blind spot for the Reformer that modern scholarship has finally corrected?
Many have followed Dunn in faulting an "old" perspective that is often
labeled "Lutheran" and associated with the Reformer. Terence Donaldson,
for instance, describes a paradigm shift away from the Reformation and
its Lutheran roots and away from the traditional opposition of human
works/guilt and grace/justification.[3] At the core of that shift is Luther's
perceived lapse in not recognizing the centrality of Paul's rejection of the
ceremonial aspects of the law.

Martin Luther spent the early part of his career reflecting on and
then breaking free from longstanding, mistaken spiritual and intellectual
assumptions—and not just from the impossible righteousness required by
a stern God of the law. Luther had already confronted a "new perspective"
reading of Paul in the writings of Erasmus, an intellectual forebear.[4] The
Dutch humanist of Rotterdam had interpreted God's Old Testament law
as a series of ceremonial obligations from which Christ and the apostles

---

2. Note the critique of Luther in an early essay from 1982 outlining the "new perspective":
James D. G. Dunn, "The New Perspective on Paul," in *Jesus, Paul, and the Law: Studies in Mark
and Galatians* (Louisville: Westminster John Knox, 1990), 183–214, esp. 185; originally published
in *Bulletin of the John Rylands University Library of Manchester* 65 (1983): 95–122; Dunn, *The
Theology of Paul the Apostle* (Grand Rapids: Eerdmans, 1998), 336–37; Dunn, *The New Perspective
on Paul*, rev. ed. (Grand Rapids: Eerdmans, 2007), 18–23, esp. 22.

3. Terence L. Donaldson, *Paul and the Gentiles: Remapping the Apostle's Convictional World*
(Minneapolis: Fortress, 1998), 4–6; cf. ix.

4. A point reclaimed by modern Luther scholars; see the helpful essay by Timothy J.
Wengert, "Example: Luther Interpreting Galatians 3:6–14," pages 92–122 in *Reading the Bible
with Martin Luther: An Introductory Guide* (Grand Rapids: Baker, 2013), 93–94.

freed New Testament believers, leaving behind the purer moral obligations. Paul was advocating the acceptance of gentiles as gentiles into the early Christian communities.[5] Erasmus was not innovating in his reading of the apostle but was promoting a popular view from the Middle Ages.

Erasmus's stress on the law's ceremonial obligations as the focus of Paul's critique was not the only inherited notion the young Luther questioned. Luther had started his career steeped in a salvation-historical reading of Scripture. His lectures on the Psalms in 1513 and 1514 faithfully reproduced the contours of this line of thought. Before Christ, the "old" law served as a sign or type, a mere shadow of what it pointed toward. Life "under the law" was a life under its ceremonial aspects. Those "under grace," on the other hand, were no longer under the law's ceremonial demands but adhered to the spiritual demands of the *nova lex*, the new law, in the same relation as a type to the antitype, as prophecy to its fulfilment, or as letter to spirit.[6] To be "under grace" included also the obligation to the new law.

Luther struggled with the deeper, more profound demands of this new law. He ultimately realized that law and gospel did not belong to merely different eras of salvation, with the gospel in continuity with the law and its demands. Far more is at stake. With his 1515 lectures on Romans and then on Galatians in 1516, law and gospel function not merely as markers of different eras but as two distinct messages entirely. They were really two different ways God engages humanity existentially. The law can only accuse, imprison, and enslave. What ended with the new era in Christ was the law's condemnation and death, although Luther stressed that the individual continues to struggle daily between the two ages, with the gospel ushering in freedom, forgiveness, and sonship.[7] Against the "new perspective" teaching of his day, Luther was offering a "newer" perspective, a reclamation of the Scriptures' distinction between law and gospel.

---

5. Luther complains in a letter to Spalatin about Erasmus's relegation of Paul's critique of the law to its ceremonial or figurative aspects rather than of a person's own righteousness (Rom 10:3); WABr 1:70, 4–8 (no. 27); Johannes Kunze, *Erasmus und Luther: Der Einfluß auf die Kommentierung des Galaterbriefes und der Psalmen durch Luther 1519-1521*, Arbeiten zur Historischen und Systematischen Theologie 2 (Münster: LIT Verlag, 2000), 52–54.

6. Erik K. Herrmann, "A Lutheran Response to the Reformed Tradition," pages 155–82 in *God's Two Words: Law and Gospel in the Lutheran and Reformed Traditions*, ed. Jonathan A. Linebaugh (Grand Rapids: Eerdmans, 2018), 163.

7. Herrmann, "A Lutheran Response," 164.

Luther's first commentary on Galatians was published in 1519 and introduced the world to his "newer" perspective. Scholars quickly grabbed it
off the press, digested it, and made it their own, as Melanchthon's 1521 *Loci
Communes* and Johannes Buenhagen's 1524 commentaries attest.[8] Luther's
objections to the Middle Ages' version of the modern Pauline "new perspective" were not just to the existential striving to gain a perfect God's
favor through the law.

Although the early Luther drew heavily on Erasmus's popular
Annotations, he complained to Georg Spalatin already by October 1516 that
the humanist had interpreted Paul's "works of the law" as referring to the
ceremonial.[9] His own reading of Galatians had pointed him in a different direction. At the same time, he had abandoned medieval interpretive
approaches to seek instead the *argumentum*, the biblical author's central
argument. He wanted to ascertain the trajectory of Paul's Letter to the
Galatians, which he had come to view as a conflict with false apostles not
just over Jewish ceremonies but also, and more importantly, over trusting
in one's own righteousness. Christ in Galatians 3:13 could not have suffered
death and redeemed the gentile Galatians from the curse of the ceremonial law, in whole or in part, since the gentiles had never been under those
aspects of Moses' law. Rather, the Galatian gentiles had been redeemed
from the curse of the law in its entirety, including its moral demands.[10] In
Galatians 3:10 the law pronounces a curse on any who do not do *all* that it
requires. How does the apostle end up concluding the exact opposite—that
those who rely on the law are inevitably under its curse? In both his 1519
and 1535 Galatians commentaries, Luther supplied the missing premise in
Paul's logic: no one does all that the law requires, and thus all people end
up under its curse, including the gentile Galatians.[11]

Luther's abandonment of the salvation-historical reading of the ceremonial law not long after completing his 1513-1515 Psalms lectures coincided

8. Herrmann, "A Lutheran Response," 166.

9. Wengert, "Example," 96-97.

10. Wengert, "Example," 105.

11. For a modern defense of this way of reading Galatians 3:10, see A. Andrew Das,
"Galatians 3:10: A 'Newer Perspective' on an Omitted Premise," in *Unity and Diversity in the
Gospels and Paul*, ed. Christopher W. Skinner and Kelly R. Iverson (Atlanta: Society of Biblical
Literature, 2012), 203-23; Das, *Paul, the Law, and the Covenant* (Peabody, MA: Hendrickson,
2001), 145-70.

with other departures from medieval interpretive traditions. His newfound focus on a central, or literal, meaning left behind the *Quadriga*, the four-fold allegorical method of his scholastic predecessors.[12] Luther wanted to identify and follow the *argumentum*. That literal sense throughout the Scriptures is ultimately Christ-centered. The Psalms thus include literal prophecies of Christ as their rightful, sole meaning.[13] Luther stressed the living voice of the Scriptures as God continues to speak through his word both to condemn and to promise, to re-create and to save. The apostle sought to reassure his readers of their salvation from the curse of the law and from sin. This was no mere transition from ceremonial law to a new law with its even more demanding obligations. That would be, for Luther's apostle, a return to slavery.

PAULINE INTERTEXTUALITY:
AUDIENCE COMPETENCE

Since nothing is new under the sun, Luther may be helpful in other modern Pauline discussions as well. Luther was appointed at the University of Wittenberg a professor of Bible, but he proved, in practice, more a student of the Old Testament.[14] Despite the early influence of Paul on his doctrine of justification, Luther did not spend most of his time with Paul, if his academic career is any indication. Of Luther's thirty-two years teaching at the university, he devoted only three or four to the New Testament: Romans, Galatians (twice), and Hebrews. His academic lectures were mostly on the Old Testament.

1513–1515	First Psalms Lectures (*Dictata super Psalterium*)
1515–1516	Romans
1516–1517	Galatians
1517–1518	Hebrews

12. Augustine (354–430): historical, allegorical/figurative, analogical (the correlation of Old Testament and New Testament), and aetiological/causal. John Cassian (360–430/435): literal, allegorical (foreshadowing Christ, the sacraments, and the church), tropological (moral application to lives), and anagogical (pointing to heavenly mysteries). Robert Kolb, "In Via Vittermbergensis: Luther Develops His Hermeneutic," pages 42–71 in *Martin Luther: Confessor of the Faith*, Christian Theology in Context (Oxford: Oxford University Press, 2009), 44.

13. Kolb, "*In Via Vittermbergensis*."

14. Heinrich Bornkamm, *Luther and the Old Testament*, trans. Eric W. and Ruth C. Gritsch, ed. Victor I. Gruhn (Philadelphia: Fortress, 1969; German edition, 1948), 7.

1518–1521	Second Psalms Lectures (Operations in Psalmos)
1523–1525	Deuteronomy
1524–1526	The Twelve Minor Prophets
1526	Ecclesiastes
1527	1 John
1527	Titus
1527	Philemon
1528	1 Timothy
1528–1530	Isaiah
1530–1531	Song of Songs
1531	Galatians
1532–1535	Psalms 2, 45, 51, 90, 120–34
1535–1545	Genesis
1543/1544	Isaiah 9
1544	Isaiah 53[15]

He preached 176 sermons from 1523–1529 on the Pentateuch, his preferred section of the Old Testament. From 1523–1534 Luther led a team translating the Old Testament. He was, in short, a student of the Old Testament who also made journeys through Galatians and Romans and the rest of the New Testament.[16]

Returning to Luther's visit to the modern classroom, he would have learned that after a long period in which New Testament scholars ignored the Old Testament roots of the Christian faith, that neglect began to be rectified in the years after World War II. The last three decades, in particular, have witnessed an incredible surge of interest in the wake of Richard Hays's *Echoes of Scripture in the Letters of Paul*.[17] Hays reveled in the parallels between Paul's own logic and that of the Scriptures he had cited. Paul's

---

15. This list does not include Luther's lectures on Judges on account of the difficulty of fitting them in a chronology. The editors of the Weimar edition see them as falling somewhere from 1516 to 1518; see WA 4:527–29.

16. Siegfried Raeder, "The Exegetical and Hermeneutical Work of Martin Luther," in *Hebrew Bible/Old Testament: The History of Its Interpretation, II: From the Renaissance to the Enlightenment*, ed. Magne Sæbø (Göttingen: Vandenhoeck & Ruprecht, 2008), 363–406, esp. 378–81; cf. Heinrich Bornkamm, *Luther and the Old Testament*, 2nd ed., trans. Eric W. and Ruth C. Gritsch (1969; Mifflintown, PA: Sigler, 1997), 269–83.

17. Richard B. Hays, *Echoes of Scripture in the Letters of Paul* (New Haven, CT: Yale University Press, 1989).

quotations served merely as the tip of the iceberg of a literary figure called "metalepsis". Hays's provocative readings of Paul in light of his scriptural roots not only inspired still more readings of Paul as an interpreter of Scripture but also the development of a more refined methodology for detecting those influences.[18] Hays was relatively conservative in the application of his own method. He tended to limit himself to citations of the Old Testament. Many of those citations are even explicitly signaled by the apostle. Hays noted how the larger contexts of citations regularly align with and reinforce Paul's message. In examining the original biblical contexts, one soon begins to appreciate the reverberations across the Testaments. Studies since Hays have gone beyond quotations to address allusions and even fainter echoes where the Old Testament signal is not as strong.

Literary theorists have explained that, as the signal grows weaker from an explicit citation, the next level of engagement with the Old Testament Scriptures is the allusion. An allusion still targets the intended audience. The author is attempting to *do* something with language *for the sake of the audience.*[19] "In order for the allusion to be successful, the audience must *recognize* the sign, *realize* that [it] is deliberate, *remember* aspects of the original text to which the author is alluding, and *connect* to one or more of these aspects with the alluding text in order to get the author's point."[20] An author's intention for the audience to grasp an allusion raises the question of audience competence.

Hays was comfortable reading Paul and the Scriptures in a twentieth and twenty-first century setting. The "echoes" of his book's title could refer to even weaker intertextual connections than the intended allusion.[21]

---

18. For those criteria, see Hays, *Echoes*, 29–32; A. Andrew Das, *Paul and the Stories of Israel: Grand Thematic Narratives in Galatians* (Minneapolis: Fortress, 2016), 16–20.

19. Carmela Perri, "On Alluding," *Poetics* 7 (1978): 300.

20. Michael B. Thompson, *Clothed with Christ: The Example and Teaching of Jesus in Romans 12.1–15.13*, Journal for the Study of the New Testament: Supplement Series 59 (Sheffield: Sheffield Academic Press, 1991), 29, drawing on Perri, "On Alluding," 301.

21. Hays would use "echo" for all manner of biblical appropriation, but in other places he would distinguish between an echo and an allusion: an allusion would be an obvious intertextual reference whereas an echo would be a subtler, more subliminal reference bordering on "the vanishing point"; Hays, *Echoes of Scripture*, 23; cf. Stanley E. Porter, "Further Comments on the Use of the Old Testament in the New Testament," in *The Intertextuality of the Epistles: Explorations of Theory and Practice*, ed. Thomas L. Brodie, Dennis R. MacDonald, and Stanley E. Porter, New Testament Monographs 16 (Sheffield: Sheffield Phoenix, 2007), 109.

An echo may be an unconscious appropriation of the Scriptures by a New Testament author—one that the modern reader may appreciate but that Paul's readers, and even the apostle himself, may have been unaware of. Putting aside the weaker echoes, literary theorists have reinserted the role of the author and the readers in identifying allusions to the Scriptures.

Christopher Stanley attempted to reconstruct the degree to which the original audiences of Paul's letters would have detected the quotations, allusions, and echoes that modern readers have recognized. Stanley raised a number of questions about Paul's original audiences. For instance, only five or ten percent would have possessed at least a basic level of literacy. Except for a very few, they would not have been reading Paul for themselves. Scrolls were incredibly costly and not in abundance. Gatherings of Christ-believers in homes would not have access to the scrolls of a local synagogue, if even the synagogue possessed an extensive set. If the Christ-believers were meeting separately from the synagogues, they would not benefit from the weekly synagogue instruction, were that a significant factor in the first century.[22] With few exceptions, the original, ancient audiences would not have been capable of detecting Paul's unsignaled quotations, allusions, or echoes. Even their designated teachers would not have had the advantages of later readers of the apostle, especially after the invention of the printing press. Christopher Stanley therefore sought to show that the ancient reader could follow Paul's reasoning without regard for the original contexts of his quotations or allusions.[23]

Paul's explicit quotations in Galatians indicate that he did not expect his original audience to possess an in-depth understanding of the Scriptures. The scriptural texts that he quotes appear to have originated in the instruction of rival teachers. For instance, in Galatians 3:10, Paul cites Deuteronomy 27:26 ("it is written"): "Cursed is everyone who does not abide by everything written in the book of the Law to do them." The Deuteronomy passage threatens a curse for anyone who *fails* to do the law. Paul's own point, on the other hand, expressed at the beginning of the verse, is that those who

22. Christopher D. Stanley, *Arguing with Scripture: The Rhetoric of Quotations in the Letters of Paul* (New York: T&T Clark, 2004), 38–61; Stanley, "'Pearls Before Swine': Did Paul's Audiences Understand His Biblical Quotations?," *Novum Testamentum* 41 (1999): 124–44; see also Das, *Paul and the Stories of Israel*, 16–28, 220–21, 236–38.

23. Stanley, *Arguing*, 114–35 for Galatians.

rely on the law are under a curse. Paul is employing a passage for support of his point that, on the surface, is at odds with his own message. Normally, no one would cite Deuteronomy 27:26 in support of the point Paul wants to make. He appears to be explaining a key proof text employed by the rival teachers at Galatia to encourage law observance.[24] The same dynamic is at work a few verses later in Galatians 3:12, where Paul cites Leviticus 18:5: "The one who does these things will live by them." The Leviticus passage promises life to those who do the law's works. The scriptural quote, like Deuteronomy 27:26, is apparently at odds with the apostle's own conclusion: "No one is justified before God by the law" (Gal 3:11). Paul is not using such poor texts for his position by choice. He is reinterpreting another of the rivals' key passages. The apostle usually indicates to the Galatians that he is quoting the Scriptures, even though he is drawing on passages that would have figured in the teaching of the rivals. Perhaps Paul is *anticipating* the rivals' scriptural arguments in support of law-observance. Note that he does not appeal to a body of scriptural teaching that he shared while still with them.

LUTHER'S CONTRIBUTION TO
PAULINE INTERTEXTUALITY

Martin Luther may at this point be profitably brought into a dialogue with the modern discussion that he encountered thanks to that imagined time machine. Unlike the very first gentile hearers of Paul's letters, who had encountered the Scriptures, at least initially, on an occasional (weekly?) basis in the synagogues, Luther was a much more knowledgeable reader, having lectured on much of the Old Testament and the books from which Paul draws. He refers to Old Testament passages over two hundred times in both his 1519 and his 1535 commentary on Galatians. The density of Luther's Old Testament references in the 1519 commentary is higher because of the shorter length of the commentary. References to Isaiah and the Pentateuch are frequent, but the most frequent are his references to the Psalms. Over one-third of his Old Testament references are from the Psalms. This reflects Luther's early lectures and continued interest. Nevertheless, he

---

24. This verse therefore offers proof that Paul is aware of some of the rivals' instruction at Galatia.

demonstrates a knowledge of the full range of the Old Testament: the rest of the Writings, especially Proverbs, the Former Prophets, Jeremiah, and even the Minor Prophets. As a reader, he is more than competent of detecting the apostle's use of the Scripture.

Paul quotes the Scriptures in Galatians eleven times: Galatians 2:16 (Ps 143:2); 3:6 (Gen 15:6; unmarked, but with explicit mention of Abraham); 3:8 (Gen 12:3; cf. 18:18; marked by a shift to second-person singular); 3:10 (Deut 27:26; 28:58[?]; marked by a quotation formula); 3:11 (Hab 2:4; unmarked); 3:12 (Lev 18:5; marked by demonstrable syntactical tension with its context); 3:13 (Deut 21:23; marked by a quotation formula); 3:16 (Gen 13:15; agrees with the LXX); 4:27 (Isa 54:1; agrees with the LXX); 4:30 (Gen 21:10); and 5:14 (Lev 19:18). Of those eleven, Luther identifies ten of them.[25]

At a weaker level of intertextual signal, to what extent does a sixteenth-century professor of the Old Testament detect the allusions and echoes in the Pauline texts that modern scholars have recognized? Two modern scholars may serve as representative dialogue partners. Roy Ciampa reviewed Galatians 1 and 2 for as many possible allusions or echoes of the Old Testament Scriptures to which Paul may have referred or that might illumine his patterns of thought.[26] The most prominent of Ciampa's discussion of Old Testament allusions and echoes in Galatians are:

VERSE(S)	SUBJECT	OLD TESTAMENT BACKGROUND
Gal 1:1-2	*Shaliach*/prophetic sending	Judg 6:8; 2 Kgs 17:13; 2 Chr 25:15; Isa 6:8; Jer 1:4-8; 7:25; 20:7-12; 23:16-22; 28:9; 28:15; Ezek 2-3; Amos 7:14; Hag 1-2; Mal 3:1; 4:5
Gal 1:2	Assemblies of God	Deut 23:1-9; Judg 20:2; 1 Chr 28:8; Neh 13:1; Mic 2:5
Gal 1:3	Grace and peace	Isa 40-55

---

25. Luther identifies (1) Ps 143:2 in his 1519 commentary but not in his 1535 commentary; (2) Gen 15:6 in his 1535 commentary; (3) Gen 12:3 in both 1519 and 1535; (4) Deut 27:26 in both 1519 and 1535; (5) Hab 2:4 in 1519 and 1535; (6) Lev 18:5 in 1519; (7) Deut 21:23 in 1519 and 1535; (8) Gen 13:15 in *neither* commentary; (9) Isa 54:1 in 1519 and 1535; (10) Gen 21:10 in 1519 and 1535; and (11) Lev 19:18 in 1519 and 1535. Thus Luther identifies all but one (Gen 13:15 in Gal 3:16).

26. Roy E. Ciampa, *The Presence and Function of Scripture in Galatians 1 and 2*, Wissenschaftliche Untersuchungen zum Neuen Testament 2.102 (Tübingen: Mohr Siebeck, 1999), 37–220.

Gal 1:4	Christ's saving work	Isa 53:6
Gal 1:4	According to the will of God	Isa 14:26; 25:1; 44:25–28; 46:10; 48:14; Ezek 24:14; Dan 4:35; Jer 49:20; 50:45; Mic 4:12; Job 23:12; Pss 37:23; 115:3; 135:6
Gal 1:5	Doxology	1 Sam 6:5; Pss 29:1–2; 96:7–8; Isa 53:12; Jer 13:16; Mal 2:2
Gal 1:6–7	Echoes of Israel's apostasy and the golden calf	Exod 32:8; Deut 9:12, 16; 11:13–21; Judg 2:17; Hos 11:1–2
Gal 1:6–7	Troublers/Achan	Josh 6:18; 7:25; Judg 11:35; 1 Sam 14:29; 1 Chr 2:7; Job 19:6; Isa 51:5
Gal 1:8–9	Anathema	Deut 11:28; 13:13–14
Gal 1:10	Persuading/pleasing God	Num 22–24; Deut 13
Gal 1:10	Persuading Yahweh's servants	1 Kgs 14:18; 18:36; 2 Kgs 9:7; 14:25; 17:13, 23; 21:10; Ezra 9:11; Jer 7:25; 25:4; 26:5; 29:19; 35:15; 44:4; Ezek 38:17; Dan 9:6, 10; Amos 3:7; Zech 1:6
Gal 1:15–17	Messenger's calling	Exod 3:11; Isa 6:5; 49:1–6; Jer 1:5–6; Ezek 1:28–2:2
Gal 1:15–17	Elijah	1 Kgs 19:5 (or Elijah in 1 Kgs)
Gal 1:18–20	No oaths	Deut 6:13; 10:20
Gal 1:21–24	Glorified God in me	Isa 49:1–6
Gal 2:1–2	Running in vain	Isa 49; Hab 2:2–3
Gal 2:3–4	Spiritual vs. literal circumcision	Lev 26:41; Deut 10:16; 30:16; Jer 4:4; 9:25 (24 LXX), 26 (25 LXX); Ezek 44:7–9
Gal 2:5	Not yielding	Deut 13:8 (9 LXX)
Gal 2:6	No favoritism	Deut 10:17; 2 Chr 19:6–7
Gal 2:7–8	Paul's apostleship	Isa 49:6
Gal 2:9	Grace given	Gen 39:21; Exod 3:21; 11:3; 12:36

Gal 2:9	Give the hand	2 Kgs 10:5; 1 Chr 29:24; 30:8; Ezra 10:19; Jer 50:15; Lam 5:6; Ezek 17:18
Gal 2:11	Resist to the face	Deut 7:24; 9:2; 11:25; 31:21; Judg 2:14; 2 Chr 13:7–8
Gal 2:12	Separating oneself	Gen 13:9–11; Num 6:2–12; Ezra 6:21; Isa 45:24; 56:3; Ezek 14:7
Gal 2:14	Walking straight	Lev 26:13
Gal 2:16	Psalm citation	Ps 143:2 (142:2 LXX); also Gen 6:9
Gal 2:16	Justification	Gen 15:6; Hab 2:4
Gal 2:18	Building up/tearing down	Jer 1:10; 12:16–17; 18:9; 24:6; 38:4, 28; 40:7; 49:10; 51:34
Gal 2:20	Christ's saving work	Isa 53:6; Hab 2:4

Ciampa does not identify whether he thinks his connections represent allusions or mere echoes.

By way of comparison, Luther likewise refers to Jeremiah 23:21 for Paul's "sending" in Galatians 1:1–2. In relation to Galatians 1:3, Luther refers to Isaiah 48:22 about the wicked enjoying no peace. Luther explains Christ's saving work in relation to Isaiah 53 (vv. 6, 8)—a favorite chapter in Isaiah for Luther—in Galatians 1:4. He identifies the unmarked quotation in Galatians 2:16, as he does for almost all of Paul's other's quotations. On the other hand, whereas the Reformer regularly comments on Paul's quotations, he does not appear to have noticed the vast majority of Ciampa's Old Testament allusions and echoes.

Matthew Harmon published a dissertation on Paul's use of Isaiah in the Letter to the Galatians.[27] He developed a cline with four categories that ranged from greater shared vocabulary and syntactical parallels to lesser: citation, allusion, echo, and thematic parallel. Harmon distinguished an allusion from an echo, in part, on the basis of author intentionality. Unlike citations and allusions, echoes are "such subtle appropriations of scripture that intentionality is often extremely difficult to determine. ... The category

---

27. Matthew S. Harmon, *She Must and Shall Go Free: Paul's Isaianic Gospel in Galatians*, Beihefte zur Zeitschrift für die neutestamentliche Wissenschaft 168 (Göttingen: De Gruyter, 2010).

of echo allows for the possibility that the influence of a previous text is so pervasive upon an author that its influence may be present even when the author does not necessarily intend the audience to see the connection."[28] Harmon's distinction between allusions and echoes is not novel but relies on the prior work of Stanley Porter. Harmon does, however, depart from Porter in endorsing a still weaker category: "With thematic parallels we are dealing with ideas/concepts shared between texts that transcend precise verbal relationships. In such cases it is often difficult to determine whether the shared thematic parallels originate from a specific text or are instead part of the larger shared scriptural background that shaped the very conceptual framework of Paul."[29] Harmon's "thematic parallels" may be due to a particular antecedent or may be derived from a larger literary tradition or intellectual milieu. A thematic parallel does *not* reflect a clear connection between two literary texts. With that fourfold classification system, he reviewed Galatians for all possible citations (c), allusions (a), echoes (e), and thematic parallels (tp), summarizing his results near the end of his study as follows:[30]

Verse(s)	Subject	Isaianic Background
Gal 1:1	Apostleship	Isa 52:7; 61:1 (tp)
Gal 1:2	Peace	Isa 40–66 (tp)
Gal 1:4	Christ's death	Isa 53:10 (a)
Gal 1:8–9	Gospel	Isa 52:7; 60:1–3; 61:1 (tp)
Gal 1:10	Slave of Christ	Isa 42:1–8; 49:1–8; 52:13–53:12 (tp)
Gal 1:15	Called from the womb	Isa 49:1 (a)
Gal 1:16	Reveal his son	Isa 49:3 (e); 49:6; 52:5, 7 (tp); 52:10; 53:1 (e)
Gal 1:16	Preach the gospel to the Gentiles	Isa 42:6; 49:6, 8; 52:5, 7, 10; 53:1 (tp)
Gal 1:17	Travel to Arabia	Isa 42:11 (tp)
Gal 1:23–24	Glorifying God in me	Isa 49:3 (e)

---

28. Harmon, *She Must and Shall Go Free*, 29.

29. Harmon, *She Must and Shall Go Free*, 30.

30. Harmon, *She Must and Shall Go Free*, 265.

Gal 2:2	Running in vain	Isa 49:4 (e)
Gal 2:2, 8–9	Ministry to the Gentiles	Isa 42:6; 49:6–8; 52:5–7 (tp)
Gal 2:16–21	Righteousness language	Isa 40–66 (tp)
Gal 2:20	Christ lives in me	Isa 49:3 (e)
Gal 2:20	Gave himself for me	Isa 53 (a)
Gal 3:2–5	Hearing of faith	Isa 53:1 (a)
Gal 3:6–9	Look to Abraham	Isa 51:1–8 (a)
Gal 3:8	Gospel preached	Isa 52:7–10 (tp)
Gal 3:13	Christ as a curse for us	Isa 53 (a)
Gal 3:14–16	Blessing, see of Abraham, Spirit	Isa 44:3–5 (a)
Gal 3:16	Singular seed —> plural seed	Isa 41:8; 53:10; 54:3 (tp)
Gal 3:15–18	Covenant, promise, seed, inheritance	Isa 54:3–10 (e); 61:7–10 (tp)
Gal 4:1–7	New exodus, (1) new creation, (2) Servant, (3) Abraham/seed	Isa 41:17–20; 43:16–21; 51:9–10 (new creation); Isa 52:11–12; 52:13–53:12 (Servant); Isa 41:8, 17–20; 51:1–8 (Abraham/seed) (a/e)
Gal 4:11	Labor in vain	Isa 49:4 (e)
Gal 4:19	Paul's birth pangs	Isa 45:7–11 (a); 51:1–2 (e); 54:1 (tp)
Gal 4:27	Rejoice, barren one	Isa 54:1 (c)
Gal 5:5	Waiting for righteousness in the Spirit	Isa 32:15–17 (tp)
Gal 5:13	Freedom	Isa 40–55 (tp)
Gal 5:13	Serve one another through love	Isa 40–66 (tp)
Gal 5:18	Led by the Spirit	Isa 63:11–15 (tp)
Gal 5:22–23	Fruit of the Spirit	Isa 32:15–20; 57:15–21 (a/e)
Gal 6:15	New creation	Isa 40–66 (a)
Gal 6:16	Peace and mercy on the Israel of God	Isa 54:10 (a)

By way of comparison again, Luther identifies the quotation of Isaiah 54:1 in Galatians 4:27. At the weaker levels of allusions, echoes, and thematic parallels, Luther only notices parallels to Isaiah 53, a favorite chapter of his: Isaiah 53:6–8/Galatians 1:4; Isaiah 53:3/Galatians 2:16–21; Isaiah 53:1/ Galatians 3:2, 5; and Isaiah 53/Galatians 3:13. Luther does not appear to have recognized any of Harmon's other allusions and echoes.

CONCLUSION

Martin Luther offers a useful test case for modern Pauline scholarship as an accomplished student of Hebrew and a longstanding lecturer on the Old Testament. Tellingly, he did not identify the vast majority of allusions and echoes that modern exegetes have noticed. If as learned a student of the Old Testament as Luther did not recognize these potential Pauline uses of the Old Testament, it is even more unlikely that the gentile Galatians would have, with their more limited exposure to the Jewish Scriptures. While the modern enterprise may illumine Paul's own conscious and unconscious appropriations of the Scriptures, to project such abilities onto the ancient reader likely represents a blind alley in modern scholarship. Paul usually *signals* the Galatians, whether by a formula or a break in syntax, when he is quoting the Jewish Scriptures. He did not expect them to recognize the quotes.

Interestingly, just as Paul can be understood by his ancient readers, and even today, without knowledge of the context of his citations, the same might be said of Luther's use of the Old Testament. He regularly mentions Old Testament verses, but he does so to illustrate points that he is making, and the Old Testament verses typically function for him without regard to their larger contexts. A key idea or word in the Old Testament verse comes to mind for Luther in relation to a point he is making as he explains the New Testament text. Luther does not require more of his reader. Modern recognitions of metalepsis in Paul deepen appreciation for the connections between his message and the Jewish Scriptures, but the vast majority of these connections were likely lost on ancient readers.

7
—
SOUNDINGS ON *SIMUL IUSTUS ET PECCATOR*

Evidence in the Pauline Epistles for Our Continuing Struggle with Sin

Thomas R. Schreiner

My goal in this essay is to show from a wide sweep in the Pauline Letters that a continuing struggle with sin characterizes the lives of believers.[1] One could show from a number of fruitful angles in the Pauline Letters that sin continues to infect even the best things we do. Here I explore one avenue that shows from the Pauline Epistles the truth that we are *simul iustus et peccator* (justified and at the same time sinners).

Certainly the whole truth of the Christian life is not expressed in this formula, and no attempt is made here to speak to other dimensions of our lives as believers. Our ongoing battle with sin should not be used to promote sin. Romans 6:1 still applies: the grace of God in Christ does not excuse sin. Still, we see in the Pauline Letters that perfection will not be

---

1. I am delighted to contribute to a Festschrift for Mark Seifrid with whom I served as a colleague at The Southern Baptist Theological Seminary for seventeen years. I dedicate this small essay on *simul iustus et peccator* to Mark. As I write this, many wonderful memories of our time together at Southern flood my mind. In our early years we prayed together in Mark's office for the school and for churches along with Greg Wills. We were excited about the work the Lord was doing at Southern and in the churches as a new day was commencing at the school under Al Mohler's leadership. In addition, I will never forget Mark's wonderful sense of humor and his hearty laugh as he recounted anecdotes and stories from his own life. Most of all, I learned from Mark about the gospel of grace. His words and his writings were full of the aroma of the gospel, reminding me that our righteousness isn't in ourselves but in Jesus Christ crucified and risen. See the helpful essay by Timo Laato, "*Simul Iustus Et Peccator* Through the Lenses of Paul," *Journal of the Evangelical Theological Society* 61 (2018): 735-66.

ours until the day of resurrection. In the meantime, in the interval between the already and not yet, we struggle with sin. Every text mentioned in this essay could be explored in more detail, so preliminary soundings are suggested here.

EXPOSITORY TEXTS

ROMANS 7:14–25

If we discuss the continuing presence of sin in believers, Romans 7:14–25 immediately and rightly comes to mind. It isn't my purpose to try to untie this knot (though I have attempted to explain this text in detail elsewhere), but to make a couple of observations.[2] The trend today is to see the person described here as unregenerate, but there are good reasons to think that the battle of believers with sin is described here as well.[3] The present tense verbs and the emphasis on the fleshiness of the "I" call attention to the state of the human being as he or she encounters the law. The intrinsic incapacity and inability of human beings is painfully evident, especially when we consider the prohibition against coveting (7:7–11). We don't have the whole picture here of those indwelt by the Holy Spirit, but the eschaton has not yet arrived in its fullness, and thus those who enjoy the work of the Holy Spirit are also keenly aware of their own fleshiness, their own propensity to evil, and their spiritual incapacity. The deliverance "from this body of death" (Rom 7:24) won't be ours fully until the day of resurrection, and in the interval, believers continue to struggle with the flesh.

GALATIANS 5:16–18

When we look at Galatians 5:16–18, the parallel to Romans 7:14–25 is striking, though the accent in Galatians is on the new life of believers. We live new lives by the power of the Spirit. At the same time, however, there is

---

2. For a fuller analysis of the text, see Thomas R. Schreiner, *Romans*, 2nd ed., Baker Exegetical Commentary on the New Testament (Grand Rapids: Baker, 2018), 369–82.

3. See recently Mark A. Seifrid, "Romans 7: The Voice of the Law, the Cry of Lament, and the Shout of Thanksgiving," in *Perspectives on Our Struggle with Sin: Three Views on Romans 7*, ed. T. L. Wilder (Nashville: B&H, 2011), 111–65; Will N. Timmins, *Romans 7 and Christian Identity: A Study of the "I" in Its Literary Context*, Society for New Testament Studies Monograph Series 170 (Cambridge: Cambridge University Press, 2017); Jeffrey D. W. Dryden, "Revisiting Romans 7: Law, Self, and Spirit," *Journal for the Study of the New Testament* 5 (2015): 129–51.

a recognition of the continuing presence of sin in believers since there is an ongoing conflict between the flesh and the Spirit. Believers aren't completely new because they still experience the desires of the flesh. Paul doesn't reflect on whether those desires are actualized in Galatians 5:16–18, but the message of the whole letter should inform our reading of Galatians 5:16–18. The Galatians were on the verge of departing from the gospel of Christ (Gal 1:6–7) and were seriously considering circumcision for their salvation (Gal 5:2–4). It was as if a spell had been cast over them, and they had forgotten that they were saved by faith in Christ and not by works of the law (Gal 3:1–5). Paul also calls upon those who are spiritual to restore those who have gone astray (Gal 6:1). We don't have a two-tiered Christianity here, as if some in the church were spiritual and others were fleshly. All believers are by definition spiritual in that all believers have the Spirit. Still, the fact that some believers have gone astray points to the truth of *simul iustus et peccator*. Indeed, even those who have not wandered must pay heed to themselves since the danger of pride and falling into sin is ever present, and self-righteousness is never completely absent. It is evident from the letter as a whole that the Galatian believers were justified, but at the same time they were sinners, and their sin was evident in their temptation to stray from the gospel. Galatians 5:16–18 reminds us that we are in a fight against sinful desires as long as we live in this present evil age (Gal 1:4; cf. 6:8).

LIVING IN THE MORTAL BODY AND PHILIPPIANS 3:12–16

The continuing presence of sin is evident as well in Paul's theology of the body. We can only consider a few texts here. For instance, Romans 8:10 says that the "the body is dead because of sin, but the Spirit gives life because of righteousness" (CSB). Believers are new and transformed since they have the Spirit, but at the same time they are mortal, dying because of the continuing presence of sin in them. Paul doesn't restrict himself to past sin. As long as believers are in the body, sin continues to bedevil us, and thus we await the day of resurrection (Rom 8:11).[4]

---

4. See David Wenham, "The Christian Life: A Life of Tension? A Consideration of the Nature of Christian Experience in Paul," in *Pauline Studies: Essays Presented to Professor F. F. Bruce on His Seventieth Birthday*, ed. D. A. Hagner and M. J. Harris (Grand Rapids: Eerdmans, 1980), 80–94.

Philippians 3:12–16 confirms our reading of Romans. Paul contrasts himself with Jewish teachers who advocate righteousness that comes from the law (Phil 3:2–11), and it is possible that they were even claiming some kind of perfection. We see in verse 11 that Paul looks forward to the eschaton, to the day of the resurrection. He follows that up immediately with the words, "Not that I have already reached the goal or am already perfect" (Phil 3:12). Paul acknowledges that he has not attained perfection, and the close association with verse 11 indicates that perfection will only be his on the day of the resurrection. Paul plainly teaches that believers continue to struggle with sin until the final day, reaffirming this truth in Philippians 3:13: "I do not consider myself to have taken hold of it," by which he means the final goal or the day of resurrection. In this life we continue to pursue the eschatological goal, recognizing that we fall short of attaining all that is required (Phil 3:14). Verse 15 is probably ironic; those who are *teleioi*, those who are perfect, should recognize that they aren't perfect! Those who have a right estimate of the Christian life recognize that they fall short in many ways. Perfection is only ours on the day of resurrection.

GODLY BELIEVERS CONTINUE
TO STRUGGLE WITH SIN

We have seen that godly believers continue to struggle with sin, and as we survey the Pauline Letters, such a judgment is confirmed in a number of texts. These texts are especially interesting because it wasn't Paul's main purpose to illustrate the ongoing battle with sin, but when we step back from these texts, it is clear that they support such a claim.

EUODIA AND SYNTYCHE

A fascinating example of *simul iustus et peccator* is the quarrel between Euodia and Syntyche (Phil 4:2), where Paul exhorts other believers to help them reconcile (Phil 4:3). Paul doesn't mention Euodia and Syntyche because they were especially bad examples of believers, but because they were especially good! They had played a significant role in the spread of the gospel and in the Pauline mission. Paul doesn't severely rebuke them, nor does he write them off as failures because they were at odds with one another. He doesn't excuse sin, but he recognizes that sin may crop up in the lives of believers, even in mature believers like Euodia and Syntyche.

THE FAILURE TO SUPPORT PAUL AT HIS TRIAL

I would suggest that 2 Timothy 4:16 should be interpreted similarly where Paul remarks, "At my first defense, no one stood by me, but everyone deserted me. May it not be counted against them." Paul reflects on his trial at Rome where his life was at stake. Clearly, forsaking Paul in his hour of need was a sin. Indeed, in the case of Demas, his desertion may be a sign that he didn't belong to Christ at all (2 Tim 4:10). But Paul recognizes in 2 Timothy 4:16 that the failure to stand by him during a trial was forgivable; it seems doubtful that Paul is suggesting that those who didn't stand by him were destined for final judgment. Paul recognizes that fellow believers may let us down at crucial moments in our lives, and we are called to extend forgiveness to them. We realize that other believers are not all they should be and that they continue to need forgiveness from the Lord and from us. Such an understanding comes from self-awareness since it is evident that we all continue to fall short of God's glory (Rom 3:23).

THE IMPERFECTION OF THE CHURCH IN THESSALONICA

We find several illuminating texts that relate to our topic in 1 Thessalonians. Paul gives thanks for the church (1 Thess 1:2–10; 2:13; 3:6–10) and is pleased with their progress in the faith. At the same time, he prays that he will be able to come in person and "to complete what is lacking in your faith" (1 Thess 3:10). Paul compliments them for keeping the commands and instructions he gave them but exhorts them to further growth (1 Thess 4:2). God himself has taught them to love one another, which is evident from the quality of love which they have shown to other believers. Even in this case, however, they are exhorted "to do this even more" (1 Thess 4:9–10; cf. 1 Tim 4:15). What we find in 1 Thessalonians is instructive, for Paul is clearly happy with the church. At the same time, he doesn't think the church has arrived. It seems fair to conclude from this that even believers who are doing well in their spiritual lives can always do better. No one "arrives" in this life; no one reaches perfection or comes to a place where they don't need to grow in their love for the Lord and for others. Another way of putting this is that sin continues to afflict us as believers even when we are making progress in the faith. We should not think that the continuing presence of sin is limited to immature believers, as if some believers leave behind any need for further growth. Instead, all believers—even the most godly Christians—still struggle with sin and still fall short of all that God requires. Pride continues to linger in us all until the day of final redemption.

THE NEED FOR EXHORTATIONS

The Pauline Letters often contain exhortations to live in a way that pleases God. Paul encourages believers to walk in the Spirit (Gal 5:16), be led by the Spirit (Gal 5:18), march in step with the Spirit (Gal 5:25), sow to the Spirit (Gal 6:8), and be filled with the Spirit (Eph 5:18). He gives such exhortations because believers, even the most mature believers, are in danger of straying, of relying upon the flesh instead of the Spirit. Such commands and exhortation would be unnecessary if sin didn't continue to lurk within believers. It is not convincing to see the desires of the flesh as something external to believers, as if they are something outside of us. Desires, after all, come from persons! They are not imposed from without but arise from within. Believers are justified in Christ and are at the same time sinners in the sense that they still have desires for evil within them.

In Ephesians 4:3, believers are to maintain and preserve the unity of the Spirit. Paul does not instruct believers to *create* unity, for the unity of believers has already been accomplished through the death of Jesus Christ (Eph 2:11–12). Still, Paul recognizes that, because of the presence of sin in believers, the unity of believers could be damaged or perhaps even lost. Along the same lines, believers are a new creation in Christ (2 Cor 5:17); they have put off the old person and put on the new (Col 3:9–10). As those who are baptized and converted, they have put on Christ (Gal 3:27), and the old person, who we were in Adam, has been crucified with Christ (Rom 6:6; cf. Gal 6:14). And yet the newness of believers has an eschatological qualification or reservation. The threat to sin remains, and thus they must put off the old person and put on the new person (Eph 4:22, 24), even though the old person has already been put off and the new one put on! Even though they have put on Christ at baptism, they must put Christ on and resist the desires of the flesh (Rom 13:14). Believers have died with Christ, and yet they must put to death sinful desires (Rom 8:13; Col 3:5). We see again that believers are both new in Christ and yet not entirely free from the old. It is not convincing to see the impetus to sin as coming from the environment or to see the flesh as something outside of us. Such approaches are rather gnostic, failing to appreciate the complexity of the human being in Christ.

We would not need exhortations if we were free internally from sinful desires and inclinations. In the new creation that is coming, and in our heavenly existence, there will be no need for exhortations since believers will be perfected. The urgent exhortations Paul gives to believers testify to the truth that believers are justified and are still sinners.

Another instructive example of the divided existence of believers is suggested by the admonitions to think in a new way. In Romans 12:2 Paul calls upon believers to be transformed as their minds are renewed. Paul says to the Romans in Romans 15:14, "My brothers and sisters, I myself am convinced about you that you also are full of goodness, filled with all knowledge, and able to instruct one another." Freedom from sin includes the notion of thinking rightly about life, though, of course, such freedom includes much more than thinking properly about reality. Paul has confidence that believers are, as new creatures in Christ, "full of goodness" and are able to instruct each other as those filled with knowledge. Still, believers must at the same time be renewed in their thinking as well, or as Ephesians 5:10 says, they are to test what is pleasing to the Lord. If we are to test and determine what is pleasing to the Lord, the right course of action isn't immediately apparent to us. Such testing doesn't mean that lack of knowledge per se is sinful, as if the process of determining what is right is necessarily blameworthy. On the other hand, the partiality of our understanding, since we are whole persons and not just abstractions, is due in part to the continuing presence of sin in believers. Our minds need to be continually renewed because, as sinners, we are disposed to construe the world in ways that are shaped by our fallenness.

We see something quite similar in 2 Corinthians 8, where the Corinthians are complimented for excelling in "in faith, speech, knowledge, and in all diligence, and in your love for us." Such words remind us that the *simul* is not the whole reality for believers. Still, Paul wrote to the Corinthians because he was concerned about them completing what they started so that they would donate a financial gift to the church in Jerusalem. We see here the complexity of the human being in Christ. We have new desires and inclinations, and the desire to do good testifies to God's work in us. On the other hand, our desire to do what is good may not be translated into actions. The desire may evaporate and not produce any concrete good in the life of the world. We find a similar phenomenon in 2 Thessalonians 1:11, where Paul prays for the Thessalonians that God would "by his power fulfill your every desire to do good and your work produced by faith." The fulfilling of desires to do good should probably be understood along the lines of the discussion here. Our desires to do good may, because of the sin, fail to become a reality, and thus Paul prays that such desires would be translated into actions. The reason godly desires don't come to fruition is the presence of sin.

ESCHATOLOGICAL PRESENTATION

We also have a number of texts that zero in on the eschatological perfection of believers. For instance, in Ephesians 5:25–27 the work of Christ on the cross is set forth, and his goal "is to present the church to himself in splendor, without spot or wrinkle or anything like that, but holy and blameless" (Eph 5:27). The beautiful perfection of the church, where it is lovely and as spotless as a bride on her wedding day, is reserved for the last day, for the eschaton. Presently, the church, as anyone with eyes to see can testify, is full of spots and wrinkles and blemishes. And if we know ourselves at all, if we have any self-awareness, we realize that self-absorption, narcissism, and self-worship continue to stain us. We see the same truth in Colossians 1:22: "But now he has reconciled you by his physical body through his death, to present you holy, faultless, and blameless before him." The church is not yet faultless or blameless; her day of perfect loveliness won't become a reality until the day of Christ's return, the final day that we believers await eagerly.

PERFECT SANCTIFICATION AT THE SECOND COMING

The important text of 1 Thessalonians 5:23–24 doesn't speak of an eschatological presentation, but it should also be understood in terms of the final eschaton: "Now may the God of peace himself sanctify you completely. And may your whole spirit, soul, and body be kept sound and blameless at the coming of our Lord Jesus Christ. He who calls you is faithful; he will do it." Some in the history of interpretation have read the prayer for sanctification as if complete sanctification can be ours in the present era, as if perfection can be ours during this life. Such a reading fails to read the text in context. We have already seen in 1 Thessalonians that, although the Thessalonian Christians were doing well, they hadn't arrived at perfection.

Paul's pray for perseverance, sanctification, and blamelessness should be interpreted carefully. He does pray for the Thessalonians in this life, asking that they will be preserved and kept in the faith until the end. Such a prayer fits with one of the great concerns that animates Paul in the letter, as we see clearly in 1 Thessalonians 3:1–10. At the same time, the final words, "he will do it" (1 Thess 5:24), should not be understood as promising perfection or complete sanctification in this life. Paul speaks eschatologically here, as the reference to Jesus Christ's coming indicates, showing that complete sanctification is reserved for the day of Christ's appearance.

EVIDENCE OF CONTINUING SIN IN THE PAULINE LETTERS

THE DIVISIONS IN CORINTH

There are also instances in the Pauline Letters where believers sin, sometimes quite dramatically, and they are not written off as unbelievers. The discussion must be nuanced since, in some instances, Paul threatens believers with eschatological destruction if they continue to sin. Still, he recognizes that believers can fall into significant sins, and he doesn't in every instance threaten them with final judgment. We think, for instance, of the divisions that were rending the unity of the Corinthian church (1 Cor 1:10–4:21). Paul is distressed by the behavior of the church, but he addresses them as "saints" and "sanctified" (1 Cor 1:2), and he is also thankful for God's work in their midst (1 Cor 1:4–9).

The discussion of the Lord's Supper is also most interesting in this regard (1 Cor 11:17–34). In this case, those who were rich were excluding the poor. They were eating and drinking and even getting drunk, perhaps in the triclinium of the house, while the poor were going hungry in the atrium.[5] Paul was outraged that the poor were so blatantly being discriminated against at the Lord's Supper. As a result of such behavior, some were sick, and some had even died (1 Cor 11:30). Some think that the death of

---

5. See Otfried Hofius, "The Lord's Supper and the Lord's Supper Tradition: Reflections on 1 Corinthians 11:23b–25," in *One Loaf, One Cup: Ecumenical Studies of 1 Cor 11 and Other Eucharistic Texts*, ed. B. F. Meyer (Macon: Mercer University Press, 1993), 75–115.

some indicates final judgment,[6] but such a reading is not convincing for two reasons. First, Paul uses the expression "fall asleep" (*koimaō*), which invariably refers in the New Testament to the death of believers (Matt 27:52; Acts 7:60; 13:36; 1 Cor 7:39; 15:6, 18, 20, 51; 1 Thess 4:13–15; 2 Pet 3:4). It is quite remarkable that when the verb "sleep" is used for death, whether in Matthew, Luke, Paul, or Peter, it always refers to the death of believers. The verb is used for the death of believers on five other occasions in 1 Corinthians, as noted above. The verb "asleep" indicates that the death of believers is temporary, that death will not last forever, and that a day of resurrection is coming. The second reason for concluding that Paul refers to believers is found in 1 Corinthians 11:32, where he says, "But when we are judged by the Lord, we are disciplined, so that we may not be condemned with the world." The death of sinning believers was a judgment, but it should not be equated with eternal condemnation since the purpose of the judgment was so that they would not face condemnation along with the world. What is of interest for our purposes is that believers may sin in dramatic ways, and yet they still belong to the Lord, showing that they are justified by faith, but at the same time they are sinners. The severity of the judgment shows that the sin is grievous, and yet salvation is still the final outcome.

FURTHER EXAMPLES OF SIN IN CORINTH

We see other examples in 1 Corinthians of significant sin. Paul doesn't guarantee salvation to the man guilty of incest, for true repentance will indicate whether he will finally belong to the Lord (1 Cor 5:1–13). The continuing presence of sin in believers doesn't mean that Paul doesn't warn believers about apostasy.[7] Those who practice the works of the flesh listed in Galatians 5:19–21 will not inherit the kingdom of God. The Corinthians were suing one another over trivial matters (1 Cor 6:1–8), and Paul doesn't conclude that they are unbelievers. On the other hand, he warns them that those who continue to live unrighteously, who engage in a pattern of sinful

---

6. James M. Hamilton Jr., "The Lord's Supper in Paul: An Identity-Forming Proclamation of the Gospel," in *The Lord's Supper: Remembering and Proclaiming Christ until He Comes*, ed. T. R. Schreiner and M. R. Crawford (Nashville: B&H, 2010), 92–99.

7. Thomas R. Schreiner and Ardel Caneday, *The Race Set before Us: A Biblical Theology of Perseverance and Assurance* (Downers Grove, IL: InterVarsity, 2001).

behavior, won't inherit the kingdom (1 Cor 6:9–11). Persistence in blatant evil calls into question whether one will receive an eternal reward. Thus, the truth of *simul iustus et peccator* doesn't open the door wide to sin in churches, as if there is no danger for those who indulge in sin. Nevertheless, we also face the danger of overemphasizing such warnings, which could lead to the conclusion that believers are more righteous in their lives than they actually are. Some of the Corinthians in Paul's second letter—particularly those addressed in 2 Corinthians 12:19–13:10—face dangers, and Paul requires repentance. But their slippage up to this point, though harmful, isn't irrevocable. Paul doesn't identify them as unbelievers but calls upon them to repent.

Not all sins, however, are blatant. Paul chides and instructs the Corinthians about spiritual gifts in 1 Corinthians 12–14. They are guilty of immaturity, narcissism, arrogance, and self-absorption. As chapter 13 indicates, they had forgotten that the most important matter was love, thinking that remarkable gifts were an indication of maturity. Those entranced with their spiritual gifts weren't on the verge of apostasy, but they had veered from the center and focused on themselves rather than others. What Paul writes to the Corinthians speaks to us all because, if we are honest, we have to admit that we are all prone to self-preoccupation and that we all fail to love as we should. Such words don't deny the transformation in our lives and the newness of our life in Christ.

THE WEAK AND STRONG IN ROMANS

We see something rather similar with the weak and the strong in Romans 14:1–15:6. Both sides of the debate concentrated on their point of view and had become rather myopic. Consequently, the strong, who had robust consciences and felt free to eat foods that were unclean according to the Old Testament law, were prone to despise and mock the weak for being so restrictive (Rom 14:3). Conversely, the weak were tempted to judge the strong for having a more liberal stance and for transgressing proper limits in the name of freedom (Rom 14:3). Both sides needed to mature and to welcome one another (Rom 14:1, 3–4; 15:7), for love recognizes the genuine faith of those who differ from us on matters of indifference.

SLACKERS IN THESSALONICA

We have noted more than once that the Thessalonians are commended for their godliness. Yet a problem with idleness surfaces briefly in 1 Thessalonians (1 Thess 4:11–12; 5:14) and bursts out in full flame in the second letter (2 Thess 3:6–12). The problem is serious, and discipline may be warranted (2 Thess 3:14). Paul, however, doesn't jump to the conclusion that those who were idle were not believers. He acknowledges that believers can fall into such sins.

BELIEVING OPPOSITION TO PAUL

The last example comes from Philippians 1:12–18 and is most interesting. Paul had arrived in Rome (or possibly Caesarea) and was imprisoned for preaching the gospel. Because of Paul's boldness in proclaiming the gospel, those around him were inspired to do the same. Nevertheless, not everything was right with the world because some proclaimed Christ "out of envy and rivalry" (Phil 1:15). They were motivated by "selfish ambition" and hoped to "cause [Paul] trouble in my imprisonment" (Phil 1:17). There is no suggestion that these people were preaching a deviant gospel. In fact, we are told twice that they proclaimed Christ (Phil 1:15, 17), and Paul rejoices in their preaching Christ. It is hard to imagine such rejoicing if they were spreading a false gospel. No suggestion is given that those who were preaching the gospel "out of envy and rivalry" were unbelievers. Certainly their behavior is not commended, and the whole message of Philippians is that the interests of others should take precedence over our own desires. Still, the continuing presence of sin is evident in this text since some were preaching the good news with bad motives. Paul is not shocked by the situation; he does not dismiss them as unbelievers, and he even finds a silver lining in adverse circumstances.

CONCLUSION

In this brief essay I have attempted to show that sin continues to bedevil believers—that even the most mature believers are still stained by sin, selfishness, and narcissism until the day we die. The ongoing presence of sin is also evident since warnings about sin, sometimes quite severe, are given in almost all of the Pauline letters. Such sin is never excused, but neither does Paul write off those who are struggling with sin as unbelievers. He recognizes that all Christians everywhere are engaged in a struggle and battle with sin until the day we die. Luther's recognition of this truth is one of his most profound, and if we lose this truth, we can fall into pride and discouragement. Pride may surface because we may begin to think that we are much better than we really are. The other danger is that we may become depressed and discouraged because we overestimate how godly we can be until the day of resurrection. The continuing presence of sin doesn't excuse sin, but it keeps us humble and it reminds us of our future hope in Christ. We aren't what we should be, and we aren't what we shall be, but the promise that we shall be what we should be gives us unshakeable hope.

8

THE CENTRALITY OF ROMANS IN THE LIFE AND THEOLOGY OF MARTIN LUTHER

Benjamin L. Merkle

The formation of Luther's theology was centered on Paul's epistle to the Christians at Rome.[1] This essay will discuss the importance or centrality of the book of Romans in Luther's life and theology. Specifically, I will consider the influence of Romans on Luther's conversion and in his teaching and writings.

THE CENTRALITY OF ROMANS
IN LUTHER'S CONVERSION

Although it might not be possible to determine the precise date of Martin Luther's conversion (somewhere between 1513 and 1519),[2] we know that the insights regarding his transformed thinking occurred in 1519, as he was beginning his second exposition of Psalms.[3] In his *Preface to the Complete*

---

1. I have the distinct privilege of being Mark Seifrid's first doctoral student to graduate. During my PhD studies, I took two seminars with Dr. Seifrid, including Romans. I am grateful for having had the opportunity to learn from someone who is both a careful exegete of the Bible and someone who greatly appreciated the life and theology of Martin Luther. Luther's passion for the gospel of Jesus Christ is a passion that Dr. Seifrid shares.

2. Holding to an early date (1514), Lohse asserts, "Dating the Reformation breakthrough in the year 1514 in no way militates against the fact that even in the following years Luther still made significant progress in his theology as a whole, as well as in his statements about God's righteousness and our justification" (Bernard Lohse, *Martin Luther's Theology: Its Historical and Systematic Development*, trans. and ed. Roy A. Harrisville [Minneapolis: Fortress, 1999], 94).

3. E.g., Timothy George claims, "The context makes clear that this insight occurred in 1519 when Luther began his second exposition of the Psalms" (*Theology of the Reformers*, rev. ed. [Nashville: B&H Academic, 2013], 63).

Edition of Luther's Latin Writings (1545), the Reformer records his remarkable discovery. He reflects,

> I had indeed been captivated with an extraordinary ardor for understanding Paul in the Epistle to the Romans. But up till then it was not the cold blood about the heart, but a single word in Chapter 1 [:17], "In it the righteousness of God is revealed," that had stood in my way. For I hated that word "righteousness of God," which according to the use and custom of all the teachers, I had been taught to understand philosophically regarding the formal or active righteousness, as they called it, with which God is righteous and punishes the unrighteous sinner.[4]

For Luther, the gospel of God's righteousness was not good news—it was utterly terrifying. He viewed the gospel merely as declaring that God will punish sinners (God's active righteousness). He continues,

> Though I lived as a monk without reproach, I felt that I was a sinner before God with an extremely disturbed conscience. I could not believe that he was placated by my satisfaction. I did not love, yes, I hated the righteous God who punishes sinners. ... Thus I raged with a fierce and troubled conscience. Nevertheless, I beat importunately upon Paul at that place, most ardently desiring to know what St. Paul wanted.[5]

Luther seemed to be without hope. But he did not give up seeking to find the truth and comfort for his soul. He continued searching the Scriptures for answers.

> At last, by the mercy of God, meditating day and night, I gave heed to the context of the words, namely, "In it the righteousness of God is revealed, as it is written, 'He who through faith is righteous shall live.' " There I began to understand that the righteousness of God is that by which the righteous lives by a gift of God, namely by faith. And this is the meaning: the righteousness of God is revealed by the gospel, namely, the passive righteousness with which merciful

---

4. Luther, "Preface to the Complete Edition of Luther's Latin Writings," in *LW* 34:336.
5. *LW* 34:336–37.

God justifies us by faith, as it is written, "He who through faith is righteous shall live." Here I felt that I was altogether born again and had entered paradise itself through open gates. There a totally other face of the entire Scripture showed itself to me. Thereupon I ran through the Scriptures from memory. ... And I extolled my sweetest word with a love as great as the hatred with which I had before hated the word "righteousness of God." Thus that place in Paul was for me truly the gate to paradise.[6]

Luther had rediscovered the doctrine of justification by faith alone through grace alone. The passage that he once hated became to him more precious than he could have imagined. The book of Romans became the spark that ignited the Reformation through the life and ministry of Martin Luther. Leon Morris asserts, "The Reformation may be regarded as the unleashing of new spiritual life as a result of a renewed understanding of the teaching of Romans."[7]

THE CENTRALITY OF ROMANS IN
LUTHER'S TEACHING AND WRITINGS

COMMENTARY ON ROMANS (1515–1516)

Luther lectured on Romans from 1515 to 1516. From his and his students' records, it appears he taught on Romans for three semesters: (1) Spring-Summer 1515: Romans 1:1–3:4; (2) Fall 1515-Winter 1516: Romans 3:5–8:39; and (3) Spring-Summer 1516: Romans 9:1–16:27. Although Luther did not formally lecture on Romans again, that epistle became the center of his theology and a major component of his writing.[8]

As Luther lectured on Romans, he produced a commentary—notes from which he taught. Following medieval method, these notes consisted of two

---

6. LW 34:337.

7. Leon Morris, *The Epistle to the Romans* (Grand Rapids: Eerdmans, 1988), 1.

8. As Richard Marius states, "[Luther] never again lectured on either Romans or Hebrews, although he cited Romans again and again in lectures, sermons, and polemics" (Richard Marius, *Martin Luther: The Christian between God and Death* [Cambridge, MA: Harvard University Press, 1999], 118). Perhaps the reason he did not lecture on Romans more was due to the presence of Melanchthon, who arrived at the university in 1518 and lectured on Romans at least five times.

types: (1) glosses and (2) scholia. The glosses were notes or comments on words or expressions, and the scholia were comments on the theological content of a passage. Because Luther wrote these early in his career—near or during the time of his conversion—these notes do not necessarily reflect Luther's more developed beliefs.

In both his glosses and scholia, he addresses the main purpose of Romans. He writes, "The chief purpose of this letter is to break down, to pluck up, and to destroy all wisdom and righteousness of the flesh."[9] He further elaborates,

> The whole purpose and intention of the apostle in this epistle is to break down all righteousness and wisdom of our own, to point out again those sins and foolish practices which did not exist (that is, those whose existence we did not recognize on account of that kind of righteousness), to blow them up and to magnify them (that is, to cause them to be recognized as still in existence and as numerous and serious), and thus to show that for breaking them down Christ and His righteousness are needed for us.[10]

He continues by explaining that people are not made righteous by doing works of righteousness; only when someone has been made righteous does he do works of righteousness.

It is no secret that Luther affirmed that the doctrine of justification by faith alone was the central doctrine of the Christian faith. He is attributed to have said that justification is "the article by which the church stands or falls." Although those exact words (in their German or Latin equivalent) are not found in Luther's writings, he did state, "If this article [of justification] stands, the church stands; if this article collapses, the church collapses."[11] Luther would later assert that the doctrine of justification "is indispensable in the church" and is the one teaching that "creates true theologians."[12]

---

9. Luther, *Lectures on Romans*, in LW 25:135 ("Scholia").

10. *LW* 25:3 ("Glosses").

11. The original Latin reads, "*Quia isto articulo stante stat Ecclesia, ruente ruit Ecclesia*" (WA 40/3:352, 3). Luther also states the following: "If the doctrine of justification is lost, the whole of Christian doctrine is lost" ("Galatians," in LW 26:9), and "For by this doctrine alone and through it alone is the church built" (*LW* 26:10).

12. Luther, *The Disputation concerning Justification*, in LW 34:157. He also states, "The article of justification is master and prince, lord, leader and judge of all kinds of teachings, which

Again, he writes, "Nothing in this article can be given up or compromised, even if heaven and earth and things temporal should be destroyed."[13] For our purposes we will consider perhaps the two most important texts in Romans regarding justification by faith alone: Romans 1:16–17 and 3:21–26.

Romans 1:16–17 can be considered the thesis statement of Paul's epistle: the gospel is good news because it contains the power of God that leads to salvation for both Jews and Greeks since it reveals God's righteousness, which people receive by faith. In Paul's statement that the gospel reveals the "righteousness of God," Luther understood θεοῦ ("of God") as a genitive of source. That is, it is a righteousness that comes from God and is given to the sinner. Thus, as demonstrated in the section on his conversion, Luther understood the righteousness of God as that "by which God justifies us."[14] In his discussion of the righteousness of God in his lectures on Romans ("Glosses"), Luther references Augustine's On the Spirit and the Letter: "[It is] not that righteousness by which God is righteous but that righteousness with which he covers man when He justifies the ungodly."[15]

In contrast to human teachings, which reveal the righteousness of people and how people become righteous before themselves and before others, the gospel reveals the righteousness of God and how people become righteous before God. Luther also clarifies that Paul is not referring to God's active righteousness (for which he must judge sin) but to the righteousness that is the cause of salvation in sinners. Luther states, "By righteousness of God we must not understand the righteousness by which He is righteous in Himself but the righteousness by which we are made righteous by God."[16] Again, he quotes Augustine (On the Spirit and the Letter): "It is called the righteousness of God because by imparting it He makes righteous people, just as 'Deliverance belongs to the Lord' refers to that by which He

preserves and guides all churchly teachings and establishes our consciences" (quoted in Lohse, Martin Luther's Theology, 258; WA 39/1:205, 2–5).

13. As quoted in Paul Althaus, The Theology of Martin Luther, trans. Robert C. Schultz (Philadelphia: Fortress, 1966), 224 (Smalcald Articles [1537]; WA 50:199). Althaus maintains that, perhaps with the exception of the Lord's Supper, "Luther throughout his life devoted more theological work, strength, and passion to this doctrine than to any other" (Theology of Martin Luther, 225). Lohse writes, "There is no doubt that the heart and soul of Luther's Reformation theology is the article on justification" (Martin Luther's Theology, 258).

14. Luther, Lectures on Romans, LW 25:30.

15. LW 25:30.

16. LW 25:151 (see also p. 249).

delivers."[17] At this point, Luther's theology of justification was not fully developed. At times he seems to acknowledge progressive justification.[18]

Some modern commentators view Romans 3:21–26 as the very heart of the letter.[19] But how did Luther view this key passage, especially in relation to the doctrine of justification?

First, justification is a work of God, not a work of man. Justification cannot come about by law-keeping since the law's purpose is to reveal our sin, not redeem our soul. Works do not save anyone, just as performing the duties of a priest (without first being ordained to the office) does not make someone a priest. A monkey who imitates humans is not made or considered human simply because it performs human tasks. Performing the actions of a person will never change the monkey's nature. It will always still be a monkey. But if God made the monkey into a man, he will necessarily act like a man since his nature has been changed. Similarly, people are justified by faith and only then receive a new nature so as to perform works in accordance with God's commandments. "Therefore," writes Luther, "justification does not demand the works of the Law but a living faith which produces its own works."[20]

Second, justification is received only by faith in Christ. One cannot have access to peace with God without first receiving Christ by faith. True faith is not merely believing some truths about Christ; true faith is believing all things that pertain to him. Saving faith involves a commitment of the

---

17. *LW* 25:151–52.

18. Luther would later change the language of justification from "make righteous" to "declare righteous." Yet, even later in his life, Luther acknowledged that, in one sense, justification was a life-long process. In his *Disputation concerning Justification* (1536) he writes, "For we perceive that a man who is justified is not yet a righteous man, but is in the very moment or journey toward righteousness" (*LW* 34:152). Again, he comments, "Sin remains, then, perpetually in this life, until the hour of the last judgment comes and then at last we shall be made perfectly righteous" (*LW* 34:167).

19. For example, C. E. B. Cranfield calls these verses "the centre and heart" of Romans (*Romans: A Shorter Commentary* [Grand Rapids: Eerdmans, 1985], 68). Martin Lloyd Jones likewise affirms that this text "is the acropolis of the Bible and of the Christian faith" (*Romans: An Exposition of Chapters 3.20–4.25, Atonement and Justification* [Grand Rapids: Zondervan, 1971], 65). Leon Morris describes it as "possibly the most important single paragraph ever written" (*Epistle to the Romans*, 173). John Piper comments that this passage "is the Mount Everest of the Bible. … There are great sentences in the Bible, and great paragraphs and great revelations, but it doesn't get any greater than this paragraph in Romans 3:21–26" ("The Demonstration of God's Righteousness, Part 3," preached May 23, 1999).

20. Luther, *Lectures on Romans*, in *LW* 25:235.

entire person: "For to believe in Christ is to reach out to Him with one's whole heart and to order all things in accord with Him."[21] Faith is not a work because it looks outside to another. Rather, faith is disavowing one's performance as a means of seeking God's favor and trusting in the complete and perfect work of Christ. Additionally, faith itself is the work of God.[22] It is a gift given by God. God, therefore, justifies someone by giving him faith.[23] Faith is that which grasps or takes hold of Christ.[24]

Additionally, Paul's reference to being saved "through the faith of Jesus Christ" (διὰ πίστεως Ἰησοῦ Χριστοῦ) should be understood as an objective genitive: "through faith in Jesus Christ."[25] Thus, writes Luther, Paul "is describing what or of what nature the righteousness of God is, namely, that it is not something by which He Himself is righteous or by which a person could be righteous, but it is that which can be possessed in no other way than through faith."[26] Later, in his "Preface to Romans," he states that "faith alone makes a person righteous and fulfils the law. For out of the merit of Christ it brings forth the Spirit." It is "a divine work in us." It "is a living, daring confidence in God's grace."[27] God's forgiveness and justification demand that atonement be made. God cannot simply wipe away our sin without complete satisfaction of his justice. Thus, God's demand requires a payment: one that either we pay or, by faith, trust in the sacrifice made by Christ and the redemption he provides through his blood.

Third, although justification is not based on works, works result from justification. For Luther, the "works of the Law" include all works that people seek to perform and should not be limited to, for example, ceremonial laws. It is all "those [works] which are regarded in themselves as being sufficient for righteousness and salvation."[28] Such works can never bring

---

21. *LW* 25:238.

22. "Faith ... is a divine work in us which changes us and makes us to be born anew of God" ("Preface to the Epistle of St. Paul to the Romans," in *LW* 35:370).

23. See Althaus, *Theology of Martin Luther*, 231.

24. Luther later wrote, "Therefore faith justifies because it takes hold of and possesses this treasure, the present Christ" (*Lectures on Galatians*, in *LW* 26:130).

25. Luther, *Lectures on Romans*, in *LW* 25:242. See also *Luther and Erasmus: Free Will and Salvation*, Library of Christian Classics, trans. and ed. E. Gordon Rupp and Philip S. Watson (Philadelphia: Westminster Press, 1969), 309.

26. Luther, *Lectures on Romans*, in *LW* 25:31.

27. Luther, "Preface to the Epistle of St. Paul to the Romans," in *LW* 35:368, 370.

28. Luther, *Lectures on Romans*, in *LW* 25:241.

salvation because salvation is a work of God. Again, it is not the works we do that make us righteous; rather, having been saved by grace through faith, we receive a new nature whereby we are able to do good works. Luther explains, "For we are not made righteous by doing righteous works, but rather we do righteous works by being righteous. Therefore, grace alone justifies."[29] Luther understood justification as a gift from God received by faith in Christ; it is not based on works, though works naturally flow once a person is justified.

SERMON ON TWO KINDS OF RIGHTEOUSNESS (1519)[30]

Although this sermon is formally based on Philippians 2:5-6, its content and rationale are often based on Romans. For example, Luther references Romans seven times, including Romans 1:17 and 3:28. Luther probably preached this sermon in early 1519,[31] and in it he affirms two kinds of justification: (1) a forensic,[32] alien righteousness and (2) a proper or personal righteousness.

---

29. *LW* 25:242. Elsewhere Luther states that "works of the law do not justify; and if they do not justify, they prove those who work them to be ungodly, and leave them so; and the ungodly are guilty, and merit the wrath of God!" He then adds, "These things are so clear that none can whisper a word against them" (*Bondage of the Will*, 284).

30. See Luther, "Two Kinds of Righteousness," in *LW* 31:297–306. Luther also preached a sermon titled "Three Kinds of Righteousness." Scholars debate which sermon was preached first. For those who affirm that the "Two Kinds of Righteousness" came after "Three Kinds of Righteousness," see Daniel E. Keen, "Two Early Sermons by Martin Luther: An Examination of the Theological Implications of the Dating of Luther's *Sermon on Three Kinds of Righteousness* and His *Sermon on Two Kinds of Righteousness*," *Perichoresis* 2, no. 1 (2004): 97–107; David A. Lumpp, "Luther's Two Kinds of Righteousness: A Brief Historical Introduction," *Concordia Journal* 23, no. 1 (1997): 30; Robert Kolb, "Luther on the Two Kinds of Righteousness: Reflections on His Two-Dimensional Definition of Humanity at the Heart of His Theology," *Lutheran Quarterly* 13, no. 4 (1999): 457. The theology represented in "Two Kinds of Righteousness" is consistent with Luther's later theology. For example, in his commentary on Galatians, Luther notes, "This is our theology, by which we teach a precise distinction between these two kinds of righteousness, the active and the passive, so that morality and faith, works and grace, secular society and religion may not be confused. Both are necessary, but both must be kept within their limits. Christian righteousness applies to the new man, and the righteousness of the Law applies to the old man, who is born of flesh and blood" ("Galatians," in *LW* 26:7).

31. Some argue that the sermon was preached on Palm Sunday, March 28, 1518 (see, e.g., Else Marie Wiberg Pedersen, "Sermon on Two Kinds of Righteousness," in *Word and Faith*, vol. 2 of *The Annotated Luther* [Minneapolis: Fortress, 2015], 9).

32. Luther's view of "forensic" righteousness was influenced by his understudy Melanchthon.

Regarding the former, he writes, "The first is alien righteousness, that is the righteousness of another, instilled from without. This is the righteousness of Christ by which he justifies through faith."[33] This type of righteousness is received by faith in Christ and is the only kind that saves. He states, "Through faith in Christ, therefore, Christ's righteousness becomes our righteousness and all that he has becomes ours; rather, he himself becomes ours."[34] For Luther, justification is a gift that is imputed to the believer from outside himself (an alien righteousness) since personal righteousness can never meet God's perfect standard.[35] Luther would later explain how a person is at once righteous and a sinner (*simul iustus et peccator*). He is righteous because he has received the forgiveness of sins through faith in Christ, who experienced God's judgment. But he is still a sinner because he still lives a fallen existence. These are not true in degrees but are both completely true: we are at the same time completely righteous and completely a sinner.

The second type of righteousness, proper righteousness, is merely the product or result of the first type of righteousness. Thus, it is "its fruit and consequence." Because believers exist in Christ, it is impossible for them to remain in sin. Nevertheless, the first type of righteousness is primary since "it is the basis, the cause, the source of all our own actual righteousness."[36]

PREFACE TO THE EPISTLE OF SAINT PAUL TO THE ROMANS (1522)

Luther wrote the preface to the book of Romans for his translation of the Bible into German. At the time, Luther was being kept hidden for his own safety by Duke Frederick. In his translation of the Bible, Luther included prefaces to some books, which introduced the book to the reader, provided a brief overview and, in the case with Romans, defined key concepts. Written several years after he lectured on Romans and after he posted his 95 *Theses*, Luther's preface to Romans offers a more mature reflection of his view of this epistle and its contents than his lectures.

---

33. Luther, "Two Kinds of Righteousness," in *LW* 31:297.

34. *LW* 31:298.

35. Earlier he stated that "we must be taught a righteousness that comes completely from the outside and is foreign" and that "all our good is outside of us, and this good is Christ" ("Lectures on Romans," in *LW* 25:136, 267).

36. Luther, "Two Kinds of Righteousness," in *LW* 31:298.

Luther believed that Paul's epistles, especially Romans, were among the most important New Testament books since they best clarified the nature of the gospel. He explains, "This epistle is really the chief part of the New Testament, and is truly the purest gospel. It is worthy not only that every Christian should know it word for word, by heart, but also that he should occupy himself with it every day, as the daily bread of the soul. We can never read it or ponder over it too much; for the more we deal with it, the more precious it becomes and the better it tastes."[37] He continues by stating that Romans "is a bright light, almost sufficient to illuminate the entire holy Scriptures."[38]

One might think that Luther is exaggerating, using inflated language that pastors and teachers are prone to use. But upon reflecting on Luther's life and thought, we see that Luther wholeheartedly embraced and modeled his very words. At the end of the preface, he again returns to the significance of Romans: "It appears that [Saint Paul] wanted in this one epistle to sum up briefly the whole Christian and evangelical doctrine, and to prepare an introduction to the entire Old Testament. For, without doubt, whoever has this epistle well in his heart, has with him the light and power of the Old Testament. Therefore let every Christian be familiar with it and exercise himself in it continually."[39]

Luther also briefly, but carefully, defines key terms found in Romans. He believed that the people of the day misunderstood many of these theological terms—terms such as "law," "sin," "grace," "faith," "righteousness," "flesh," and "spirit." Luther contends that if we do not properly understand Paul's meaning of these concepts, then we are wasting our time reading Romans. For instance, by "law" Paul does not simply mean that certain acts are permitted whereas others are forbidden. Instead, God's law requires obedience from the heart since God is the judge who knows the hearts of all. Therefore, even our attitudes and convictions must be pure. According to Luther, "If, now, there is no willing pleasure in the good, then the inmost heart is not set on the law of God."[40] This is why the law is spiritual; it

---

37. Luther, "Preface to the Epistle of St. Paul to the Romans," in *LW* 35:365.

38. *LW* 35:366.

39. *LW* 35:380.

40. *LW* 35:366.

requires obedience from our inmost being, from a heart that is given to us only by the Holy Spirit. The only way to fulfill the law "is to do its works with pleasure and love,"[41] which can only come from the joy and love put into our hearts by God's Spirit.

Luther spends less time defining other terms. "Sin" is not merely external acts done by the body but includes "the inmost heart, with all its powers."[42] Consequently, "even if outward acts of sin do not occur, they can still lead to the destruction of body and soul." And the root of all our sin is unbelief. "Grace," according to Luther, is "God's favor, or the good will which in himself he bears toward us, by which he is disposed to give us Christ and to pour into us the Holy Spirit with his gifts."[43] Although we need God's grace daily since we battle the old desires that still linger in us, his "grace does so much that we are accounted completely righteous before God."[44]

For Luther, "faith" is not a dream or illusion that we conjure up by our own resources and call "belief." Rather, faith "is a divine work."[45] It is something that "is a living, busy, active, [and] mighty thing" and thus does what is good.[46] Those who claim to believe but do not pursue good works have not truly believed. Therefore, "it is impossible to separate works from faith, quite as impossible as to separate heat and light from fire."[47] "Righteousness" is a gift from God that, once received by faith, sets us free from sin and allows us to delight in God's commandments.

Finally, Luther explains "flesh" and "spirit." "Flesh" is not simply related to moral impurity whereas spirit relates to our hearts. Rather, flesh includes our whole being (body and soul) that is fallen. In contrast, "spirit" (or "spiritual") is applied to someone who "lives and works, inwardly and outwardly, in the service of the Spirit and of the future life."[48] Luther comments that unless people understand the concepts mentioned above

---

41. *LW* 35:368.
42. *LW* 35:369.
43. *LW* 35:369.
44. *LW* 35:369–70.
45. *LW* 35:370.
46. *LW* 35:371.
47. *LW* 35:371.
48. *LW* 35:372.

in the way he explains them, they "will never understand this letter of St. Paul, nor any other book of Holy Scripture."[49] He then warns his readers to beware of others who use such terms differently, be they Augustine, Ambrose, Origen, or others.

DISPUTATION CONCERNING JUSTIFICATION (1536)

Luther wrote several disputations concerning justification related specifically to Romans 3:28 ("For we hold that one is justified by faith apart from works of the law," ESV). These disputations, which centered on Paul's teachings on Romans, answered objections to his view of justification by faith alone. Luther clearly indicates that "we are considered righteous on account of Christ" and that "justify" means "to impute."[50] The one who is justified and therefore considered fully or perfectly righteous is still a sinner. Since the righteousness of Christ is an alien righteousness and is therefore outside of or foreign to us, it cannot be obtained by our works. Rather, it is only by faith that we can comprehend and trust in Christ. Faith should not be considered a work since it is of divine origin. Consequently, we are justified by faith alone apart from works. Justifying faith is that which "comprehends Christ."[51]

Although Luther readily affirmed the necessity of good works, he carefully articulated their role in God's plan for redeeming humanity. First, a mere claim to be a Christian without the accompanying fruit demonstrates that one has not made a credible profession of faith. He writes, "For those who glory that they are Christians and do not show this faith by such good works ... are not Christians at all."[52] Second, works are the fruit and not the root of justification: "Works only reveal faith, just as fruits only show the tree, whether it is a good tree. I say, therefore, that works justify, that is, they show that we have been justified."[53] Or, to put it differently, "Works ... show evidence that we are righteous and that there is faith in a man."[54]

---

49. *LW* 35:372.

50. Luther, *The Disputation concerning Justification*, in *LW* 34:153, 167.

51. *LW* 34:153.

52. *LW* 34:161. He also comments, "He who says that he believes and still whores, drinks, and is covetous, does not truly believe."

53. *LW* 34:161.

54. *LW* 34:165. Luther also maintains, "We can, therefore, ascertain and recognize those who have true faith from the effect or from what follows" (183; see also 189).

Justification is the efficient cause of salvation, whereas works are the effect of salvation and subsequent justification. Third, works are still necessary for salvation. Luther explains, "True faith is not idle. Works are necessary to salvation, but they do not cause salvation, because faith alone gives life."[55] Although it is true that faith alone justifies and saves a person, works are the necessary evidence that demonstrates that true faith is indeed present. In sum, "works are necessary in order to prove that we are righteous."[56] Or as Althaus summarizes Luther's thoughts, "If faith is the actual basis of the work, then work becomes the basis for knowing we have faith."[57] Thus, Luther affirms the necessity of works as found in the Letter of James.

CONCLUSION

According to Timothy George, "Luther's doctrine of justification fell like a bombshell on the theological landscape of medieval Catholicism."[58] Not only did Luther overturn the merit-based system of penance, he also paved the way for later Reformers who would expand on his teachings. The impact of Luther's writings continued for centuries.

Luther's legacy also continues today. Mark Seifrid follows in the line of those who have been greatly impacted by both Paul's Epistle to the Romans and the works of Martin Luther. In his comments on 2 Corinthians 5:21, Seifrid states:

> According to Paul ... our righteousness is found only in an abiding relationship of communication with Christ. ... Justification is not found in a *bare* declaration ... but in a relation, an apprehension or grasping of the crucified and risen Christ. Or in terms closer to those of Paul here [in 2 Cor 5:21], justification is found in the "transfer" of our person into Christ, through the exchange that has taken place in him. God's justifying declaration remains, so to speak, clothed in the crucified and risen Christ and is not to be found outside of him. ... To be justified *by* faith is to be justified *in* the very form of faith. ... In Paul's understanding, then, justification is fully

---

55. *LW* 34:165.
56. *LW* 34:166.
57. Althaus, *Theology of Martin Luther*, 246.
58. George, *Theology of the Reformers*, 72.

forensic and declaratory. As an *event*, however, it includes the reality of the new creation that has been effected by God in Christ, apart from any work or quality in us—indeed, in spite of who we are and what we continue to do in our unbelief.[59]

Like Luther, Seifrid affirms that faith is a work of God and that justification is a forensic event whereby God creates a person anew in Christ. He writes, "Luther understands 'justification' as a forensic *act* of God by which he creates the human being anew in Christ by the word of the Gospel. Correspondingly, 'faith' for Luther is not finally a performance of the human being but a performance of God within the human being, an act of creation."[60] God is the founder and perfecter of our faith (Heb 12:2), and he is the one who works in us both to will and to do his good purpose (Phil 2:13). Thus, it is fitting to end with Luther's last words: "We are beggars. That is true."[61]

59. Mark A. Seifrid, *The Second Letter to the Corinthians*, Pelican New Testament Commentaries (Grand Rapids: Eerdmans, 2014), 266. Emphasis original.

60. Seifrid, *The Second Letter to the Corinthians*, 264–65n555.

61. Luther, "Table Talk," in *LW* 54:476. After the quote from Luther, it reads, "These were the last thoughts of Dr. Martin Luther on the day before he died" (as recorded by Jerome Besold).

9

(RE-)CENTERING RIGHTEOUSNESS IN CHRIST

A Reflection on Luther's "Two Kinds of Righteousness"

Brian Vickers

Justifying righteousness is found in a person.[1] All discussion about righteousness must begin with and never stray from the one who is the revelation of God's righteousness: Christ, our righteousness.[2] The word of God in justification is indeed forensic, and must be so, but God's word of justification is declared *only* through his righteousness enacted and embodied in Christ Jesus in his cross (judgment) and resurrection (vindication). Only if we maintain that Christ himself is our righteousness can we speak biblically of God's declaration of righteousness, of imputed and forensic righteousness, of righteousness as a status, and of the gift of righteousness—all of which are "on account of faith, or on account of Christ, who is

---

1. This chapter is a constructive appreciation of both Luther's *Two Kinds of Righteousness* (1519) and for Dr. Mark A. Seifrid, teacher, colleague, friend, and brother in Christ. By "justifying righteousness," I mean God's declaration in the gospel that, through faith in Christ, sinners, apart from all works, having died and risen in Christ though faith, are both legally and actually made right with God through Christ's righteousness. God's judgment and condemnation of sin and the sinner, the Creator's case against his rebellious creation, passed to Christ on the cross, is the ultimate display of the righteousness of God. As Seifrid puts it, "'God's righteousness' is his 'vindicating act' of raising Christ from the dead *for us*." Mark A. Seifrid, *Christ, Our Righteousness: Paul's Theology of Justification*, New Studies in Biblical Theology 9, ed., D. A. Carson (Downers Grove, IL: IVP Academic, 2000), 47. Note that the emphasis lies clearly on God's *act* in justification.

2. A purposeful nod to the title of Seifrid's seminal work on justification in Paul, and to the fulfillment of Jeremiah 23:5-6: "Look, the days are coming—this is what the Lord declares—when I will raise up a righteous Branch for David, and he shall reign wisely as king, and administer justice and righteousness in the land. In his days Judah will be saved, and Israel will dwell in security. This is the name he will be called: The Lord is our righteousness" (CSB).

present within faith."[3] Likewise, if righteousness is in any sense "ours," and if we want to connect justifying righteousness to sanctification, Christian living, hope, virtue, or whatever else, then we must ground it all in Christ, our righteousness.

When justifying righteousness is detached from the *person* of Christ, then one metaphor or aspect—imputation or obedience, for instance— may become the center of our talk about justification. The tricky thing is that the aspect emphasized is often, if not always, a core piece of the overall biblical picture of righteousness. For instance, Paul, following Genesis 15, speaks of righteousness in accounting terms: "Abraham believed God and it was counted (λογίζομαι) to him as righteousness" (Rom 4:3; cf. Gen 15:6). The doctrine of imputation is built upon this text, but λογίζομαι captures just one aspect of justifying righteousness.[4] If it is allowed to become the central or controlling idea, then, practically speaking, righteousness may be conceived of and/or expressed as a commodity—as a thing that is transferred to the positive side of the ledger or an item that is exchanged for sin and condemnation. Yet righteousness before God is greater than the sum of its parts, and the parts themselves are not synonymous with righteousness.[5]

---

3. Mark A. Seifrid, *The Second Letter to the Corinthians* (Grand Rapids: Eerdmans, 2014), 264n555. Seifrid comments here on Luther's view of the imputation of righteousness in distinction from the evolution from Melanchthon to debates among Protestants with Osiander's view of justification "based upon the divine presence of Christ." Note the vital distinction between Christ "present in faith," and justification on the basis of "divine presence."

4. I am in no way diminishing the place of imputation but rather emphasizing that biblical teaching on justification is greater than any one aspect and/or metaphor and any one text of Scripture. Locating imputation across a variety of texts, none of which contain the entire doctrine in themselves, motivated my first writing on the topic. See Brian Vickers, *Jesus' Blood and Righteousness: Paul's Theology of Imputation* (Wheaton: Crossway, 2006). Though I still hold essentially to the conclusions reached in that book, I find after several years of reflection that my language regarding the imputation of Christ's righteousness in that work tilts more toward righteousness as an objective *thing* possessed by individual believers (once given by God) than it would if written today.

5. There is beyond doubt an exchange of our sin for righteousness, as Paul makes clear in 2 Corinthians 5:21: "He made him sin who knew no sin in order that we might become the righteousness of God in him." The exchange of sin for righteousness, however, is not a simple trade of one *thing* for another but "the work of God, who has acted in and through Christ. Furthermore, it entails something more than *work*. It involves the very person of Christ, who, in his suffering and death, 'was made sin' for us.'" Seifrid, *The Second Letter to the Corinthians*, 261.

Likewise, in Romans 5, Paul says that "many will be made (καθίστημι) righteous" through Christ's act of obedience just as many "were made (καθίστημι) sinners" as a result of Adam's disobedience (Rom 5:18–19). Here the emphasis is on the status God grants on the basis of Christ's obedience. If, however, this text is separated from Christ himself as our righteousness and raised to the defining aspect of righteousness, then justifying righteousness may become only an impersonal status granted by God. Righteousness, then, loses its dynamic and living sense and can become static, focused on the status of the individuals in themselves rather than God's work in Christ. In that case, it is easily detached from the reality of what such a status looks like in terms of obedience and new life (Rom 6).

If we sever righteousness from the person of Christ, we lose the Bible's emphasis on *alien* or extrinsic righteousness in justification. At no point is righteousness inherent to the believer. Mark Seifrid sums it up best:

> We do not have our righteousness in ourselves, but only in relation to the crucified and risen Christ, who has made us his own. Against its own intention, however, the traditional Protestant understanding can lead to the false assumption that "justification" has become an inherent possession of the Christian. Once justification is understood as a bare imputation or declaration, the righteousness credited to the believer may be regarded wrongly as "money in the bank." It may become a sort of intrinsic possession, even if it is not based on an intrinsic moral quality. The very concern to affirm the extrinsic nature of justification may then be undermined.[6]

On the other hand, if Paul's discussion of righteousness in terms of the Christian life in, say, Romans 6 becomes the center, or if the fruit of faith (Matt 7) becomes synonymous with God's justifying righteousness in Christ, then things shift in the other direction.[7] Now the emphasis is on the believer's *actions as proof*, rather than God's *act* in Christ grasped in faith. In that case, the essential forensic and declarative nature of justifying righteousness fades into the background, even if first granted an obligatory

---

6. Seifrid, *The Second Letter to the Corinthians*, 265.

7. The point is not to relegate such texts and vital biblical emphases to second-string status but to point out that inseparable things such as faith and obedience are nonetheless distinguishable.

nod. Not only does such an emphasis lead to ideas of imparted or infused righteousness, but, more commonly, it leads to the shattering of hope, joy, and assurance among many people who regularly repeat every *sola* of the Reformation. In this case, individual believers turn to themselves as the measure of righteousness and subsequently become piously self-righteous or grief stricken in self-loathing. The evidence of true conversion, whether positive or negative, takes the place of faith as God's gift of life in union with Christ. The common denominator in all imbalanced views of justifying righteousness is this: the individual person becomes, for all practical purposes, the focal point of that which only Christ must be center.

Re-centering righteousness in Christ, righteousness as Christ, is the way to avoid carving out doctrines of justifying righteousness that overemphasize single aspects of the whole and lead to locating or identifying righteousness as a personal possession.[8] With that in mind, Luther's "Two Kinds of Righteousness" points both the way back and the way forward.

"TWO KINDS OF RIGHTEOUSNESS"

Though not as well-known as such works as *The Freedom of the Christian*, *The Babylonian Captivity of the Church*, *The Bondage of the Will*, or his lectures on Romans and Galatians, Luther's "Two Kinds of Righteousness" is among the most significant and foundational of his works—not only for understanding Luther, but also as a faithful expression of biblical teaching.[9]

At first glance, Luther's introduction appears somewhat loose in terms of the texts cited, perhaps even on the verge of proof-texting. Readers may well wonder why, in a sermon entitled "Two Kinds of Righteousness,"

---

8. What I'm proposing is that the Bible teaches justifying righteousness as a multifaceted work of God in Christ through faith. It is much the same as pointing out that the larger biblical teaching regarding salvation necessarily has many aspects and cannot be reduced down to an order even though we may distinguish a logical order for the sake of discussion and/or clarity. If, however, soteriology becomes *only* a matter of ordering, then individual experience of salvation takes center stage rather than God's work in Christ. The question of *when* salvation is experienced individually (even if the "when" is logical) must not take priority over *how* and *why* the Creator reconciles his creation to himself in Christ, in whom all things reach their appointed fulfillment.

9. Luther wrote and preached this sermon on Palm Sunday in 1518 or 1519. Pedersen, like others, supposes Palm Sunday, March 28, 1518, is most probable. The sermon was published in 1519. Else Marie Wiberg Pedersen, *Word and Faith*, vol. 2 of *The Annotated Luther* (Minneapolis: Fortress, 2015), 9. See also the introduction to the sermon in Timothy Lull, ed., *Martin Luther's Basic Theological Writings* (Minneapolis: Fortress, 1989), 150–51.

Luther cites a series of texts, only one of which mentions righteousness. On closer examination, however, the introduction provides a foundation that Luther constructed carefully as the basis for his following discussion. Luther gives nothing less than a holistic picture of Christian identity *in Christ*. Before unpacking righteousness, Luther contextualizes righteousness in Christ in a broad perspective of the believer's life and existence. He does so on the basis of three texts: 1 Corinthians 1:30, John 11:25–26, and John 14:6.

Luther establishes the broad spectrum of salvation in Christ with 1 Corinthians 1:30: "And because of him you are in Christ Jesus, who became to us wisdom from God, righteousness and sanctification and redemption, so that, as it is written, 'Let the one who boasts, boast in the Lord'" (ESV).[10] With these words, Paul concludes his contrast of the world's wisdom and God's wisdom. God's wisdom shows itself in the cross, which confounds and condemns the world. In John 11:25–26 Jesus declares that he is the resurrection and the life, and in John 14:6 Jesus proclaims that he is "the way, the truth and the life." Together, these three texts establish Christ as the source and substance of Christian identity. In him we have salvation, freedom from death, and the gift of life. Christ himself is the foundation and focus for Luther's two kinds of righteousness. The first is "alien," a righteousness that comes to us from without. The second, "proper" righteousness, flows from the first and out to others.

"ALIEN" RIGHTEOUSNESS

Today, the term "alien righteousness" is about as alien sounding as possible.[11] Hidden behind that term, however, is arguably the most essential concept of Luther's biblical teaching on justification. The idea is that

---

10. Unless otherwise noted, all Bible quotes in this essay are from the ESV.

11. I have not thought up a better alternative, though I've tried a few. "External righteousness" is really no better because it sounds as if righteousness is never *in* us. "Outside righteousness" is either *outside of* righteousness or righteousness that has to do with the great outdoors. Something like "righteousness from without" is hopelessly out of touch with human communication. I like the phrase "Jesus righteousness" that Deines uses with regard to the Sermon on the Mount but, without explanation, the content is, at best, vague. Besides, he's referring to what *might* correspond to Luther's second type of righteousness. Roland Deines, "Not the Law but the Messiah," in *Built upon the Rock: Studies in the Gospel of Matthew*, ed. Daniel M. Gurtner and John Nolland (Grand Rapids: Eerdmans, 2008), 81. Ultimately whatever phrase we use has to be explained—and the explanation is what matters. Perhaps the terms "Christ

justifying righteousness comes from outside us and is not intrinsic to us. Christians from various, though not all, backgrounds affirm this idea when they speak of being justified by grace through faith in Christ, apart from works. As Robert Kolb and Charles Arand put it: "The righteousness that we receive is an 'alien' righteousness, a righteousness that is acquired by someone else and belongs to someone else. It is given to us from outside us."[12] We cannot speak in an unqualified way of justifying righteousness as "ours" in the same way we say that sin is "ours." This righteousness is, and always remains, a gift. The gift of righteousness is not owned or possessed outright, but ever remains a gift.[13] That is not to say that righteousness is on loan, as if it were temporary or provisional; much less is it some sort of legal fiction, as alleged by some opponents of anything remotely identified as a "traditional" view. To be fair, though, the responsibility for the legal fiction allegation lies in part, albeit unintentionally, with some narrowly communicated formulations of justification. When righteousness is primarily conceived as a thing (even when the word "gift" is used), as an impersonal commodity, as a bare legal decision practically divorced from the reality of a just God justifying sinners through his *word of justification in Christ*, or as simply a piece of divine accounting, then the charge of legal fiction is likely inevitable.

Luther's conception of this righteousness cannot rightly draw criticism as a legal fiction because he conceives of righteousness as wholly centered

---

our Righteousness," "Christ's righteousness," or simply "righteousness" are all that's needed these days. Better to explain "righteousness" biblically (difficult enough already) than have also to explain an English word like "alien" in the twenty-first century.

12. Robert Kolb and Charles P. Arand, *The Genius of Luther's Theology* (Grand Rapids: Baker, 2008), 39.

13. Grasping this righteousness as a gift and not as "our own" righteousness is essential for understanding how justification and sanctification relate. If the "alien" nature of justifying righteousness is lost, then sanctification will become a matter of self-reference—what *I must do* to become *more* holy or *more* pious or to prove *my* salvation. In other words, sanctification becomes a work in which I *prove* to myself or others that my salvation is genuine. Bayer concludes that, in order to keep sanctification from "becoming enthusiastic and fanatic," we must preserve the *alien* and *prior* nature of righteousness in Christ: "We are continually referred to the pronouncement of the gospel and therefore to the 'alien' righteousness that is given to us in Christ. This righteousness is appropriated and imparted. But it is never our own. We could never think of it or recollect it ourselves. This kind of self-reference, even on the part of those who are devout and want to observe their growth in faith and love, is in constant contradiction of the communion that the gospel grants us." Oswald Bayer, *Living by Faith: Justification and Sanctification*, Lutheran Quarterly Books, ed. Paul Rorem, trans. Geoffrey W. Bromiley (Grand Rapids: Eerdmans, 2003), 68.

in Christ's person and work and our union with him. Connecting God's promise to Abraham that the nations will be blessed through his seed (Gen 12:3) to Isaiah's promise of a child born and given "to us" (Isa 9:6), Luther emphasizes the "to us" as ensuring that "he is entirely ours with all his benefits if we believe in him."[14] Recounting Paul's word in Romans 8:32 that God "did not spare his own son, but gave him up for us all, will he not also give us all things with him?" Luther concludes: "Therefore everything which Christ has is ours, graciously bestowed on us unworthy men out of God's sheer mercy, although we have rather deserved wrath and condemnation, and hell also."[15] Notice that the mercy and grace given to humanity under God's justified wrath and condemnation is not a pardon by divine fiat but is thoroughly and only Christ in fulfillment of God's promises. The gift of righteousness is complete because God declares and grants the believer Christ himself as all righteousness. While it is true that the benefits (namely, forgiveness of sins) of Christ's atoning work come to the believer, Luther goes one step further to ensure that righteousness is understood as both a result of Christ's work *and* Christ himself in faith:

> Through faith in Christ, therefore, Christ's righteousness becomes our righteousness and all that he has becomes ours; *rather he himself becomes ours*. ... This is an infinite righteousness, and one that swallows up all sins in a moment, for it is impossible that sin should exist in Christ. On the contrary, he who trusts in Christ exists in Christ; he is one with Christ, having the same righteousness as he. It is therefore impossible that sin should remain in him. This righteousness is primary; it is the basis, the cause, the source of all our own actual righteousness.[16]

That quote contains the bridge, so to speak, between the righteousness that comes from outside the sinner through faith and the righteousness that may be called the believer's own righteousness. Note that the righteousness remains the same. Christ's righteousness—which cannot

---

14. *LW* 31:298.
15. *LW* 31:298.
16. *LW* 31:298. Emphasis added.

be separated from Christ himself—is given in the forgiveness of sin.[17] Not only is sin forgiven and exchanged for righteousness, but the decisive power for sin's defeat in the ongoing life of the believer is given simultaneously. Luther is not drawing a hard and fast separation between justifying righteousness in the forgiveness of sins and the new righteousness of the believer. Christ, by faith, is "the basis, the cause, the source" of all righteousness, including both kinds of righteousness.[18]

Though Luther emphasizes the external work of God in Christ that comes to us as righteousness by faith, he does not see "alien" righteousness as an impersonal or static transaction—God actually gives us Christ as our righteousness! Luther's emphasis on Christ himself through faith as the believer's righteousness is vital for understanding how he can go on to speak of that same righteousness in dynamic terms as it displays itself progressively in a believer's life.[19] Progress, however, is not, from the believer's perspective, a matter of sensing or seeing quantifiable growth in personal piety or holiness; rather, it is progressively less trust in themselves and deeper reliance on and faith in Christ.[20]

---

17. "Luther is explaining how the alien righteousness, *iustitia aliena*, becomes the proper righteousness, *iustitia propria*, of any Christian." Pedersen, 15n2.

18. Luther links Christ's work to and in contrast with Adam's failure. Christ's righteousness replaces that righteousness Adam "would have accomplished." This is not a case of simple recapitulation, however, for Christ's righteousness "accomplishes more." Similarly, Luther contrasts the alien righteousness of Christ to "original sin, likewise alien which we acquire without our works by birth alone." Here it seems Luther is highlighting the status and reality resulting from Adam's sin. Such an emphasis is in keeping with Paul in Rom 5:12–21.

19. Faith is not, either in total or even just from the outset, simply a mental assent to information about Jesus. Faith is not a starting point upon which the individual adds his or her works (including works "of the Spirit") to assure and secure salvation through sanctification. Seifrid states it best: "Faith for Paul cannot exist as a mere assent to facts which must be shaped by love in order to be savingly effective. It is rather the reflection of Christ's cross and resurrection within us, which cannot be supplemented but can—and must—only continue and increase." *Christ Our Righteousness*, 132.

20. Kittleson and Wiersma point out "two great dangers" faced by Christians: "On the one side lay the peril of repeated failure and then of despair. ... But on the other side lay the more common pitfall of apparent success, together with a complacency that bred self-righteousness. Luther understood that sinners who were declared righteous might begin to think that they were righteous within themselves rather than righteous on account of Christ. Worse still were those sinners who thought they no longer had to struggle against sin. ... He flatly denied that there was any possibility of becoming better in the presence of God. As time passed, Christians could hope, only to become ever radically dependent on the righteousness of Christ." James M. Kittleson and Hans H. Wiersma, *Luther the Reformer: The Story of the Man and His Career*, 2nd ed. (Minneapolis: Fortress, 2016), 59–60.

OTHER-CENTERED RIGHTEOUSNESS

The second sort of righteousness is that which Luther calls our "proper righteousness." This righteousness is distinguishable but inseparable from the first. Our righteousness, says Luther, is not something we do in and of ourselves, but that which we "work with that first and alien righteousness."[21] On the surface this may appear to be a kind of synergism or partnership between Christ and the believer, with each doing their part. However, he clearly has no such thing in mind. Luther does not intend a cooperation of two kinds of righteousness leading to sanctification; he means that the second kind (our righteousness) flows from and is the fruit of the first: "This righteousness is the product of the righteousness of the first type, and actually its fruit and consequence."[22] The idea can be summed up like this: the alien righteousness, the righteousness of Christ that is present in faith, brings the believer into a new existence. The believer, filled by Christ's righteousness, is now free and empowered to kill remaining sin and follow in Christ's footsteps by loving others. Just as justifying righteousness comes from outside the believer, it points the believer outside his- or herself to others.

If readers of Luther's sermon came away with just *one* key idea, it would be this: from first to last, all talk of righteousness must point away from the individual and his or her righteousness and focus squarely on Christ and others.[23] The first type of righteousness, Christ himself, delivers us from condemnation, guilt, and sin, with the result that we no longer need to make ourselves righteousness before God or others. Because of this type of righteousness, we have no need to pledge or resolve to do better tomorrow than we did today; to make our works the standard of our assurance and hope; or to enslave ourselves either to prideful ambitions or debilitating shame. Believers are free from all forms of making

---

21. *LW* 31:299.

22. *LW* 31:300.

23. Though Luther does not develop the idea in his sermon, what he describes is the reality of the new age into which believers enter in Christ. Luther's second type of righteousness, like the first, is the righteousness of the new creation in Christ that comes as a result of Christ becoming sin for us (2 Cor 5:17, 21). Seifrid's comment on 2 Corinthians 5:21 is fitting: "Paul here describes the new life given in Christ as 'the righteousness of God,' echoing his description of the new covenant that brings life and righteousness (3:6–11). In so speaking, he obviously refers to the new creation that has broken into the world in Christ, which he has already announced in v. 17." Seifrid, *The Second Letter to the Corinthians*, 263.

themselves devout, pious, holy, or acceptable.[24] This is the freedom of the gospel—believers are free from slavery to and obsession with the "I," the self apart from, and standing against, God and all others. Working "with" the first kind of righteousness means believing that God speaks the truth in our justification and welcoming the freedom to love others as Christ, our righteousness, loved us.

Luther uses marriage imagery to show the intimate link between the two kinds of righteousness. He builds upon Paul's teaching in Romans 6, which contrasts sin and righteousness—specifically, the incompatibility of sin in the new reality of righteousness. Now that sin no longer reigns, the believer, filled with Christ's righteousness, is free to be that righteousness: "For just as you once yielded your members to impurity and to greater and greater iniquity, so now yield your members to righteousness to sanctification" (Rom 6:19). Yielding to righteousness is then linked to the believer yielding to Christ as bride to bridegroom:

> Therefore through the first righteousness arises the voice of the bridegroom who says to the soul, "I am yours," but through the second comes the voice of the bride who answers, "I am yours." Then the marriage is consummated; it becomes strong and complete in accordance with the Song of Solomon (2:16): "My beloved is mine and I am his." Then the soul no longer seeks to be righteous in and of itself, but it has Christ as its righteousness and therefore seeks only the welfare of others.[25]

Once yielded to Christ as righteousness, the believer embodies his righteousness by becoming Christ to others—that is, by putting away self-interest in the best interest of the neighbor.[26] "Two Kinds of Righteousness"

---

24. My thoughts here reflect Bonhoeffer's insight that being righteous in Christ "does not mean to be religious in a particular way, to make something of oneself (a sinner, a penitent or a saint) on the basis of some method or other, but to be a man—not a type of man, but the man Christ creates in us." Dietrich Bonhoeffer, *Letters and Papers from Prison*, Dietrich Bonhoeffer Works 8, ed. John W. de Gruchy, trans. Reinhard Krauss, Nancy Lukens, Lisa E. Dahill, and Isabel Best (Minneapolis: Fortress, 2010), 235.

25. *LW* 31:300.

26. As Pedersen puts it: "As the bridegroom's alien righteousness is given to the bride against her alien original sin, it prompts the bride's righteousness to sanctify her through faith. Hence, the marriage is consummated as the righteousness that seeks the welfare of

invites us to look to God and to others. To put it another way, it invites us to live *in Christ*, and to grasp that "to live is Christ" (Phil 1:21).

LIVING RIGHTEOUSNESS

Luther calls the second kind of righteousness the "manner of life spent profitably in good works." He also divides it into two parts.[27] These are the results—the natural and necessary outflow—of the first kind of righteousness. First is the battle against the self. Luther's conception here is undoubtedly based on Paul's teaching in a text such as Romans 6:6: "We know that our old self was crucified with him." Though crucified, the old self, identified as the vestiges of the former person outside of Christ, remains. Now, having "learned Christ"—that is, having heard the gospel—the call to the new self in Christ is "to put off your old self, which belongs to your former manner of life and is corrupted through deceitful desires, and to be renewed in the spirit of your minds and to put on the new self, created after the likeness of God in true righteousness and holiness" (Eph 4:22-24).[28]

Of the two results of the first righteousness displayed in the second, warring against sin and loving neighbor, Luther gives more attention to

---

the others in the exclamatory exchange of bridegroom and bride: 'I am yours' (Song of Sol. 2:16)." Pederson, 12.

27. Luther's sermon is straightforward, and he doesn't qualify or nuance every statement. The section dealing with the second kind of righteousness is filled with examples that I will not smooth over or explain away. One of the most refreshing aspects of Luther's sermon, and I'd say of reading Luther generally, is that he is not always concerned to say everything about every subject at every time, particularly in his sermons. When he needs precision, he is more than capable of it. We should learn a lesson from him. In an effort to guard salvation by faith apart from works from beginning to end, we often end up creating vocabulary or terms that are at once correct and also made nearly nonsensical through qualifications, caveats, and other verbal safety nets. For instance, it is absolutely correct to say that faith is passive—faith is a gift received from God and receives God's work in Christ for salvation. At the same time, faith can be said to "act" or be "active" (Jas 2:22) insofar as it is the basis or foundation for our actions and is shown or displayed in works. Are the actions "faith"? No, not strictly speaking, but faith and works are inseparable. Or as someone said, faith without works is dead (Jas 2:17). We do not need simply to fall back on phrases like "passively active" or "actively passive" in attempts to alleviate tension from reading the Bible. Likewise we do not always need to qualify faith and obedience to the point where we fail to say anything biblical about either one. I'm not arguing the virtues of theological imprecision, but simply saying that some contexts call for plain, biblical speaking with the understanding that there is always more to say on every topic.

28. I could wish that Luther cited these texts since they fit perfectly with the themes of his sermon. Nevertheless, the presence of such texts that dovetail so well with Luther's theology of the two kinds of righteousness point to the authentically biblical character of his sermon.

love.[29] This emphasis makes sense, considering that his text is Philippians 2:5-1, a text that emphasizes Christ's servanthood on the cross as *the* foundation for love and service among believers.

The depth of content in Luther's treatment of proper righteousness with regard to the mortification of sin and self, however, is more profound than what is indicated by mere word count. First, as cited above, in the section on the first type of righteousness, Luther provides the necessary theological framework for dealing with sin in the Christian life. The presence of Christ through faith in the believer destroys sin because sin cannot "exist in Christ," and so it cannot exist in the one who believes in Christ. The way to deal with sin, therefore, is to believe that Christ's righteousness means the forgiveness of sin. By faith, sin is "swallowed up" in the one who believes in Christ.

When Luther comes to the second kind of righteousness, the "proper righteousness," he builds on Christ's defeat of, and the incompatibility of his presence with, sin. He makes clear that mortifying ongoing sin is not simply a second step moving toward sanctification. Killing sin and "crucifying the desires with respect to the old self" means believing Galatians 5:24: "And those who belong to Christ have crucified the flesh with its passions and desires." Old Adam is confronted not simply with newfound power to defeat sin, but the power to defeat sin rooted in the belief that Christ has destroyed sin utterly.

The other result—and the one Luther emphasizes most—is righteousness demonstrated in love for others.[30] It turns out, however, that waging war against the old self and loving neighbor are not separate steps but complimentary actions. Just as alien and proper righteousness are inseparable,

---

29. Luther had much to say elsewhere about the ongoing presence of sin in the Christian life. For an excellent discussion of *simul justus et peccator* ("at once righteous and sinner") in Luther's theology, see Thomas R. Schreiner's chapter in this book.

30. Here Luther, citing Galatians 5:22, identifies this righteousness as the fruit of the spirit but, contrary to most interpreters, takes "spirit" as the new "spiritual man, whose very existence depends on faith in Christ." This agrees with his Galatians lectures from the same year (1519) in which he expressly says that "'spirit' in this passage (despite Jerome's insistence to the contrary) does not mean Holy Spirit; it means the spiritual man," LW 27:373. It seems Luther changed his mind. In his 1535 lectures on Galatians 5 he does not qualify "spirit" as "spiritual man" in Galatians 5:22 but simply the "fruit of the Spirit" (the capital letter, I assume, indicates that Pelikan interpreted Luther to mean Holy Spirit), LW 27:93. Luther must take the word to mean the Holy Spirit, for, commenting on the same verse, he speaks of "the indwelling of Christ and the Holy Spirit."

so also the parts of our proper righteousness are inseparable. The Christian life is not divided into deprivation (battling sin) on the one hand and an active pursuit of loving neighbor on the other. Hating the old self—that is, hating the self that is contrary to and at war with Christ and others—is the way toward loving others. Once this connection is made, the link between the two kinds of righteousness becomes even clearer. Luther says that our proper righteousness "goes on to complete the first [alien righteousness] for it ever strives to do away with the old Adam and to destroy the body of sin. Therefore it hates itself and loves its neighbor; it does not seek its own good, but that of another, and in this its whole way of living consists."[31] By "complete," Luther is not saying that Christ's righteousness is not enough, or that he provides a portion and then we provide the rest. Christ's defeat of sin and God's gift of righteousness in Christ necessarily results in a new person who hates sin, because it is contrary to Christ, and loves others, because Christ loved sinners and gave himself for them.

Righteousness demonstrated in love for others is nothing less than the display of Christ's love for sinners according to Philippians 2:5-11, Luther's sermon text. "Do nothing from selfish ambition or conceit, but in humility count others more significant than yourselves. Let each of you look not only to his own interests, but also to the interests of others" (Phil 2:3-4). Paul's exhortation is met in Christ. He chose, in obedience to the Father, to serve rather than seek his own welfare or exert his divine identity for his own gain (Phil 2:6-7). This obedience led all the way to his ultimate service of self-sacrifice on the cross (Phil 2:8). Luther reads this text the way Paul intended, not as a christological abstraction but as the foundation for the Christian life—or what Luther terms as our "proper" or "actual" righteousness. Grounding Christian ethics in Christ means not only providing an example for imitation (though of course it does) but also the embodiment of Christ's righteousness. Our righteousness is the work of Christ, who is also our righteousness at work in us.[32]

Here is how I sum up Luther's teaching in this sermon. If we, by faith, were crucified with Christ (Gal 2:20) and died with him on the cross under God's curse (Gal 2:19; 3:13), and if we were raised with him (Eph 1:6), and

---

31. LW 31:300.
32. See "Short Instruction" in LW 75:7-12.

his presence now lives in us by faith (Gal 2:20), then our new self in Christ is free from sin (Rom 6:7; 18).[33] For Luther, in this sermon, mortifying sin means believing Christ is our righteousness. Where Christ is present by faith, sin has no place and therefore will be killed.

CONCLUSION

The distinction in "Two Kinds of Righteousness" is Luther's answer to the age-old perceived dichotomy of faith and works, trust and obedience, justification and sanctification, indicative and imperative, or any such expression seeking to grasp God's work and human responsibility. By distinguishing but not separating God's declaration of justification by faith in Christ—who is our righteousness—and *our* righteousness—which flows from that declarative word of the gospel in Christlike love and service to others—Luther left us a simple yet profound insight through which we may live by faith in the one who loved us and gave himself for us (Gal 2:20). God's declarative word of righteousness in Christ frees us from the works of sin and self and in turn sets us free to pursue living out this *Christ-righteousness* in the world.[34] With Christ himself as our righteousness, whom we have by faith always as a gift, believers are "free from having to find their own identify or achieve self-fulfillment" and seek the good and fulfillment of others.[35] The subject and object of the two kinds of righteousness are God in Christ and the world around us. The "I" is wonderfully and finally put aside.

---

33. Prothro makes a convincing argument that "one who died has been set free (justified) from sin" (Rom 6:7) refers to Christ's resurrection as his vindication "over against sin"—a vindication "that will be shared by those who have been united to his death in baptism, when they will finally be conformed to his resurrected image at the eschaton (6:8–10; cf. 5:18; 8:29–30)." James B. Prothro, *Both Judge and Justifier*, Wissenschaftliche Untersuchungen zum Neuen Testament, 2 Reihe 461, ed. Jörg Frey (Tübingen: Mohr Siebeck, 2018), 210.

34. In justification there is a shift from works of and for ourselves to the works that flow out to and for others—not, however, as "proof" of salvation or for our assurance. The pursuit of "proof" and assurance by works (even works by "the Spirit") is sub-Christian and marks a return to slavery to sin. The works of faith are a gift to others; the Christian is free in and through Christ, provided he or she *believes* and accepts that freedom. Commenting on Luther's view of Christian freedom and service, Bayer provides the following summary: "Christian or *evangelical freedom is that freedom though which the conscience is free of works*—not in the sense that none take place but in the sense that one does not rely on any of them." Emphasis original. Oswald Bayer, *Martin Luther's Theology: A Contemporary Interpretation*, trans. Thomas H. Trapp (Grand Rapids: Eerdmans, 2007), 289.

35. Bayer, *Living by Faith*, 39.

10
—
IN TROUBLE AND IN GOOD HEART

Oswald Bayer

I.

Dear congregation, moments ago, we joined in the cry of lament: "My God, why have you forsaken me?"[1] In marked contrast, *he* is not at a loss for words at all—*he* being the poet and composer of the Trinitarian doxology we heard in the Ephesians reading (Eph 1:3–14).[2] This powerfully eloquent poet and composer (Johann Olearius) is able to convey the fullness of God's Trinitarian being in a very articulate manner. He is able to assert the threefold distinction between Father, Son, and Holy Spirit while maintaining both their oneness and uniqueness. And, in the Greek original, he does all of this with just one single sentence. It is perfect, complete, lovely, transparent, capturing the totality of it, leaving no question unanswered. On the contrary, all our questions appear to be answered—and fully answered at that: Where do we come from? Where are we going? What are we? Answer: The Father chose us before the foundation of the world was laid, the Son redeemed us and lavished upon us the riches of his grace, and the Holy Spirit seals us and assures us of the glorious future that awaits us.

---

1. What follows is the transcript of a sermon preached by Oswald Bayer on Trinity Sunday, May 27, 2018, at Collegiate Church (Stiftskirche) in Tübingen. It has been translated by Karl Böhmer. Bayer's sermon text was primarily Genesis 32:23–32 with Ephesians 1:3–14. The editors of this volume have retained the original spacing of the manuscript to preserve various points of emphases throughout the sermon and added footnotes.

2. Johann Olearius, "The Lord, My God, Be Praised," Hymn 794 in *Lutheran Service Book* (St. Louis: Concordia Publishing House, 2006).

Perfect, complete, lovely, transparent, capturing the totality of it, leaving no question unanswered. Should we not take joy in such effusive praise of God?

Even so: "Oh, that we were there!"[3]

II.

But we are *not* yet there in that bright light. Instead, often enough, we find ourselves in darkest night, deserted and all alone—like Jacob at the Jabbok:

> The same night [Jacob] arose and took his two wives, his two female servants, and his eleven sons, and crossed the ford of the Jabbok. He took them and sent them across the stream, and everything else that he had. And Jacob was left alone. And a man wrestled with him until the breaking of the day. When the man saw that he did not prevail against Jacob, he touched his hip socket, and Jacob's hip was put out of joint as he wrestled with him. Then he said, "Let me go, for the day has broken." But Jacob said, "I will not let you go unless you bless me." And he said to him, "What is your name?" And he said, "Jacob" [i.e., *deceiver*]. Then he said, "Your name shall no longer be called Jacob, but Israel [i.e., *he strives with God*, or *God strives*], for you have striven with God and with men, and have prevailed." Then Jacob asked him, "Please tell me your name." But he said, "Why is it that you ask my name?" And there he blessed him. So Jacob called the name of the place Peniel [i.e., *the face of God*], saying, "For I have seen God face to face, and yet my life has been delivered." The sun rose upon him as he passed Penuel, limping because of his hip. (Gen 32:22–31 ESV)

It is an intensely riveting, immensely dramatic story—a story about a life-and-death battle for recognition. It is a difficult story that, in a subtle, even inscrutable fashion, speaks about how our life is threatened, but also—thanks be to God!—about how we are saved.

After all, the story of Jacob, the patriarch of Israel, is our own life story, characterized by more or less threatening and perilous transitions: out of

---

3. Arthur T. Russell, "Now Sing We, Now Rejoice," Hymn 386 in *Lutheran Service Book* (St. Louis: Concordia Publishing House, 2006).

the narrow uterus into life on this earth under open skies, kindergarten, school, starting a career, marriage, childbirth, having our lives interrupted by sickness, by the death of those closest to us, and by whatever other turning points and transitions there may be in our various uniquely personal life stories. At any rate, inescapable and unavoidable for each of us is the final transition: crossing the ford, crossing through the water, perhaps at night, perhaps alone.

That prospect may well strike fear and terror into your heart, especially when, as was the case with Jacob the deceiver, your past catches up with you and you are overcome by fear—yes, when you have reason to fear that Esau, the brother you deceived, will now finally take revenge, that the wicked deed will come back like a boomerang, and that, as a result of its curse, you will not be blessed, but accursed. Fear that you will not be one for whom the sun rises, but one for whom the sun does not shine and who falls into darkness instead.

That prospect may well strike fear and terror into our hearts "when the foe shall taunt and assail us," when the great accuser and killjoy whispers, "It was all useless, your life was not worth it. Throw it away!"[4]

Do not pretend that you never have such dark thoughts, as if your life is nothing but sunshine and roses and you always come away smiling. None of us can say that. We live in a world marked by deception and fear, by threats, terror, torture, murder, and war, a world in which there is no getting around the question asked in Wolfgang Borchert's "The Man Outside," where he returns from the eastern front to a bomb-gutted Hamburg and asks: "Did you dearly love us in Stalingrad, dear loving God, did you dearly love us then, huh?"[5] Instead of God's clear love and grace, instead of the bright sun of his mercy, a dark, mute, implacable fate seems to prevail. Not a person whom you could address by name, but some nameless thing. And I cannot ignore it or walk on by. It bothers me, badgers me, afflicts me, attacks me. "A man wrestled with him" (Gen 32:24). Jacob doesn't know *who* it is. Yet this uncertainty and namelessness is precisely what makes

---

4. Martin Luther, "To God the Holy Spirit Let Us Pray," Hymn 768 in *Lutheran Service Book* (St. Louis: Concordia Publishing House, 2006); citing Rev 12:10.

5. Wolfgang Borchert, *Draußen vor der Tür* (1947); for an English translation, see Wolfgang Borchert, "The Man Outside," in *The Man Outside: Play and Stories*, trans. Kay Boyle (New York: New Directions, 1971).

it so unbearable. Just who is this enemy attacking me? Who is attacking me with external tribulations, blows of fate, with hostilities, harassments, character assassination? Or with internal *Anfechtungen*, with the guilt and burden of my own past and the fear of my own future? Or is it perhaps—in, with, and under these external and internal hostilities—the destroyer of life, the devil attacking me? Or is it God himself, who, as it sometimes seems, does *not* let his face shine on me, but hides it from me—who does *not* hear me, does *not* answer me, does *not* help? As it says in the hymn, "Nor to thy supplication an answering be found." Or, "God, my God, why, oh why do you not answer?"[6]

III.

In the darkness of this tribulation and uncertainty, Trinity Sunday, with its clarity and certainty, is far away. As we sing, "Oh, that we were there!"[7] perhaps, in our *longing* for clarity and certainty, we are there—there at the goal. Perhaps not *only* in our longing, but already when we lament and cry out: "I will not let you go unless you bless me."[8]

Let us look to Jacob. What does he do? Does he throw in the towel? Does he give up? Does he grow hard and bitter? Does he become silent? Does he become depressed or frivolous? Jacob knows that it's all or nothing; passionately, he *goes for broke*: "If I die, I die; but first I will fight for my life and defend myself." Jacob wrestles with curses and damnation, wrestles for grace, for a blessing; he wrestles for these things in desperate defiance and wrings a blessing from his enemy: "I will not let you go unless you bless me" (Gen 32:26). He essentially says, "If you will *not* bless me, if you will *not* turn your face to me, if you will *not* give me courage and strength, then I am done for." This Jacob is *wrestling* with a terrible power; he refuses to let go of his enemy, but at the same time, he throws himself at his mercy: "Just bless me!"

---

6. Paul Gerhardt, "Commit Whatever Grieves Thee," Hymn 520 in *The Lutheran Hymnal* (St. Louis: Concordia Publishing House, 1941); Friedemann Gottschick, "Gott, mein Gott, warum hast du mich verlassen," Hymn 381 in *Evangelisches Gesangbuch* (Göttingen: Vandenheock & Ruprecht, 2014).

7. Russell, "Now Sing We, Now Rejoice," Hymn 386.

8. Russell, "Now Sing We, Now Rejoice," Hymn 386.

IV.

He *does* bless Jacob. This life-threatening power, the God who hides himself in such terrible ways, has allowed himself to be compelled, to be overcome. "[You, you God-fighter,] you have striven with God … and have prevailed" (Gen 32:28).

How can this be? How can a finite, mortal human overpower the infinite, immortal God? How can he turn his enemy into a friend who no longer threatens, but actually blesses and recognizes him?

That can only happen when the infinite, immortal God himself provides the finite, mortal human being with the key to compel him. *God allows himself to be overcome.* Earlier, he had promised Jacob that he would bless him and his descendants (e.g., Gen 28:13–15; 32:13). And now, Jacob is able to appeal to that promise—just like we are able to appeal to the promise specifically given to each of us in baptism. In baptism, God has promised himself into our power, has delivered himself into the word of his pledge: "I am with you always: in my goodness I will give you whatever you need; in my mercy I will deliver you out of all your troubles!"

And now God stands in the word; he wants to be taken at his word, his pledge. You may—yes, you *should*—hold God to this pledge. Rub it in his face, as it were. Yes, grab hold of him by clinging to his pledge, appeal to it as you grapple with his hiddenness, when he—along with the whole world and your own heart—grows dark before you in the times of transition and crisis in your life, when he hides his face from you and *does not* intervene. Then—yes, then—you must not, may not in any way give in and surrender to defeat and the weariness of the world. On the contrary, you may and you should put up resistance, using precisely that weapon which God himself placed into your hands when you were baptized—or, more precisely, which he placed into your ears and heart: his pledge to be there, to encompass you on all sides with his protection and to hold you in the palm of his hand. In short: his promise to bless you.

This promise God gave to us when we were baptized in his name, when he delivered us from all darkness and all uncertainty and placed us before him in the light of his face. The sun shining on us is the Father who chose us in him before the foundation of the world was laid, the Son who redeemed us and lavished upon us the riches of his grace, and the Holy Spirit who assures us of the glorious future that awaits us. So he who is cheerful, as it says in James 5:13, should sing psalms of praise like the Trinitarian doxology at the beginning of Ephesians, which is perfect, complete, lovely, transparent, capturing the totality of it, and leaving no question unanswered. But if there is anyone suffering among you, the very same verse of James directs him to lament and pray as he impatiently longs for God to intervene with judgment and salvation: "Give, Lord, this consummation to all our hearts' distress."[9]

In the face of the evil in us and around us, we keep on choking on the effusive praise of the Triune God. But even when it is dark and murky around us and we cannot understand why we have to keep on waiting, why God does not take away the pain and suffering, it is then—yes, *especially* then—that God's baptismal pledge to us holds true: his promise to be with us and to go with us. His promise gives us the strength to hold up in the distress of unanswered prayers, of ongoing illness, and of ongoing disability, and to praise him even in suffering: "Through my crying I will praise you."[10] Then, with God's unconditional pledge in your ears and in your heart, as you fight the ongoing earthly battle with him, the battle that will cease only at death, you will emphatically, defiantly cling to this promise.[11] "Lord, when the shadows lengthen and night has come, I know that you will strengthen my steps toward home."[12]

The night will not last forever. Ultimately, enlightenment will come. Full enlightenment. Clarity. The narrow straits will ultimately open up, and it will grow light. At the end of that day, when you will have no complaints left to make to God (cf. John 16:23), when you will no longer need to struggle and to strive with him, it will be said of you: "The sun rose upon you as you passed Peniel" (cf. Gen 32:31)—namely, the sun of Easter. And it will never set again. Your praise of the Triune God will not be afflicted by tribulation any longer. It will be lovely, and it will be complete. Even so, you will retain some reminder of your striving with God—just like Jacob,

9. Gerhardt, "Commit Whatever Grieves Thee," Hymn 520.

10. Walter Börner, "Herr, lass deine Fahnen wehen," Hymn 82 in *Jesu Name nie verklinget* (Stuggart: Friedrich Hänssler, 1965). The English title of the hymn is "Lord, Let Your Banner Wave" in the hymnal *Jesus's Name Never Fades Away*.

11. Walter Börner, "Herr, lass deine Fahnen wehen."

12. Julie von Hausmann, "Lord, Take My Hand and Lead Me," Hymn 722 in *Lutheran Service Book* (St. Louis: Concordia Publishing House, 2006).

"limping because of his hip" (Gen 32:31), and just like the Crucified One, who has been raised from the dead and is coming in glory, bears the marks of his wounds for all eternity. Amen.[13]

Let us pray: Lord, I believe; help my unbelief! How often do we try to avoid striving with you and curl up into a ball inside of ourselves instead— in depression, frivolousness, resignation, or apathy. Attack us when we are apathetic; shake us up when we are sluggish, so that we must run into you, take a stand before you, and—like Jacob at the Jabbok—experience you in tangible ways and become assured of your physical proximity. Lord, have mercy!

Wake us up so that we join in the lament of the oppressed, the homeless, the victims of violence and war, the children being abused and killed, of all those dishonored and despised, and so that we cry out: "Why do you not judge, why do you not save? Why do you allow evil to have free reign? How long will you stand back and watch? (Rev 6:10) Why so much senselessness, so much futility? So much suffering? So many injuries? So much pain? Why all this ongoing sickness? These incessant disabilities? These never-ending conflicts? Give, Lord, this consummation to all our hearts' distress!" Lord, have mercy![14]

And so, in our opposition to the distress of the world, we pray to you for peace in the face of conflict (and not only in Syria). In the face of shortsightedness and the bankruptcy of ideas in politics and economics, in education and academia, in social institutions and in the media, we pray for responsible, mindful, and sustainable action. In the face of broken relationships in so many families, we pray for people to be considerate and sincerely devoted to one another. In the face of the loneliness and isolation of those who mourn, those who are ill, and the dying, we pray for helping words and hands. Lord, have mercy!

Graciously take us into your care, bless our lives until our last hour comes, and gather us together before your face, where you will wipe away every tear from our eyes and where there will be no mourning, nor crying, nor war, nor pain anymore.

---

13. At this point in the sermon text, Bayer inserts "EG 381, 3–4," which is a reference to Friedemann Gottschick, "Gott, mein Gott, warum hast du mich verlassen," Hymn 381 in *Evangelisches Gesangbuch* (Göttingen: Vandenheock & Ruprecht, 2014).

14. Gerhardt, "Commit Whatever Grieves Thee," Hymn 520.

Hear us as we dare even now to address you as our Father through your Son by the Holy Spirit: *Our Father* ...

SUBJECT INDEX

—

SCRIPTURE INDEX

—

Old Testament

New Testament